Environmental Protection In The United States

Industry
Agencies
Environmentalists

Library of Congress No. 87-060733

ISBN No. 0-936434-21-X (Cloth)
ISBN No. 0-936434-22-P (Paper)

Illustrations: Hans Ticha

Editing, Design, Production: San Francisco Study Center
Editor: Geoffrey Link
Design: Nancy Hom
Type and Production: Keren Dick, Drew Sproul, Cindy Fong

San Francisco Study Center
1095 Market Street, Suite 602
San Francisco, CA 94103
415/626-1650

Environmental Protection In The United States

Industry • Agencies • Environmentalists

Joseph M. Petulla

San Francisco Study Center

*Dedicated to those who
have been entrusted with the work
of environmental protection
in the United States.*

CONTENTS

Preface   1

Introduction: Several Sets of Problems.   5

PART I: The History
Chapter One: Environmental Protection History.   13
The Industrial Revolution and Public Health (chart)   34
Chapter Two: The Politics of Pollution   39
Environmental Pressures and Legislation Since WWII (chart).   60
Attitudes on Environmental Concerns Early 1980s (graph)   67

PART II: In the Trenches
Chapter Three: Industry   71
Trends In Industrial Commitment (chart)   85
How Much Are Future Benefits Worth? (chart).   89
Chapter Four: Government Agencies   93
Goal Definition In Industry and Government (chart). 106
Chapter Five: Environmental Groups. 109

PART III: Root Problems
Chapter Six: Professional Standards 127
Chapter Seven: Ethical Responsibilities 147
Chapter Eight: The Federal Role. 165
Elements of Risk Assessment and Risk Management (chart) 180

Epilogue: What Can Be Done 187

Index 191

This book builds on my earlier work on environmental history (*American Environmental History* 1977, revised 1987) and the intellectual traditions of environmental thought (*American Environmentalism* 1980). It focuses on contemporary groups and institutions that are creating that economic history and those intellectual ideals—in industry, government and environmental groups—to develop a picture of the state of environmental protection in the country today. It goes beyond historical generalizations and philosophical typologies to explain the specifics of work in environmental protection through questionnaires and interviews of more than 300 specialists—the people in industry, public agencies and environmental activists who are involved in the work from day to day—who are able to bring abstractions down to the concrete, messy reality rather quickly, showing why environmental protection in the United States is an elusive goal.

I found that each sector is part of a subculture, which drives the way they see environmental protection, solve problems and perform daily tasks. Environmental specialists seem to be shaped in their thinking more by their jobs than whatever training they might have had. They expect to take sides rather than look at the science or merits of an environmental question. Those working in industry, agencies and environmental groups accept the system of adversary relationships as the way we solve problems in this country. Yet, largely because of this system, things do not seem to be working for the benefit of Americans.

We need to develop some new institutions without adversary relationships to solve environmental problems in the future. We need a corps of well-trained environmental professionals who will interact on a new level in the regulation, control and planning of modern environmental problems. These people could act as a leaven in the diverse, sometimes contentious, social environments in which they work.

At the same time, the institutions of environmental management must adapt to a new social environment. The impetus must be provided by the federal government. Past environmental policy has primarily been based on political pressure from business or environmental groups often buttressed by uncertain science. If environmental quality is to advance, the federal government must bring business and environmental groups into rule-making at the beginning of the research process.

There are many incentives for positive responses to environmental challenges. Business must change because it is threatened by liability costs and credibility losses. Government and agencies need a new modus operandi because their work grows and their budgets do not; moreover, their policy objectives, implementation strategies and inconsistencies of practice are under increasing scrutiny. And environmental organizations cannot afford to keep spending more of their resources with less results, or with no actual involvement in policy-making than a generation ago. The federal role in environmental management must become more efficient and more effective, especially in ensuring a large role in public policy-making by corporate and environmental specialists, particularly in research and rule-making.

To clarify the present, we must understand the past. The historical section of this book is crucial for many reasons, especially because it helps to understand that the problems are complex, took many years to reach their current proportions, and that tens of thousands people have been concerned about them for more years than the modern movement. Knowing history develops a sense of proportion and helps define the boundaries of contemporary problems. Knowing environmental legislative history further illustrates the connection between (disastrous) events, human or political reactions and the development of regulations.

The final section of the book is evaluative, drawing out the implications of the interviews, addressing the root causes of environmental protection, especially for professionals in the field. We can readily see how and why the field of environmental management is lacking in professional standards, since few people recognize it as a distinct field. Its practitioners come out of dozens of different disciplines and have an amazing variety of skills, perceptions, biases and commitments. Environmental studies can teach the need to integrate many disciplines into ecosystems study, but the problem of professional standards is far more complex than a theoretical approach. Environmental professionals need a distinct identity and professional purpose based on the ability to do technical negotiation, the term I use to describe their work.

Environmental management demands standards and clearly defined professional training; it also should reflect on its ethical responsibilities. For the same reasons the three groups need to change their mode of interrelationships, they have to look at the ethical dimensions of common societal goals that can improve the status of each of them in the short term and future generations in the long term. As I write this preface, a minor wave in the media has been created because W. R. Grace & Co. has produced a commercial that the major TV networks would not air because, they maintain, it is too controversial and might provoke demands for equal time. The commercial takes us into the future where people are huddling in rags in a dark, foreboding courtroom, where an old man is on trial. A child prosecutor is asking the oldster how he possibly could be so cruel as to leave his children and later generations with so much debt. Grace, of course, was referring to the national deficit, but we may justifiably ask this question regarding the natural environment of future generations.

The future of environmental protection will largely be determined by our response to this question and the political will to answer it together with our current "adversaries."

What I learned during the several years I've worked on this project, as well as teaching graduate students who worked in environmental management, gradually shaped the way I think about environmental problems and their solutions. I can see that environmental specialists hold the key to the future of environmental protection.

I began to research historically persistent environmental problems "laterally," through identifiable concerns of workers in the field. As I explored the ramifications of what my respondents were telling me, the dissonance I found at the center of American pollution control efforts "in the trenches" led me to the history and a critical evaluation of the basic institutions of environmental management.

Along the way I received a great deal of help from many people. First, it was an interdisciplinary study grant from the National Science Foundation and National Endowment for the Humanities that enabled me to do the first round of study and interviews that helped define the project and provide a lot of data. Dr. Rachelle Hollander at the National Science Foundation and Professor Kristin Shrader-Frechette were very helpful at various stages of the project.

Nancy Litterman Howe, an unusally sensitive reader of my work for many years, went beyond her customary excellent criticism and developed the graphics for the text. With an ability to cut through the mass of detail and come up with a synthesis that captures its meaning in a small box, she has proven that good graphics not only assist the process of learning but also are able to provide new insights in themselves. I am especially grateful for her contributions to the book.

In the historical section I have stood on the shoulders of Joel Tarr, George Rosen, Martin Melosi and many others who have focused on environmental history in general and urban environmental history in particular. The faculty of the graduate program in environmental management at the University of San Francisco have contributed to many parts of the manuscript. Richard Zelenka, Daniel Reidy, Nick Sundt and Jim Van Sant kept me from going off the deep end a few times. Present and past students in the graduate program, most of whom work in the field and come to Saturday classes, have been my best critics in and out of the classroom. I feel very indebted to them. Elizabeth Nichols, whose study on personnel in the nuclear industry is unusually illuminating, provided solid sociological advice. Special thanks to Geoff Link and the staff of the San Francisco Study Center for their outstanding work publishing the book.

The University of San Francisco itself has been continuously supportive of the project and provided a sabbatical to complete the manuscript. Finally, I am particularly grateful to the several hundred respondents who took the time and trusted me enough to answer my questions. It was extraordinarily difficult to pry much of the information loose from those stodgy institutions of environmental management in industry and government, but it certainly was worth all the trouble, and I hope that my new colleagues in the project will appreciate the results of our discussions.

Several Sets
of Problems

Do Americans today enjoy greater environmental protection than they did a generation ago? One would hope so, given the hundreds of billions of dollars spent by the federal government and private industry just for pollution control since that time. And, in fact, most data indicate cleaner air and water throughout the nation. Yet, many environmental analysts argue, neither the dozens of environmental laws nor a strong environmental movement has slowed the degradation of the natural environment. And we are not at any less risk from the life-threatening technologies that generate nuclear and toxic waste which contaminate the groundwater, surface water and the air. We know more now than a generation ago about the dangers to our health and environment and, realizing that we have not regulated the most dangerous pollutants, we have scarcely begun to do the major work of environmental protection.

Still another large group of informed scientists and policymakers hesitates to calculate the gains in environmental protection. Environmental quality undoubtedly would be worse, they say, without the legislation during this period, but they also point out more serious risks and problems that have eluded an easy solution, such as widespread groundwater contamination, indoor air pollution, chemical plant safety risks and acid rain. And, they correctly state, many other air and water quality standards established over a decade ago still have not been implemented or enforced in many regions of the country. A large number among this group wonder whether environmental gains have exceeded losses in the last 20 or more years.

There are various reasons it is difficult to find easy answers to the question of environmental protection. The notion itself encompasses many sets of problems that are not easily related. What is the common denominator for two such basic environmental concerns as wilderness protection and indoor air pollution? Which deserves regulatory priority? How should priorities be established? How much regulatory weight should be given to the business costs of a regulation? Should human health concerns be given regulatory precedence over ecological

5

problems of a wilderness area, because of limited budgets? Often popular ideas that are grouped under the notion of environmental protection range from complex scientific theories about problems like acid rain to personal feelings for the rights of animals.

Another cause of disagreement over answers to the questions of environmental protection is that personal interests shape the way we look at the issue. These personal (special) interests and values are usually legitimate viewpoints, but just as frequently can be self-serving propaganda. How is possible to sort out the difference?

Business interests generally value environmental considerations far less than a growing and strong economy. How valid is this view? On the other hand, many natural scientists and conservationists deplore the ruin of so many scenic and wilderness areas. Hunters and fishermen have joined their ranks when development or pollution have eliminated fish and game populations. How much consideration should be given to this position? Lots of people have become instant environmentalists when hazardous wastes and toxic air emissions have threatened their lives and health. How much must industry be regulated to protect potentially endangered populations?

As the environmental movement has grown, its influence has increased proportionately in the political arena. During the 1970s, an unprecedented amount of environmental legislation was passed. With the new environmental laws came mandates to government agencies to develop environmental standards, then to implement and enforce them upon an unwilling industrial community, which has challenged them on technical and legal grounds. Under the pressures, the regulations sometimes have been watered down or difficult to enforce. Enforcement agencies across the country have significantly differed in their degree of cooperation with industry or attempts at tough enforcement methods. At the same time, environmental groups have become increasingly vocal, taking their case to the courts and the media.

Environmental protection has become a monumental tug-of-war among the institutions involved. Industry, agencies, environmentalists have not been able to agree on environmental goals, means or standards. Each has defined the environmental protection problem from its own viewpoint: the economic hardship of unattainable or uneeded standards (industry); the necessity of complete environmental protection and health or safety (environmentalists); an attempt to combine disparate political and scientific factors to balance all interests or politically motivated shifts toward one or the other side (government agencies). Each approach may be legitimate, but at what point are they irreconcilable, unfair, propagandistic or illegal?

The history of environmental regulation is the evolution of a cumbersome, federal-state-local vehicle of overlapping jurisdictions, conflicting goals and political imbroglios. Industry fights with public agencies over standards and regulations, and environmental groups battle both agencies and industry over the same issues and enforcement practices. On the grass-roots level, where environmental protection relief is supposed to occur, environmental specialists working in industry and government have been at a loss to plan or implement a program of environmental protection.

What is the connection between the national debate waged in the media, legislatures and courts and the local scene where environmental specialists are attempting to implement management strategies in a day-to-day struggle with the realities of life in the environmental trenches? Simply because environmental policy questions are answered politically does not guarantee those policies will be implemented in the millions of places where pollution is generated. For example, the federal government establishes rules regarding pollution, but states and localities are responsible for the lion's share of enforcement duties—and they have their own agendas on enforcement priorities. Or industry might decide to stonewall the agencies or do the utter minimum until they can get the standards changed. Or, in many instances, environmental personnel in both government and industry are inadequately trained to do the job.

There are legitimate differences in approach among industry, government and environmental groups about what can and should be done. No one wants thousands of firms to be shut down, especially if the environmental standards violated are based on questionable scientific grounds. In the face of uncertainty, industry and government stall until a more favorable political climate prevails. No wonder the extent of progress in environmental protection during the past generation is still debated.

So this book investigates not only the societal dynamics among industry, agencies and environmental groups; also the internal dynamics of local environmental departments in industry and government, where specialists are grappling with the obstacles to environmental protection. What are their on-the-job problems or frustrations? How much support do they get from their employers or supervisors? What technical qualifications do they need to do the job well? How strong are their professional standards and personal commitments? What stands in the way of an effective environmental program?

Although the common work of environmental specialists in industry and government relates to public service and the societal good, these groups of professionals have not developed a sense of common purpose to carry out their societal mandate. There are good reasons for this unusual professional peculiarity. One is that the authority for fulfilling societal mandates comes from higher economic and political sources than practicing professionals. Nor are environmental specialists or educators in agreement about what training they need—some have no formal education at all. Another reason is that each subculture of employment in industry and agencies (and environmental groups, which act as gadflies) has its own purposes and rules distinct from whatever might be considered the common good. The main concern of every interest group is its own separate good, which, though legitimate, may not be good for other groups or society as a whole. In the end, it is the federal government that holds the key to full and fair environmental protection. Environmental professionals can assist mightily in the task. This study of environmental specialists in industry and government began in 1982 with a random sample of 1,300 firms taken from an EPA list of hazardous waste generators within a wide range of industries— primary metals, chemical, textiles, petroleum, utilities, paper, cement, electronics, electroplating, plastics and others—in seven major metro-politan regions. The initial single-page questionnaire was short and simple. It asked whether the firm was covered by the mandates of the Resource Conservation and Recovery Act of 1976; how the environ-mental section or division is organized, number and background of personnel, and whether the firm practiced any form of recycling, which recycling technologies, and how the economics worked out (positive or negative as compared with other methods). I avoided proprietary topics, and didn't request specific quantities or dollar figures. Naturally, I promised confidentiality.

I received 117 responses (9 percent), plus a few dozen that said they did not come under the requirements of RCRA. I did follow-up phone and personal interviews with 49 of the respondents in environmental departments, who put me in contact with another 70 environmental managers over the next year. By the end of 1984, I had spoken to 136 environmental specialists in close to 100 firms and also had gathered useful information on another 28 companies. In 52 companies I was able to talk to more than one person.

As time went on, my research interests broadened, and when I began to talk to environmental managers personally, I was able to inquire into many other details of environmental management in industry: besides information on their education and occupational experience, I wanted to find out what they did every day, what frustrations or problems interfered with their work, what environmental policies the firm fol-lowed, if any, problems with regulations and regulators, pollution control strategies, etc. Discussions were held in an open-ended format.

In 1984, I extended the study to include environmental specialists from agencies and engineering consulting firms that help industrial firms cope with environmental compliance problems. I sent questionnaires to 700 engineering consulting firms and government environmental agen-cies, mainly federal and state, and to about 25 local planning agencies, in 22 states. This time I received 141 responses (21 percent), 93 from agencies and 48 from private firms. The questionnaires focused on job description, educational background of specialists, problems and obstacles, and outlook for environmental progress; I also included a reprint of an article I had written for *Environment* magazine (1983) that described the research project and made some points. I did 45 follow-up personal and phone interviews with agency personnel. To this group, I added information from 13 agency personnel I had interviewed during my 1982-83 research trip to industrial respondents around the country. The 154 agency public respondents were specialists on all levels of environmental responsibility in government in 19 states.

During 1985, I phoned 41 of the key industry contacts from 1982 and was able to ask 32 of them about their firms: whether the changes were substantial or their situation remained about the same. Not surprisingly, there had been many changes, mostly toward better environmental compliance, perhaps because of the Bhopal, India, disas-ter but more likely because of the dramatic increase in toxic torts cases and potential liability claims. Furthermore, the 1984 RCRA amend-ments had expanded federal criminal enforcement powers: plant and environmental managers became liable for concealment of illegal hazardous waste activities, punishable by up to a five-year prison term; knowing endangerment could lead to a 15-year prison sentence and fines of $250,000 to $1 million.

With the environmental groups, it was not as necessary to uncover the way they do their day-to-day work as it was to see how they are organized, why they have been so successful, and their range of tactics and strategies. Therefore, I did not do many in-depth interviews, even with staff workers from the national groups, since I was looking for information that is generally available from the press and their own sources.

My material on environmental groups comes from newsletters and magazines of 10 of the more active environmental organizations in the country—the Sierra Club, the Wilderness Society, Friends of the Earth, Environmental Defense Fund, Audubon Society, Natural Resources Defense Council, Citizens for a Better Environment—plus three local ecology groups. I also discussed purposes of environmental groups and their work with about two dozen of their leaders. Here, unlike respondents in industry and government, I found a consensus about purposes and procedures.

In summary, my inquiry into the quality of environmental protection in the United States operates on several levels. The general historical/ societal level points up the interaction of primary environmental interest groups, including a number of prophetic individuals who managed to alert others about environmental dangers or who created the larger constituency for environmental protection. I also outline the labyrinthine process by which environmental regulations have become encumbered with overlapping jurisdictions, political compromises, sectarian disputes, media involvement and public fears.

Another set of questions concerns the workplace dynamics of environmental specialists in industry and government agencies in dealing with their daily problems implementing environmental legislation. Finally, there is an attempt to determine whether much can be done for environmental protection in general or the profession that implements it under the weight of historical and institutional inertia.

The final three chapters try to answer such questions as: Why are technical or performance standards uneven or rarely considered in the environmental management field? Why is it necessary to reconsider the education of environmental professionals and question their ethical responsibilities? What structural reforms are needed on a national level in the agencies and research centers if we are to encourage more cooperation among the basic institutions of environmental management? I contend that the processes of environmental management have become so divisive, counterproductive and expensive that a strong integrating institutional mechanism has to be found very quickly to begin to reverse contemporary separatist trends. Perhaps new institutions centered on environmental professionals, who would be trained together and work in all segments of society, could begin to infuse in them an interest in the needs of the common culture rather than simply one's own special interest. New institutions in the federal government are needed to integrate diverse societal segments by reorganizing into units concerned with common problems in society rather than departments and research sections devoted to the protection of their budgets and other questions of turf boundaries. The federal government's role in research leading to environmental standards and rule-making could integrate the separate factions of environmental management. The three primary parties all could have a responsible role in establishing priorities and developing policies.

Underlying the historical and contemporary struggles among business, government and environmentalists are the tools that each sector attempts to utilize in the fray: the media, the neutral public, and especially scientific understanding and environmental engineering technology. For example, during the 19th century, physicians, health reformers and government officials all blamed "bad air" or miasmas for the spread of disease and epidemics. Even after Pasteur and others demonstrated the role of bacterial contact in the incidence of disease, and the view became accepted toward the end of the century, officials utilized the same technologies—flushing away and diluting excrement into rivers and streams—that were advised by reformers 50 years earlier. The reasons are found more in the conflict among doctors or reformers vs. engineers and their employers than in scientific understanding or technological innovation. Furthermore, the same types of conflicts characterize modern environmental battles, often over the same science and the same technologies.

Thus, I have attempted to illustrate (not prove) connections (not necessarily causal ones) between environmental stalemates and environmental institutions. Because environmental problems are so multidimensional, it is especially important to avoid the impression of having "the answer." I have studied and conjoined areas that are not usually looked at together, from history, social science, philosophy, education, science and technology. The relationship among the three sections of the book is certainly neither tight nor linear.

A portrait of U.S. environmental protection is painted in this book by drawing on images of environmental managers in industry and agencies, along with gadfly environmental activists. The cultural textures that emerge are not abstract; they provoke the sights and sounds of real life. Therefore, the analysis of the institutional problems of environmental quality is not derived so much from environmental statistical data, as from the frustrations and needs of the people on whom environmental protection ultimately depends.

PART I:
The History

CHAPTER ONE

Environmental Protection History

A merican environmental history is the story of Americans and their relationship to their natural environment—land, air and water. Environmental degradation is not unique to the United States. Man-made environmental problems have plagued the world from at least the time that grazing animals scarred ancient Mediterranean hillsides. Yet the industrial revolution, with its grimy slums, brought new environmental problems and dreadful epidemics. The new era multiplied deaths from the occupational diseases caused by long workdays in primitive factories and mines. Industry's race for more energy for increased production brought waste, waste and more waste from sewage to toxic chemicals.

This section focuses on three variables: 1) America's development and the industries that shaped it; 2) the effect of this development on the land, air, water and human health, and the civic and scientific response to the impact; and 3) the political response to the impact in the form of legislation, enforcement agencies, lawsuits. From hindsight the drama is almost predictable after you understand American cultural institutions and economic rules of the game.

The Economic Keystone

The most important fact of American history is the central power of economic activity. Not long after the American Revolution, huge areas of the land were divided—into sections, half-sections, quarter-sections—and bought and sold. People wrested a living from it or moved on. Entrepreneurs made money from the forests, wildlife, gold, silver, iron ores, and coal, then also moved on when the resources were depleted.

Most of the early commercial activity took place in the seaport towns. Colonial merchants traded salt, guns, kettles, cloth and other necessities for goods from trappers, farmers and fishermen. They controlled local political policy, traded internationally with their own ships, lent money, set up distilleries and slaughterhouses, bartered guns and liquor with the Indians for furs and made money at every level of interchange.

13

Disabuse yourself of any notion of bucolic romance in your attempt to understand this period of history. Environmental conditions in early American cities were primitive. In *The New Yorkers,* Smith Hart (1938, p. 14) provides a graphic picture of living conditions in New York City at the close of the Revolutionary War:

> The problem of sewage disposal rested lightly on the city fathers. Processions of slaves from the abodes of the town's first families wended their way to the river banks at dusk each with a tub of dung perched on his shoulder. The generality, however, still disposed of excrement by flipping it through the handiest window. In accordance with a city ordinance, on Tuesdays and Fridays from April to December, all good householders scraped it biweekly from sidewalk and gutter and pushed it into the center of the streets. In winter, they let it lay where it landed. There was a pleasant fiction current that these mounds of offal (known to the jocular citizenry as "Corporation Pudding") were to be removed by cartmen in the employ of the city and occasionally a captious critic would address a newspaper broadside to the Commissioner of Streets labeled "Awake Thou Sleeper" but it was generally felt that it was a small matter to make such a fuss about. Unless there was an epidemic, the "pudding" was left in the center of the streets where in due course of time it was kicked about by the feet of unwary passersby until it got lost.
>
> The wells from which drinking water was drawn were situated for the most part in the middle of the extremely filthy streets. Much of the supply came from the famed Tea Water pump in Chatham Street (Park Row). The Tea Water was fed by seepage from the Collect Pond, once a beautiful, limpid pool surrounded by hills, which had long since become a receptacle for dead dogs and cats and the contents of slop buckets. The white and black residents of the shanties on its banks laundered their odds and ends of linen and "things too nauseous to mention" in it.

Although the window was often the point of disposal at the time, in most small cities, human wastes and waste water were deposited into cesspools, privy vaults and open lots or fields. Often the wastes were picked up and thrown into waterways or recycled by spreading on nearby fields.

Immigrants to Cities

By the time of the American Revolution, Philadelphia was the second-largest city of the British empire, with only 40,000 people. Within a generation, several dozen urban centers of 2,500 or more dotted the Atlantic coastline. In the 19th century the influx of immigrants from peasant villages of Europe accelerated. More than 30 million people came into the country during the 19th century; most stopped in the coast cities and newer ones over the mountains. In 1910, immigrants accounted for at least 70 percent of the populations of New York, Boston, Buffalo, Detroit and Chicago. In Pittsburgh, St. Louis, Philadelphia, Newark, Milwaukee and Cincinnati, the number ranged from 50 percent to 70 percent.

Between the Revolutionary War and the Civil War, cities became the magnet for tens of thousands of farmers who had tried to make a living from the land but were thwarted by the unpredictable boom-and-bust American economy as well as droughts, grasshoppers and other hardships of the frontier. After the Civil War, tenancy became common in the prairie and plains states toward the end of the 19th century. The celebrated farm movements of the period could not protect farmers from inflation/deflation, railroad monopolies, declining prices and credit problems. So they packed up what would fit on their family wagon and headed for the nearest city, where industrialists promised work for everybody. What they found were dozens of workers competing for every job, slums, tenement buildings, sewer backup (where sewers existed) oozing onto filthy streets, and a steady stream of dirt particles floating from smokestacks nearby. Unions were nonexistent, pay was meager, work hours extended into the night. They sometimes joined immigrants to live in discarded crates and other refuse in shantytowns on open land outside cities or shared rooms with other families in tenement houses that reeked with foul odors and disease.

The Road to Environmental Protection

Environmental and health problems developed in new industrial cities on the Continent before they assumed grave proportions in the United States, and efforts to control them in European cities and towns were under way during the American colonial period. German kings assumed the role of protector of the land and health of their people. Health programs included the appointment of physicians and surgeons to protect against the plague and other contagious diseases and inspect food and water.

In England, protection policies rested with each local town or village. The poor laws offered a measure of social welfare but little environmental or health protection. Residents were forbidden to throw animal or human wastes into gutters and streams, but sewage and refuse remained a continual pollution problem, even when scavengers were hired to collect it. Because of rapid population growth in emerging industrial towns, the easiest way to dispose of any waste was to dump it into the streets and gutters, where rain carried it eventually into streams. Water supplies from wells and natural springs close to town dumps were contaminated from leaching wastes. Cesspools were usually dug near tenement buildings seeping into the basements where very poor dwellers lived amid the stench and disease; in mid-19th century, at the beginning of the Industrial Revolution in Liverpool, 40,000 people lived in the cellars. Where privies existed they often served dozens of buildings; in Manchester during the same period, 33 privies were set up for about 7,000 people. Dysentery was a fact of life throughout Great Britain and the Continent.

Early Urban Improvements and Health Reformers

Some cities in England, particularly London, were improved during the last half of the 1700s. Initial efforts were directed toward draining and paving streets, which were believed to be major causes of epidemics. The Westminster Paving Act of 1762 became a model for more than 200

British communities between 1785 and 1800. At the same time, improvements were made in obtaining cleaner water supplies and disposal of wastes by new sewerage that gradually replaced wood mains with iron pipes. The iron industry was growing rapidly in England at this time.

But by early in the 19th century, the Industrial Revolution had taken hold in England and factory deaths were dramatic despite the fact that physicians had long studied occupational diseases of industrial workers, particularly in mining, metal-working factories, and textile mills. In the early 16th century, the Swiss physician Paracelsus wrote about the skin and lung disorders of miners, and in 1700, Bernardino Ramazzini of Italy wrote a book on various occupational diseases of the day.

Occupational/environmental diseases were lively topics in the press and novels of the mid-1800s. Elizabeth Gaskell, a popular novelist of the period, told the story of a young Manchester textile mill worker who was dying of byssinosis, a lung disease caused by inhalation of cotton, flax and hemp dust. Charles Dickens referred to Manchester as "Coketown," a grimy, industrial city that dehumanized its population, and in a newspaper report in 1868 he described, in the words of one of her fellow slum-dwellers, the problem of a woman working in the mills:

> The lead, sur. Sure 'tis the lead-mills, where the women gets took on at eighteen-pence a day, sur, when they makes application early enough and is lucky and wanted; and 'tis lead-pisoned she is, sur, and some of them gets lead pisoned soon, and some of them gets lead-pisoned later, and some, but not many, niver, and 'tis all according to the constitooshun, sur, and some constitooshuns is strong, and some is weak; and her constitooshun is lead-pisoned, bad as can be, sur; and her brain is coming cout at her ear, and it hurts her dreadful; and that's what it is, and niver no more and niver no less, sur. ("Small Star in the East" 1868)

Beginnings of Modern Public Health

Until later in the1800s, physicians believed that most diseases were caused by the state of the atmosphere (miasma), from foul odors from excrement, privies, sewers, decaying carcasses or corpses, filthy streets and the like. Any kind of decaying organic matter, from excrement to dead animals, was seen to cause disease-carrying miasmas. Poor sanitary conditions were believed to be especially responsible for atmospheric conditions that brought epidemics and infectious diseases. Throughout the 19th century, many studies were conducted that illustrated that animate contagion, living bacterial organisms able to reproduce themselves, caused contagious diseases, not the air, but the miasma theory directed physicians, chemists, health reformers and leaders from the mid-1700s until at least the end of the following century. At bottom, it espoused environmental factors as the primary bearers of disease.

(In *The Cycles of American History* (1986), Arthur Schlesinger points out that many Europeans in the 1700s believed that the air of the American continent was so bad that human beings could not grow in that atmosphere.)

Alain Corbin (1986) mentions in his fascinating study on the sense of smell that doctors and chemists believed that diseases could be cured by a proper control of foul odors, particularly of excrement. They went so far as to classify smells that emerged from cesspits and latrines as well as other other putrid smells such as from decaying carcasses and corpses.

The theory seemed to be confirmed by common observation. Many diseases in the factories were in fact caused by airborne pollutants. (In the quotation above, Dickens also noted that some people, because of genetic "constitooshun," were able to withstand the attack.) Furthermore, wherever epidemics spread, like the cholera epidemic of 1831 and 1832, the victims lived in poorer districts where foul smells, filth and poor sanitation were characteristic features. Poverty and filth were considered the primary threat to public health and morals as well as an ordered (free enterprise) economic system in an ordered society.

During this period, philosopher Jeremy Bentham developed a utilitarian theory that illustrated how private interests could benefit from public order. His disciples were known as Philosophic Radicals, intellectuals who proposed a series of "rational scientific" reforms to solve public policy questions. Most were concerned with environmental causes of poverty and disease, and also how scientific/utilitarian policies can promote more efficient government and industry. The group believed that these reforms could be implemented most effectively on a national level by Parliament.

One of the most influential of the group was Edwin Chadwick, who became interested in public health as secretary of the 1834 Poor Law Commission. The commission was primarily concerned with freeing a large labor pool to work in new factories by removing them from local parish welfare lists, but Chadwick was also interested in the causes of poverty and the health of those living in slums.

The Report on Sanitary Conditions

Chadwick and two other disciples of Bentham—Southwood Smith and Neil Arnott—believed that disease was caused by the conditions of poverty, and that most of the problems of both poverty and contagious diseases could be eliminated by stamping out the environmental causes of sickness, i.e., the filth and stench of the slum. Chadwick's "sanitary idea" that the physical and social environment determines health and well-being was the conclusion of the most influential environmental health document of the 19th century, his own *Report . . . on an inquiry into the Sanitary Condition of the Labouring Population of Great Britain,* appearing in 1842.

The report was commissioned because Chadwick and three medical inspectors who worked on the Poor Law Commission maintained that disease prevention could save the government and industry lots of money, a reason the remains a primary political motive for much environmental legislation. Chadwick wanted to collect public health data to find out which environmental conditions led to better health. Chadwick enlisted Arnott and Smith to the work on the report and also Philip Kay, known for his short tract, *The Moral and Physical Condition of the Working Classes of Manchester,* published at the time of the first cholera epidemic in 1832. All three were interested in epidemic outbreaks and had conducted surveys to determine their causes. The use of public health surveys (from reports of local physicians) to determine remedial action in regions, towns and factories had been common throughout the Continent for about a century.

Chadwick's monumental work was published as a report from the Poor Law Commissioners to the Home Department in London and was filled with survey material, rich in detail of environmental conditions related to mortality rates and economic conditions, as well as discussions about promising sewer technologies and disposal of sewage. The report concluded firmly that sickness and disease, especially contagious diseases, were directly connected to environmental filth and pollution from lack of drainage, polluted water supplies and excrement and garbage in homes and on the streets. Chadwick especially blamed "miasmas" from decaying animal and vegetable matter and other types of foul air. He quoted Villareme, who wrote for the Royal Academy of Medicine in Paris, that the canton of Varregio was transformed from a disease-ridden, "barbarous and miserable" district into a model of industry, "moral character" and health by simply draining the swamp whose *"aria cativa"* (foul air) polluted the inhabitants (p. 91).

He advocated the "great preventives" of "drainage, street and house cleansing by means of supplies of water and improved sewerage, and especially the introduction of cheaper and more efficient modes of removing all noxious refuse from the towns, ... (all) operations for which aid must be sought from the science of the Civil Engineer, not from the physician, who has done his work when he has pointed out the disease that results from the neglect of proper administrative measures, and has alleviated the sufferings of the victims" (p. 159).

Note that Chadwick and his collaborating physicians agreed that the solutions for environmental-medical problems would come from the engineering, not the medical, community. The primary leadership role of the physician, however, was apparent in that doctors played the diagnostic role in uncovering community medical problems in the first instance by treating patients. Throughout that century, doctors had a lower status and were often linked to health reform movements especially among the poor. Government and business hired technical experts or engineers to carry out their policies, which stayed within a tight economic budget.

The report led to a wave of concern around the country. Groups were formed to deal with working people's problems of high mortality, disease, congestion, crime and poverty—all found in slums. "The Sanitary Question" became the focus of discussion, locally and nationwide. A national Public Health Act was passed to establish a Chadwick-recommended General Board of Health, which was empowered to establish local boards of health to deal with local water supplies, sewerage, control of offensive businesses and other matters. Each board was to appoint a health officer, a legally qualified medical practitioner, to deal with the issues raised in Chadwick's report. Chadwick became leader of the first board, but found that local authorities were not so eager to implement costly reforms as he. Small water companies fought his efforts to set up central water systems, especially in London, where many members of Parliament held stock in private water companies.

In England, as early as the 1770s, the idea of using running water to carry off human wastes was born of the public concern over disease-laden miasmas. The invention of the water closet was designed to wash away foul odors as well as fecal matter and urine. Corbin (1986) calls this phenomenon the "privatization of human wastes." The notion has ancient roots (e.g., latrines of the Roman empire often were flushed by surface water) but not until Sir John Harington, a courtier and poet, published *The Metamorphosis of Ajax* in 1596, and persuaded Queen Elizabeth to install a water closet in her Richmond palace did the idea receive modern form. Sir John's book contained a complete plan of the first modern water closet. A few water closets were found in London and larger cities during the 1770s. At the time, unfortunately, the wastewater from water closets was dumped into cesspits, where it overflowed and often polluted springs, wells and other water supply sources. The London water companies eventually flourished because of increasing demand for water to flush away the wastes "out of sight, out of mind," and "out of nose" as well. However, the companies were not interested in consolidating their many systems in the interests of health reform.

Impact of the Report

Although sanitary progress in England continued in fits and starts, with much opposition raised around issues of costs of new sewerage and water systems, the report undoubtedly defined the important issues in Britain, the Continent and the United States for almost a century. One reason for its importance and acceptance was that epidemics, infected food and defective sewerage were beginning to reach crisis proportions in industrial cities. Not only were slums affected, but entire communities. The report was written at a time when it touched the nation's vital nerve.

One of Chadwick's central engineering recommendations was to apply sewage to agricultural land. He described a system of covered sewers that led from the city to a stream, which was diverted to irrigation ditches, increasing the land's productivity immeasurably. When the city attempted to divert the sewers away from the stream, the farmers fought the change in court, claiming that Edinburgh would lose the rich milk and butter from cows that enjoyed the grasses fertilized by sewage effluent (p.48).

Chadwick wanted to avoid contamination of the streams, in which towns typically dumped their wastes, so he recommended using covered sewers, flushed by water systems, to carry wastes directly to the countryside away from dense populations. Chadwick was among the first to recommend a combined water-supply and sewage-disposal system.

In 1858, the stench of sewage directly discharged into the Thames was so great (renowned as the "great stink") that members of Parliament could not bear to attend sessions. During that year they authorized the London Metropolitan Board of Works the power to build a main drainage system to intercept local sewers and transport raw sewage just far enough downstream that the incoming tide would not take the waste back to London. Within a generation, Londoners realized that the pipe simply transferred the problem downstream, and a treatment plant was authorized. The new facility left the Londoners with a huge pile of sludge, which eventually was dumped from specially constructed ships far out at sea (again transferring the problem).

Yet, throughout the 19th century, land application of sewage remained the recommended form of disposal to protect rivers and streams and the water supplies of the towns and cities of Great Britain. Royal commissions and parliamentary committees were unanimous in four reports during the 1860s. They considered the use of chemicals in water treatment, rejected the possibility, and in 1871 a commission recommended legislation that would enable towns to seize land for the purpose of "purifying" sewage. In 1876, the Rivers Pollution Act forbade the discharge of sewage into a stream.

The Rivers Pollution Act is of great interest at least because it became an archetype of the history of many environmental regulations in the United States as well as England. Since the legislation potentially could affect hundreds of municipalities and industries, virtually all of its teeth were carefully removed before passage. Alleged offenders had to be given two months notice before enforcement could proceed, during which time the court could send "skilled parties" to advise treatment. Manufacturing interests were provided preferential treatment: local governing boards had to give special permission to the sanitary authority before the latter could initiate action against industry, making certain that the enforcement actions were "reasonably practicable." Industrial interests only had to claim hardship to be exempted from the law.

Critics in and out of Parliament said minimal progress was made to curb water pollution by the end of the century in Great Britain, and that land application of wastes, the primary means by which progress could have been made, was avoided because of the expense to cities. Instead, engineers began to recommend a "dilution" or "assimilation" method. First the sewage was chemically and biologically treated, then discharged in quantities that were believed to be in proportion to the stream's capacity of assimilation. The waterway thus became the chief means of water purification in modern times. It still is, on both sides of the Atlantic.

United States' Practice

American cities developed at least as haphazardly as London and other British cities and suffered similar environmental distress. The horse-drawn omnibus was the first of a series of transportation innovations in the 1830s that led to the hectic 20th century city. Before that time cities tended to have their commercial activity clustered in one area, mostly at the waterfront, and people walked to work and back home. The physical expansion of the city then was limited to "walking city" dimensions. By 1850, commuter railroads began to appear to carry wealthier residents from newly built suburbs to their central city work place. Streetcars, electric trolleys, cable cars and, ultimately, subways and elevated railroads changed urban land use patterns from "walking cities" to sprawling, densely populated, congested metropolises. Transportation lines served the underclass as well as the rich, taking everyone to downtown shopping and business districts. Noise, dirt and smells from locomotives and other transporters were layered on the

20

traditional smells in the city of horses and pigs (which were tolerated because they ate garbage).

Although responsible for most of the transportation, hauling and much of the heavy labor of the era, horses represented a special environmental problem. There were 3.5 million of them in American cities at the turn of the century and they generated a monumental smell before and after evacuating their wastes. Every city had large horse populations: 83,000 in Chicago, 12,000 each in Milwaukee and Detroit. Environmental historian Joel A. Tarr (1971) remarked: "The faithful, friendly horse was charged with creating the very problems today attributed to the automobile: air contaminants harmful to health, noxious odors, and noise. The presence of 120,000 horses in New York City, wrote one 1908 authority, for example, is 'an economic burden, an affront to cleanliness, and a terrible tax upon human life.'" Experts at the time asserted that the normal city horse dropped 15 to 30 pounds of manure a day. The buggies spread it around and caked it to the streets. Tarr points to the calculations of health officials in Rochester, N.Y., which reported to the city that the 15,000 horses in the city produced enough manure every year to make a pile 175 feet high over a full acre of ground, enough to breed 16 billion flies and spread life-threatening sickness and disease. A strong demand for the "horseless carriage" existed very early in the large cities of America.

The Industrial City

City fathers of the time wanted flourishing, mechanized cities, so eventually horses would have disappeared from the scene even if they smelled like roses. By the 20th century, most big cities, already crammed with a large, unemployed workforce and connected to each other by an elaborate network of railroads, were ready for the influx of capital from local and British capitalists that would transform them into full-fledged industrial cities. Older, small, local foundries, refineries, tanneries and other such manufacturing plants that were financed by merchant capital were being pushed out of business by new, large corporations that strove for stable, monopolistic power in the marketplace. Municipal authorities welcomed their presence and never interfered with their operations.

New York was among the first to make the transition from a walking city to an industrialized city. Already in 1880, it had 287 foundries and machine shops, and another 125 steam engines, bone mills, refineries and tanneries. Its slums were among the most crowded in the world—more than 900 people were packed into every acre. By the turn of the century, Pittsburgh had hundreds of iron and steel plants with (according to its publicists) about 14,000 chimneys up the Monongahela Valley. As early as 1862, Anthony Trollope described Pittsburgh as "the blackest place I ever saw." Shantytowns were common in the Pennsylvania steel and coal mining districts. Chicago's stockyards combined with eight railroads, a busy port, and heavy industry to assault its residents with smelly, cough-causing black smoke.

Most industrial cities reeked of sulfur, ammonia gases, offal rendering, bone boiling, manure heaps, putrid animal wastes, fish scrap, kerosene, acid fumes, phosphate fertilizer and sludge. Garbage, kitchen slops, cinders, coal dust and other unwanted litter was piled in the streets. Many cities had no official garbage collection practice. New York hired street teams to handle its garbage, which was randomly and irregularly collected and barged for sea-dumping. Most other cities simply found a vacant lot or field in or out of the city where the open garbage lot became a breeding ground for disease, and debris blew into nearby residents' windows. The rapid and huge population increases as well as the poverty and isolation of new immigrant groups crammed into tenement houses precluded the possibility of community cooperation or peer pressure to solve these problems.

After the Civil War

Industrialization did not accelerate until the Civil War when the Union government bought arms, food and clothing, using millions of "greenback" dollars printed in lavish amounts. With this new kind of government financing of industries, cities began to spawn large companies that produced iron and steel for ordnance and later bridges and high-rise buildings as well as textiles and food processing industries for their multiplying populations. Oil refining, chemical manufacturing, machine tool shops, engines and farm machinery followed. Most large metropolises grew rapidly and randomly with diversified economies, but many cities specialized with local resources, labor and markets: steel in Pittsburgh, Youngstown and Gary; glass in Toledo; textiles in Fall River and New Bedford; flour milling in Minneapolis; brewing in Milwaukee; farm machinery in Racine; meat packing in Kansas City and Omaha, and so on. The population in the cities grew 100 times from 1850 to 1900, with little thought, let alone planning and regulations, about the human and environmental effects.

Each city developed its own pollution problems as factories, furnaces and warehouses were constructed amid a crazy quilt of streets, alleys, canals and railroads. Urban immigrants from European farms and villages had been used to feeding their garbage to farm animals and spreading human and animal wastes on their fields. Industrial cities on the Continent and in the United States grew so rapidly that most people simply tossed their wastes into common dumps, cesspools or dunghills in courts and alleys around which their tenements or houses were built. Besides excrement, in or out of cesspools, courtyards were filled with kitchen slops and other garbage, dead animals, ashes, street sweepings and sometimes industrial wastes from nearby factories. People expected scavengers to haul away their garbage for a pittance. American culture associates waste with low-life activity.

The Beginnings of Reform

So strong were the economic and cultural connections between England and the United States that the former colonies followed the economic pattern of English cities—laissez faire growth and increase in wealth accompanied by rapid development of environmental and health problems. The intellectual bond also was tight, so American reformers and politicians looked to British practice for solutions to their own health problems, including epidemics that were related to urban decay.

Newspapers in the older cities at the beginning of the 19th century blamed the accumulation of filth in the streets, poor drainage and air pollution from businesses such as slaughterhouses and soap factories for epidemic outbreaks. But at that period seaport towns still were growing too slowly to generate much action.

After the heavy waves of immigration, American cities reeled from recurring epidemics of yellow fever, cholera, small-pox, typhoid fever and typhus fever. Then the country was ready for its own Chadwick report, and two of them arrived in the same decade, from New York and Boston.

The first was done in 1845 by John C. Griscom, a physician and New York City health inspector. Griscom launched his study at the end of 1842 when he appended to his yearly health report a short essay, "A Brief View of the Sanitary Condition of the City." Three years later, he published an expanded study, *The Sanitary Condition of the Laboring Population of New York,* a title that reflects the influence of Chadwick's report. Griscom analyzed the exploitive "system of tenantage" and its resultant poverty, and explained its relationship to filth, disease and high mortality. The American Medical Association was founded in 1847 and its hygiene committee conducted sanitary surveys and collected other vital statistics that documented the need for reforms in urban practices.

Lemul Shattuck, a Boston bookseller and publisher, had already helped found the American Statistical Society in 1839. He issued a *Census of Boston,* which was prelude to another sanitary report, in 1845. The census documented the high general mortality, especially of infants and mothers, and the prevalence of communicable diseases such as scarlet fever, diphtheria and tuberculosis. From these data, Shattuck determined that a further study was needed and he convinced the Massachusetts Sanitary Commission to charge him with the task. Shattuck published his *Report* in 1850.

That study was pioneering in its attempt to standardize terminology and raise the quality of statistical material in reports of the day. He recommended establishing a state board of health and local boards of health to conduct and publish regular sanitary surveys. As did his colleagues in England and New York, Shattuck connected environmental sanitation to public health. Shattuck proved the importance of child care, school health programs, mental health, health education, teaching preventive medicine in medical schools, alcoholism and smoke control. Although little was done about these matters in his own time, Shattuck has had great influence on subsequent urban policies and reform activity.

However, politics and reform have not always gone together. While it was true that by the 1880 U.S. census more than 94 percent of the surveyed cities had set up a board of health, a health commission or hired a health officer, who controlled all aspects of environmental sanitation—water problems and sewage and garbage—these boards became political bodies, not under the control of physicians. Rather, political considerations of money and influence played more of a role in local environmental affairs than considerations of public health until the late 1880s.

Sewerage Problems

Public reaction in the late 19th and early 20th centuries increased as deteriorating air and water quality were seen to cause epidemics of typhoid, dysentery, cholera and yellow fever. By the 1880s, most cities had built sewerage systems that disposed of untreated wastes in nearby rivers, streams, lakes, harbors and estuaries. Control of air pollution caused by smoke from factories, coal and wood-burning stoves depended on heavy winds. Some cities' sewerage systems solved health problems caused by overflowing cesspools and privy vaults of their own residents, but downstream or lake cities usually drew their water supplies from these polluted watercourses. Even scavengers contracted by the cities to clean out cesspools and privy vaults (by means of buckets) often dumped the wastes into nearby rivers and streams. More often, cesspools were filled in with dirt and new holes dug, eventually contaminating water wells in all directions. At the same time, steel mills and other factories were built beside rivers or lakes because water easily purifies their products and then is handy for dumping metallic particles, oil, grease, cyanide, ammonia and other waste products. Cities with chronic air pollution problems such as Pittsburgh also suffered from dying rivers and streams.

As the demand for clean water grew, not only for household uses but also for flushing to fight epidemics and for fighting fires in the tenement districts, cities built waterworks systems out of nearby rivers. Philadelphia built the first in 1802; by 1860, 136 systems had been built in the country; in 1880, there were 598 systems.

Citizen Reaction

During the 1890s, physicians, public health officers and citizens' groups stepped up the pressure to do something about the "garbage problem," "foul smells," and resultant health hazards. Newspapers and popular and technical journals frequently featured articles about some aspect of the problem. Adding fuel to the early reform movement, William T. Sedgwick of the Massachusetts Board of Health proved the relationship between polluted water and typhoid fever. Writers and citizens groups cited the spread of diseases and stench as they appealed for action from their municipal leaders.

By the turn of the century, dozens of citizens groups, mostly made up of educated, middle-class women, were active in every large city. The Ladies' Protective Association of New York City, among the most effective of the groups, was organized in 1884 to force authorities to clean up a smelly manure pile in a neighborhood. Later, the women tackled a wide variety of urban sanitation, street-cleaning and refuse-disposal problems. So much media attention was given to these problems that most large cities had their own "public improvement" groups, very often formed by educated upper- or middle-class women. They were interested in health and aesthetics and involved themselves with littered streets, spoiled produce at markets, smoke pollution, sewage pollution and other issues. They usually did not get involved in scientific debates or even specific control measures, as this argument from the New York group—the sentiments repeated often by other improvement groups—attests:

Even if dirt were not the unsanitary and dangerous thing we know it is, its unsightliness and repulsiveness are so great, that no other reason than the superior beauty of cleanliness should be required to make the citizens of New York, through their vested authorities, quite willing to appropriate whatever sum may be necessary, in order to give to themselves and to their wives and daughters, that outside neatness, cleanliness and freshness, which are the natural complement and completion of inside order and daintiness, which are to the feminine taste and perception, simply indispensable, not only to comfort but to self respect. (Quoted in Melosi 1981, p. 36)

The contribution of women's clubs in conservation causes—particularly in reforestation, forest preservation and animal preservation—had been substantial from the mid-19th century. The suffrage and Progressive movements added a sharper political edge to their work and brought many of their leaders to Washington to lobby the Congress and members of President Theodore Roosevelt's cabinet. By 1910, hundreds of local women's organizations could mobilize hundreds of thousands of members on behalf of environmental legislation to protect the natural environment. Their day-to-day activities monitored the local environments in and around urban areas. The women's organizations' signal achievements established a solid tradition for environmental groups of the 1960s and 1970s.

Influence of the 'Apostle of Cleanliness'

One of the more influential of the late 19th century reformers, Col. George E. Waring, became involved in urban problems through his friendship with conservationist and landscape architect Frederick Law Olmsted in the 1850s. Well-known for research work in agriculture, Waring was appointed by Olmsted to do drainage and other agricultural work in New York's Central Park. Commissioned a colonel during the Civil War, and after the war continuing his studies in "scientific" agriculture, Waring gradually turned his attention to drainage and sewerage problems, about which he wrote and on which he worked.

At Lenox, Massachusetts, in 1875-76, he built the first separate sewer system, called the "Waring system," one for channeled rain water and one for raw sewage. Waring believed it was necessary to build small-diameter separate sewers, one for storm water and one for wastes from homes, because a large combined system allowed fecal matter to accumulate and generate disease-inducing sewer gas. Chadwick, who also held to the miasma theory of disease, preceded Waring in this view. Many engineers, following the work of Rudolph Hering, believed that the combined single-pipe system brought no ill-health effects, but some advocates of the separate system contended that not all urban areas needed both flood drainage lines and a different sewage disposal system, which would have priority for any city's sanitary problems. The debate was carried in most engineering journals of the day, and their conclusions were derived mainly from cost considerations.

The National Board of Health appointed Waring to examine sanitary conditions in Memphis after 5,000 of its inhabitants died from a yellow fever epidemic and more than 25,000 more residents fled in panic.

Waring was commissioned to build his separate system for the city, amid some controversy, and later built the system in other cities. His critics attacked him for promoting his own system and attempting to get rich from it (he held its patent rights), regardless of disputed sanitary value. Both separate and combined types led to a river or water course without treatment. The reason for the Waring system lay in a miasma theory of disease (influence of sewer gas), not that the sewage could be treated separately from storm water.

By the end of the century, however, Col. Waring was recognized as one of the nation's leading sanitary engineers. He worked with the short-lived National Board of Health and was able to interact with a variety of sanitarians, public health officers, engineers and civic groups. He continued to publish widely circulated articles on sewerage, drainage and other urban problems. He had worked on urban social statistics for the 1880 census, which introduced him to detailed statistics surrounding urban problems. In 1894, he was appointed to the position of New York City street-cleaning commissioner in reform Mayor William Strong's administration. Before the appointment, he was assistant engineer for the city of New Orleans.

Waring attacked problems of the city with steadfast discipline. He believed that all foul city odors had to be removed for the health of its residents: manure from the horses, sewer gas, garbage, factory wastes, human excrement. Meticulously dressed in his spotless uniform, pith helmet and riding boots on his prancing steed, the ex-military officer went to the most offensive parts of the city and gave orders to his street-cleaning corps. He checked and double-checked their work, fired them if they disobeyed or ignored his instructions, dressed them in white uniforms, had his "White Wings" march in city parades and gave them pep talks. He repeated the talks at civic meetings and to journalists, who gleefully snapped his picture on his horse and unwittingly gave Waring the publicity he wanted. The commissioner understood his position to be as much of a public educator as an engineer.

Waring reorganized every facet of the job from street sweeping and disposal collection to snow-removal and "garbage-reduction" experiments. He also used ashes and street sweepings as landfill and collaborated in experiments to recycle ashes and organic materials into fireproofing blocks. Known as the "apostle of cleanliness," Waring greatly influenced other urban engineers for decades. His books and articles on urban engineering were considered authoritative long before and after he died in 1898. His work helped bring the field of sanitary engineering from England, where Edwin Chadwick had created it, to the United States, where it became an important facet of municipal or civil engineering. Moreover, he was a media star, and he recommended cost-effective engineering solutions to a variety of sanitation questions.

Sanitary engineering developed early in the history of most cities because of the need to obtain water supplies for swelling populations, and some way had to be found to safely dispose of their sewage. By 1910, seven in 10 of the cities with 30,000 or more people owned their own water supply systems. With the flow of water into the cities, came water closets and an increase in water consumption of 50 to 100 times. Thus did privy vaults and cesspools overflow, and new environmental problems were placed on the shoulders of sanitary engineers. With these new responsibilities for building sewer lines, their influence grew in the cities. Soon they were handling the collection and disposal of garbage and refuse. It was a time that generated the hope that all these problems could be solved by good engineering and modern technology.

Influence of Germ Theory

For many centuries, philosophers and physicians debated the causes of disease, especially dread plagues and epidemics. Several early scientists—Fracastoro in 1546, van Leeuwenhoek about 150 years later, then Spallanzani in the 18th century—all suggested that a living contagion was the cause of infection. The notion remained present but under the surface until Pasteur's experiments during the mid-19th century. He was greatly assisted by improvements made on the microscope during the 1830s, as well as by the work of colleagues showing that fermentation was caused by microbes and Bassi's proof that a particular microbe causes a certain silkworm disease.

Especially interested in disproving the ancient theory of spontaneous generation of life, Pasteur confirmed Spallanzani's experiments that microbes or germs floated in the air and set on applying his work to the origins of disease. After hearing Pasteur, the English surgeon Joseph Lister, son of the founder of modern microscopy, began to investigate bacteria present in the air and found that these bacteria often caused his patients' wounds to become infected with pus. Lister also found that he could control infection by applying carbolic acid, which at the time was used to disinfect sewage. In 1867, he wrote about his "antiseptic surgery" as a means of killing germs, and soon after germs were routinely excluded from wounds by cleanliness of person and environment. At the same time, Pasteur was showing that microbes cause diseases in beer, wine, silkworms, hens, cows, sheep and men; he also developed vaccination methods to prevent diseases.

Sanitary Engineering

By the turn of the century, the germ theory of disease was commonly accepted by public health officials on both sides of the Atlantic, but public policy continued to apply the miasma as well as the germ theory. Throughout the latter decades of the 19th century, most large American cities, to contain disease, used both quarantine (implying knowledge of contagion) and environmental sanitation, usually because of abhorrence of foul smells. Paradoxically, even after Pasteur, sanitary engineers used methods to remove germs that Chadwick and others had much earlier recommended to dispel miasmas—water carriage of sewage, removal of excrement, carcasses and garbage from city streets, elaborate sewerage systems.

Sanitary engineering received respectability through the efforts of scientists and engineers associated with a number of research stations connected to state boards of health. Foremost among these was the Lawrence Experiment Station of the Massachusetts Board of Health, which brought together engineers, chemists and biologists to solve problems of water purification and sewage treatment. One engineer at the experiment station offered this early definition of a sanitary engineer: "He who adapts the forces of nature to the preservation of public health, through the construction and operation of engineering works . . . (sanitary engineering) is the application of a new science to a new product of civilization. The new science is bacteriology; the new product of civilization is 'The Modern City.'" (Tarr 1980, p. 433)

After a reasonable consensus was reached on the germ theory of disease and particularly the relationship between typhoid fever and water polluted by sewage, along with a deduction (first postulated by Englishman William Budd in 1849) made at the Lawrence Experiment Station, sanitary engineers focused their attention on sewage treatment and "purification." The laboratory experimented with methods of sewage treatment—intermittent filtration and land application of wastewater— and showed they could protect water supplies. The experiment station rejected land application of wastes because of the enormous amount of land required for even a small city.

Meanwhile other experiments with mechanical filters at Louisville, Kentucky, were proving successful. By 1900, *Engineering Record* reported: "The resources of the sanitary engineer are sufficient to bring about the purification of sewage to any reasonable degree. This costs money . . . , but not so much as is often believed." (Tarr 1980, p. 428)

The reason to treat sewage, of course, was to protect the water supplies of downstream cities. However, government and business did not favor sewage treatment, preferring water filtering and sometimes disinfection. By 1900, American sanitary engineers began to follow the British practice of water protection by combining stream dilution along with treatment of incoming water supplies. Americans developed a system of filtering water coming into the system rather than treating sewage going out, if the sewage did not create a "nuisance." The reason given was that it is more economical to purify water than treat sewage. The assumption was that sewage was diluted, dispersed and clarified as it moved down rivers and streams to the city receiving its waters. Purification measures by filtration made the water safe to drink after dispersion and dilution of sewage in waterways, they maintained. One of the first metropolitan areas to practice the method was Chicago, which first constructed a canal as an open sewer to dispose of Chicago's sewage into the Illinois River in 1848. Then, after a series of typhoid epidemics in the 1880s, a new Municipal Sanitary District decided to solve the problem by expanding drainage capacity with a new Chicago Drainage Canal in 1890. Designed by the famous engineer, Rudolph Hering, who traveled widely in England and the Continent, the canal carried sewage from Chicago to the Illinois River, which emptied into the Mississippi. Before long, growing cities around the country were emptying their wastes into nearby rivers, with water-carriage as the preferred engineering method. The water pollution or sanitary problems of the previous century were either diluted away or transferred downstream.

Until World War II, few municipalities interfered with the rights of business to dump wastes either into surface waters or on open lands. One reason was the common perception that industrial wastes did not carry the germs of disease; in fact, many believed that the wastes from factories killed germs in rivers and streams (Tarr 1985). More important was the extraordinary amount of power that industry wielded in local governments.

An example typical of the period can be traced in the Calumet area of South Chicago, which was developed during the 1870s by the Calumet at Chicago Canal and Dock Co. (Cf. Colten 1986). The company was able to receive congressional appropriations to dredge the Calumet River and wipe out a lush marsh area. Soon the river was lined with steel mills and agricultural rendering plants. Into the river were poured acids, phenols, benzene, tars, oils, fat and animal carcasses along with domestic sewage. City officials at first only were concerned about the domestic sewage, not with industrial wastes. By the turn of the century, when the volume of the wastes was multiplied by five, the stench and taste of the water made life on or near the river impossible. When local politicians realized they had to act on the crescendo of complaints, they did not consider a course of action that forced treatment of wastes or their reduction, but only further diversion and dilution.

Disputes Over Methods and Policies

Early in the 20th century, major public disputes about the need to treat sewage before discharge broke out between the engineers and public health physicians and their allies in the press. The issue was whether public health was being adequately protected. Politicians, business interests, municipal bureaucrats and civic groups all became embroiled in the dispute. The Progressive movement supported treatment over dilution, not only for health reasons but for recreational and other purposes of waterways. The multiple-resource use became a national plank in their platform. Most uses of water demand a fairly high degree of purity. Progressives also favored "rational" national planning to mediate special interests at the local level.

The federal government became involved with passage of the Public Health Service Act, which established research facilities to determine, among other things, the possibility of self-purification of interstate streams. The act intensified the states' activities, mainly in monitoring sewage disposal and water quality through their state boards of health. Many times it took disease outbreaks such as the typhoid epidemics of 1904 to galvanize state action.

A typical example of such policy struggles occurred in Pennsylvania, which passed its own law in 1905 "to preserve the purity of the waters of the State for the protection of the public health" after serious typhoid epidemics. New municipal bodies were forbidden to discharge untreated sewage into state waterways, and cities that already discharged raw sewage had to receive state permits to extend their systems. (Cf. Tarr 1980, pp. 430-31)

The industrial city of Pittsburgh in southwest Pennsylvania, with a 500,000 population and another half million around its borders in 1910, had been suffering from recurring typhoid epidemics. For a century, all domestic water had been drawn from the Allegheny and Monongahela rivers, whence these cities also dumped untreated sewage. In 1910, when Pittsburgh applied for a state permit to extend its sewer lines, the health director required a "comprehensive sewerage plan for the collection and disposal of all of the sewage of the municipality."

Pittsburgh hired the well-known engineering firm of Allen Hazen and George Whipple to do the study. Hazen and Whipple concluded that a new sewage treatment plant would offer no greater protection to downstream residents because the suburbs would continue to dump raw sewage. They also maintained that the cost of treating sewage far outweighed potential benefits. The state Health Department initially withheld the permit because the firm did not submit the comprehensive planning report the department required, but under political duress the state granted a temporary discharge permit, renewed regularly until 1939. No treatment plant was built in the region until 1959. Most engineers believed it was more cost effective for downstream systems to use sand or mechanical filtration methods developed in the 1890s at the Lawrence Experiment Station and Louisville, or to apply chlorine, which was introduced in 1908, than build new treatment plants at the source of the pollution. They agreed that a treatment plant was the better alternative when it was necessary to control floating solids and odors.

The nation's engineering community rejoiced over the victory with articles and editorials in engineering journals. *Engineering News* complained that the state board "joined blindly in . . . the doctors' or physicians' campaign against the discharge of untreated sewage into streams, with little or no regard to the local physical and financial conditions." The editors affirmed that engineering questions of water supply and sewage disposal should be left to engineers, not doctors.

After a series of typhoid epidemics in the late 19th century, several states, particularly in the East, attempted to regulate water quality, mainly by requiring cities to submit sewerage plans to the state. In the beginning, enforcement measures were rare, but after 1900, under mounting political and civic pressure and despite the difficulty in proving the source of waterborne diseases, state courts began to sue offending municipalities for creating downstream pollution. The first municipal treatment plants utilizing sand filtration and chlorine disinfectants were built during this era. During the entire period, treatment for industrial wastes was ignored or believed to be too expensive to be considered. Engineers simply did not work on treatment systems for industrial wastes as long as health problems seemed to result only from undiluted domestic sewage. Fish kills rarely were significant political issues of the day.

Air Quality

The air of large U.S. cities during this period was no better than the water. Smoke was the bane of city life. Most cities were near waterways in order to receive and send out goods to market by boat, but these locations are especially susceptible to atmospheric inversions. Then cities built rail lines for trains that used cheap, available and highly polluting bituminous coal. Soft coal was also used by factories that belched smoke and dirt so thick it covered everyone and everything, including the sun. By 1900, Dickens' "Coketown" was seen throughout America as the industrial revolution traveled at full speed.

Of course, many people became sick, and the foundations of buildings, viaducts and statuary began to crumble. Foresters around several cities said smoke was killing large numbers of trees. Civic and women's groups allied with physicians to speak out about the effects of the "smoke nuisance." Relying on metropolitan statistics of the time, Dr. J.B. Stoner, an activist physician, outlined some of the problems caused by smoke: *"There are more people subject to nasal, throat and bronchial troubles in a smoky city than in a clean city. There are also more fatalities from pneumonia, diphtheria and typhoid fever owing . . . to the lowering of the vital forces as a result of the scarcity of sunshine, caused by heavy fogs of smoke. . . Women living in sunless, gloomy houses and attired in somber clothes (were) also prone to be irritable, to scold and whip their children and to greet their husbands with caustic speech . . . Children (were apt to become) dull, apathetic and even criminally inclined."* (Quoted in Grinder, 1980).

Health officers and the American Medical Association pointed to black lungs of dead city residents as evidence of deadly smoke pollution causing consumption and various bronchial disorders. Smoke Abatement Leagues and Ladies Health Clubs were organized around the country, again run by upper-middle-class women. Most newspapers and journals took up the cause, attacking judges for being too lenient on industry, (even Andrew Carnegie rallied the Pittsburgh Chamber of Commerce against smoke), and, responding to the power of their constituencies, politicians began to make statements about the smoke of factories and railroads.

Eventually, engineers became involved and also wrote articles, claiming the problem could be avoided with technical innovations like stokers and down-draft furnaces, or electrified transportation systems. These mechanical and stationary engineers even helped draft legislation to prohibit smoke nuisance, and wrote many technical reports to civic associations and local government officials.

Of course, this was an era when smoke was equated with progress and prosperity. Some good was accomplished by these turn-of-the-century reformers, but industry generally made changes in production equipment when and where it was expedient. The most successful arguments pointed to aesthetic degradation, health decline and economic losses attributable to the pollution.

Energy and Progress

The last significant phase of American environmental history began with technological innovations in the field of energy use that magnified human exploitative capability a hundredfold. Noted geologist M. King Hubbert, who warns that 80 percent of all oil and gas reserves will be burned away in 50 years at the current rate of consumption, says that from 1850 to 1910 energy production doubled every 10 years. America's abundant supplies of coal, natural gas and petroleum, as well as geographic suitability for hydroelectric power, has made the country No. 1 in energy consumption potential.

With the U.S. agricultural base already well-established and plenty of fuel available to the proliferating industrial plants, and a population that had reached 120 million by the 1920s, entrepreneurs were ready to service the emerging consumer society. They beamed messages to the 3 million homes with radio receivers; influenced wide-eyed moviegoers

(40 million tickets sold each week) with glamorous heroes and heroines who lived luxurious lifestyles; and advertised widely in newspapers, journals and on billboards. In short, they contributed mightily to a revolution of rising expectations and to the homogenization of American culture.

The Automobile Revolution

No other product epitomized the transformation of American society during the 1920s more than the automobile, which dominated the decade. The number of cars registered jumped from 2.5 million in 1915, a few years before the Model T, to more than 9 million in 1920, to almost 20 million in 1925, to 26.5 million in 1929. The mass-production techniques of Ford, the development of sheet steel auto frames, and installment buying financed by the auto companies all played a role in the incredibly rapid saturation of the automobile into American society. The tempo of American life speeded up proportionately.

It is difficult to overestimate the car's impact on U.S. geography, environment, economy and society. The wilderness gave way to highways and their trappings—gasoline stations, roadside stands, restaurants, garages, tourist camps, wayside inns and billboards. Towns and cities began their unstoppable sprawl into the countryside. Rural children were carried in buses to central schools. Trucks hauled goods to places railroads could not reach.

Cities and suburbs were newly designed with the automobile in mind. Suburbs existed before the auto but were linked by railroads and usually did not extend farther than a mile or two beyond the stations. With the car, suburbs pushed their way into the country, divided and subdivided. Because fuel cost less than a quarter a gallon until the 1960s, the newly affluent were happy to live in the suburbs or country and commute to work. Cities remained noisy, dirty and polluted—not a pretty place to raise a family.

The 1920s gave birth to the parking problem and its never-ending attempts at solutions: more parking lots and garages; more street space for parking; widening of permanently congested streets into parkways and boulevards. The federal government became involved in highway building as early as 1916 with the passage of the Rural Post Roads Act, and local governments spent $2 billion a year for streets and highways during the '20s. Highway building seldom seems to have generated much opposition.

After World War II

The Great Depression stopped most of the growth, consumer demand and environmental impact, but World War II restarted the great American industrial machine. By 1944, half the country was engaged in production for war, bringing full employment; but, because of the scarcity of consumer goods, Americans saved their money for a better day.

After the war, corporations retooled quickly in an effort to satisfy consumer demand that was to last for more than a generation. Housing, automobiles and thousands of new appliances and gadgets were easily supplied by a larger, trained work force, supplemented by returning soldiers. More jobs meant more spendable income, through which new marketing and advertising methods and expanded consumer credit rebuilt the American dream of the 1920s. Television became increasingly important; almost 90 percent of American homes had a set by 1960. While new images for living were broadcast to the people, median family income grew steadily. At the same time, population growth and the sheer quantity of goods produced and bought in the Fifties and Sixties—along with the waste spinoffs associated with the automobile—levied their toll on the natural environment.

Many of these goods—detergents, synthetic fibers, plastics and pesticides from petroleum, natural gas and coal tar—are manufactured as synthetic products in high-temperature, pressurized and intensified-energy processes of distillation and evaporation. The manufacturing of synthetics is sometimes risky and always polluting; waste heat, toxic gases and hazardous waste are the usual byproducts. Accidents in Bhopal, India, Mexico City and Institute, West Virginia, have been widely publicized during the 1980s, but dozens of others have been recorded in the past generation. They represent an unintended but definite effect of industrial activity in a consumer society.

The 1980s

The environmental toll of the 1980s includes: acid precipitation caused by oxides of nitrogens from automobile exhaust and sulfur oxides from burning coal and oil at electric utilities; contaminated groundwater from leaking gasoline and other chemical storage tanks and abandoned hazardous waste or municipal dumps; toxic chemicals in the air from such indoor sources as pilot lights and radioactive building materials or toxic pollutants from hundreds of uncontrolled industrial contaminants; non-point source water pollution from city streets, agricultural lands and construction sites, which represents about one-half of the nation's water pollution; contaminated drinking water supplies of hundreds of cities and towns; continued soil erosion on farms and newly cut forest lands and accelerated destruction of wet-lands; and potentially extremely dangerous accidents at nuclear power and chemical plants.

These environmental and health costs of technological progress and the consumer society become less acceptable as the country grows aware of the health and environmental risks. From less complicated, but just as burdensome and risky, days in our cities 100 years ago, consciousness of the need for environmental protection blossomed. But the days of simple solutions were long gone.

In colonial days, as economic, political and social life were localized, so were the environmental problems. Until well into the 20th century, communities have attempted to deal with their own environmental problems, moreover, distrusted solutions from the outside. But as their local economies and political fortunes became integrated by energy, transportation and electronic media into the national and international fabric, problems could not be solved locally. Products poured into their homes from around the globe, and their wastes began to create problems in other states and countries.

The Industrial Revolution and Public Health

DATE	SCIENCE & TECHNOLOGY	CITIZEN GROUPS & PROFESSIONAL OPINION	GOVERNMENT ACTIVITY
1785	Iron water mains begin to replace wood in Britain.		
1830-32	Horse-drawn omnibus extends city limits beyond walking distances.	Jeremy Bentham's disciples urge utilitarian "rational scientific" reform for public health in wake of cholera epidemic.	
1842			Chadwick's monumental public health report calls for engineering solution to environmental miasmas. Griscom's New York study in 1845 reaches similar conclusion.
1847		American Medical Association founded with intent to conduct sanitation surveys.	
1848-49	Englishman William Budd links typhoid fever to water polluted by sewage. New cholera epidemic.		England's National Public Health Act passes.
1850s	Commuter railroads' smoke and noise begin to appear in U.S. suburbs.	"The Sanitary Question" gains national prominence in England. Miasma theory guides public opinion.	For two generations, Royal Commissioners recommend purifying sewage by spreading it on the land.
1860s	Pasteur experiments with microbes and vaccines.		England's Rivers Pollution Act of 1876 makes it an offense to discharge sewage into streams.

1880s	U.S. boasts 598 waterworks systems. Most sewage systems dump untreated waste into rivers, streams, lakes, harbors.	Engineering journals debate single-pipe vs. separate sewer system designed by Col. Waring.	
1884		Ladies Protective Association founded.	
1890s	Water closets present engineers with overflow, collection, disposal problems. Series of typhoid epidemics occur.	Medical community pitted against engineering societies over who should decide issues of public health.	British Commissions give up land spreading of sewage as impractical, begin to advocate treatment and dilution methods.
	Chlorine introduced to purify drinking water supplies.	Engineers prefer dilution and filtration/purification methods for economic reasons. Physicians argue for wastewater treatment.	Engineer Col. Waring appointed New York's street-cleaning commissioner.
1900	3.5 million horses living in U.S. cities, representing air/water pollution problems.		
1905-07		International Association for the Prevention of Smoke established.	Pennsylvania passes law that forbids cities to dump untreated sewage.

The general theme follows historical events, environment/health impacts, economic growth or industrial development that cause public, scientific and political reactions, and eventually societal debate. As the time-line and subsequent chapters indicate, interactions among industry (economic development), civic groups (or individuals), and government legislators (or agencies) have generated a crazy-quilt of environmental policies that reflect the respective power of each sector and scientific understanding of the age. Consensus has been a rare occurrence.

Summary

1. Environmental problems have been traced to many sources, from overgrazing, overcutting and overhunting to epidemics caused by contaminated water from densely populated cities. Most pollution problems have coincided with rapid population increases, urbanization and the industrial revolution. Their solution has been defined by 19th century utilitarians, led by Jeremy Bentham, who wanted to solve the problems by applying the same principles of rational "scientific" efficiency management as were governing the industrial revolution itself.

Chadwick's report is the prime example of utilitarianism in action. He concluded that efficient solutions to public health problems would lead to a healthier economy and a stronger England. The Progressives in the United States picked up the theme and applied it especially to resource management and multiple-use policies for rivers and streams.

2. Special industrial and environmental interests only gradually were defined in opposition to one another, and government bureaucracies saw themselves mainly as serving the needs of emerging industries, in England and the United States. A Royal Commission on Sewage Disposal report in London (1901) clearly shows the mainstream opinion in the testimony of A.D. Adrian: "You have to deal with this question from a common sense point of view. What is the object we have in view? The object is to make rivers as little of a nuisance as we possibly can. But that must be consistent with supporting industries of the neighborhood. If you go on to insist on conditions which it is impossible to carry out except to the detriment and destruction of these industries, then I say you are doing far more harm than good." (Quoted in Ridgeway, 1971, p. 30) As long as business interests and their engineers could demonstrate that their dilution and filtration technologies would prevent epidemics, they could hold back the more expensive treatment methods advocated by health reformers, conservationists and Progressives.

U.S. regulatory agencies, until World War II, were virtually dedicated to the speedy industrialization of the nation, from the Interstate Commerce Commission (1887) to agencies overseeing the building of railroads and digging of mines. During the New Deal era, new agencies were set up to shelter small businesses from corporate giants and the sweeping market swings of the economy. Although, during epidemics or resource crises, women's groups and individual environmentalists exercised some local influence on sanitation questions and wilderness issues, the utilitarians' national conservationist strategy favored development and corporate interests. Not until hunters and fishermen lost prime recreation sites in the 1930s and '40s, did the Izaac Walton League, National Wildlife Federation and hunting clubs gear up to press for a major anti-pollution campaign from the government. Sportsmen's organizations were powerful lobbies in the early conservation movement.

3. Federal intervention into local pollution control was rare until the 1970s. Even Franklin D. Roosevelt, at a time when the federal government was massively engaged in local projects, emphasized that federal participation in pollution abatement should be confined mainly to research, education, grants, loans and some help in enforcing local laws. Roosevelt, persuaded by his own "brain trust" that pollution control

should be managed by regional water- and air-shed agencies, set up the Tennessee Valley Authority as a model regional planning and management agency. The federalism suggested by the Constitution and "states rights" advocates of the South and West represented the strongest influence on environmental legislation before World War II.

4. The beginnings of professional struggle among local physicians, engineers and their relationship to the scientific community and local organizations, particularly women's clubs, also emerged at the turn of the century. Nonetheless, the multi-use, scientific managers usually won the day with "economic" arguments touting the most efficient methods to curb pollution. Industrial wastes too expensive to treat (or had no known method for clean-up) were not considered. All wastes eventually came to be cleansed, at least in part, by dilution in streams, regardless of its effect on the marine life near the outfall. "Streams are nature's sewers" was one of the engineering principles of the day.

These themes of struggle among special interest groups, including different professional classes, continue to this day—as do their conflicting arguments for "rationality." Throughout the 1970s and 1980s, discussions about amendments to the Clean Water Act and its regulatory standards have centered on whether the treatment standards should be based on the "receiving water" standards—use, temperature, assimilative or "break-down" capacity, speed of water-flow—or on technology-based standards requiring the "best" technology available.

Environmentalists have sued for best-technology standards rather than the older receiving-water standards because they have come to believe that industry pressure was causing the vast majority of streams to be reclassified downward rather than toward better water quality. Many large companies have argued in court that technology-based standards are uneconomical and often treat the wastewater to a level cleaner than the receiving waters. Agency officials have been pulled and tugged with the political winds, depending on whether the politicians maintain a conservative "economic" line or an environmentalist position.

As Joel Tarr (1985) has convincingly demonstrated, urban environmental problems originated as local community problems and were solved by transferring the "sink" into another disposal arena in another community. Thus, early wastewater problems in homes and cesspools were transported by sewers into streams and rivers, where they floated downstream to become someone else's bacterial problems. The solution to air pollution was thought to be very tall smokestacks, which delivered polluting gases and particulates far downwind where it formed acid rain. Sanitary landfills leached contaminants to groundwater. Miracle energy sources were believed to be found in nuclear power, which has bedeviled authorities seeking safe disposal of its lethal wastes. And so on. Meantime, state governments helped local governments solve their environmental problems; and, eventually, the federal government, holding financial power, stepped in with a new kind of political clout.

But, more significantly, Americans found out their democratic institutions gave them a way to organize into groups, at first local, and lobby for their own environmental interests. In the beginning, it was mostly a matter of convincing city hall something had to be done; this taste of victory spurred them to state capitals and on to Washington.

Bibliography

A basic source for this chapter is the excellent scholarship of Joel A. Tarr: "The Search for the Ultimate Sink: Urban Air, Land and Water Pollution in Historical America" in Kendall E. Bailes, ed. *Environmental History* (Lanham, Md.: University Press of America, 1985), which was based on the superb monograph with James McCurley III, Francis C. McMichael and Terry Josie, "Water and Wastes: A Retrospective Assessment of Wastewater Technology in the United States 1800-1932," published in *Technology and Culture* Vol. 5, No. 2, April 1984; see also Tarr's "Urban Pollution—Many Long Years Ago" in *American Heritage*, October 1971; and "Disputes Over Water Quality Policy: Professional Cultures in Conflict, 1900-1917" with Terry Josie and James McCurley III, *American Journal of Public Health*, Vol. 70, No. 4, April 1980; and "Historical Perspectives on Hazardous Wastes in the United States" in *Waste Management and Research*, 3 (1985), 95-102. For a good case study, see Craig E. Colten, "Industrial Wastes in Southeast Chicago: Production and Disposal 1870-1970" in *Environmental Review 10* (1986): 93-105. A basic source for the history of the "sanitary movement," especially in England but also in the United States, is George Rosen's classic *A History of Public Health* (New York: MD Publications, 1958). Hart's description of New York's streets is printed in a reference collection of documents, *Conservation in the United States: Pollution*, edited by Leonard B. Dworsky (New York: Chelsea House, 1971). Edwin Chadwick's *Inquiry into the Sanitary Condition of the Labouring Population of Great Britain* (London, 1842) still makes good reading; James Ridgeway's *The Politics of Ecology* (New York: Dutton, 1971) begins with an interesting treatment of the report and subsequent U.S. documents. The best source that documents original public works debates in 19th century London is *The Government of Victorian London, 1855-1889: The Metropolitan Board of Works, The Vestries, and the City Corporation* by David Owen (Cambridge, Mass.: Harvard University Press, 1982). Alain Corbin has written a fascinating study of the social context of the sense of smell, *The Foul and the Fragrant* (Cambridge, Mass.: Harvard University Press, 1986), which includes excellent material on the extent of public concern over the threat of miasmas. Martin V. Melosi's *Garbage in the Cities* (College Station: Texas A&M University Press, 1981) and *Pollution & Reform in American Cities, 1870-1930* (Austin: University of Texas Press, 1980) also edited by Melosi are excellent basic books; the latter contains an article by Suellan Hoy on "the role of women in improving urban sanitation practices." A special issue of *Environmental Review* (8:1 Spring 1984), edited by Carolyn Merchant, points up the achievements of women's organizations in environmental history. For a survey and bibliography on urban history, see Howard P. Chudacoff, *The Evolution of American Urban Society* (Englewood Cliffs: Prentice Hall, 1975); David Ward, *Cities and Immigrants: A Geography of Change in Nineteenth Century America* (London: Oxford University Press, 1971); and Sam Bass Warner, Jr.: *The Urban Wilderness: A History of the American City* (New York: Harper & Row, 1972). Most scholars utilize the U.S. Commerce Department study, *Historical Statistics of the United States: Colonial Times to 1970* (U.S. Govt. Printing Office) for basic statistical data.

CHAPTER TWO

The Politics of Pollution

After World War II, a new constituency began to emerge in the American environmental movement, outside of the inner circle of conservation thought. Urban sprawl and industrial pollution began to take their toll on the populace, and events pushed Americans little by little to a deeper concern for the natural environment. Conservation of natural resources gradually became transformed into environmental protection, less at the level of local politics, more on the level of a wider national consciousness.

Before the 1950s and 1960s, the policy emphasis, particularly in the federal government, was on efficient use of natural resources, especially land (soil), timber, water and minerals, rather than on environmental protection of water, wilderness and air, or even protection of human health. Very few efforts were directed toward environmental protection on a national level. It was remarkable that so few policy-makers even suggested it, considering the widespread outcries about the possibility of "timber famines" or other natural resource disasters. The vast majority of Americans did not perceive clean air and water as threatened, though many scattered local efforts were made in the cities to protect the public health by means of better and safer water systems.

But after the war, rapid population growth, increased air and water pollution and traffic congestion, and much faster consumption of dozens of new products made of new chemical compounds—these social developments took conservation consciousness into a new stage of political activity, from the efficient use of natural resources to a new politics of environmental pollution. But the fact that the federal government was not accustomed to addressing environmental problems, even those that crossed state lines, restrained its involvement in local or state problems. So the unhappy result has been two generations of uneven, overlaid environmental regulations and equally erratic state and local enforcement. The reasons can be found in the nature of environmental politics since World War II.

Urban Growth and New Consumerism

Early in the 1950s, dozens of new metropolitan areas suddenly emerged. From 1950 to 1960, U.S. cities with over 50,000 people grew by an average of 65 percent. Many cities doubled or tripled in size seemingly overnight. The forced saving during the war—consumer goods were not available—created a pent-up demand for housing, appliances and other consumer goods. This led to the quick retooling of war industries to peacetime production. On the promise of jobs, former servicemen took their families to the new large urban areas. Cheap GI loans enabled tens of thousands of ex-servicemen to buy homes, and they also received funds to attend college.

The idea that the American masses were entitled to a wide range of consumer goods was fairly new. Some among the emerging middle classes had gotten a taste of the good life and home conveniences during the 1920s with the inauguration of easy credit and the siren portrayal of consumer values in newspapers, magazines and especially the movies. A growing inventory of items—homes, wringer washing machines, gas stoves, carpet sweepers, indoor plumbing, automobiles, watches and others—became within credit reach of virtually all of the expanding middle class.

The 1950s were marked by massive federal redevelopment efforts to wipe out slums and other old sections of large cities and to spend billions on highways connecting the growing metropolitan regions. The entire country caught freeway fever, and within a generation many of the nation's old downtown sections were torn down, rebuilt or paved over.

The required land and resulting congestion of streets, highways, housing, waste disposal, airports, new factories, commercial areas and other ingredients of modern metropolitan regions soon provoked political reactions and generated new environmental controversies. Farms, increasing their production to feed a new, increasingly affluent, hungrier population, used more and more artificial fertilizers and pesticides, mainly DDT. It was a short generation before problems of the natural environment, ranging from a new burst of air, water, waste, and land-fill pollution to a variety of wilderness despoilments, touched every corner of the nation.

One of the first national battles of the decade took place over the proposed damming of the Green River at Echo Park in the 320-square-mile Dinosaur National Monument on the Colorado-Utah border. The area, designated by President Woodrow Wilson as a national monument in 1915 because of prehistoric dinosaur fossils, also was blessed (or cursed) with the kind of deep, narrow gorge at Echo Park that hydraulic engineers seek out for dams, especially in the West. As the country grew, engineers and planners kept looking for newer and larger sources of water supplies and hydroelectric power. Per capita use of water in the cities grew at exponential rates, doubling every six to 10 years.

During the 1940s, the federal Bureau of Reclamation developed a comprehensive plan for a 10-dam Colorado River Storage Project to meet the water demands of the booming Southwest. Political support for the project after the war seemed universal. Secretary of the Interior

Oscar L. Chapman held a public hearing on the Echo Park Dam in 1950 and recommended that, "in the interest of the greatest public good," Echo Park be included in the project. The entire Colorado project, however, had to be approved by Congress.

The Sierra Club and the Wilderness Society both were active during the period. Urban chapters steadily increased their memberships because people were becoming more interested in getting out of noisy, hot, congested cities for trips into more peaceful, refreshing wilderness areas. Gradually, beginning in the 1940s, more and more people were looking for non-material amenities. In an effective national campaign against the proposed Echo Park dam through articles in publications such as *Life, Newsweek, Saturday Evening Post,* as well as in conservation magazines, club leaders tapped this desire for wilderness. They used non-economic arguments in full-page newspaper ads and direct mail campaigns: "Wilderness areas have become to us a spiritual necessity; an antidote to modern living," they are needed "for our spiritual welfare;" they present a prehistoric "reservoir of stored experiences in ways of life before man;" "we deeply need the humility to know ourselves as the dependent members of a great community of life." Thousands of wilderness advocates wrote letters to Congress and the secretary of the Interior to protest damming of Echo Park.

Supporters of the dam were of course shocked that anyone would question the desirability of economic growth, but the new environmentalists managed to have Echo Park struck out of the project bill, and Congress stated its intention that "no dam or reservoir constructed under the authorization of the Act shall be within any Park or Monument." The bill became law in April 1956. The environmentalist victory spurred further efforts for wilderness protection and other issues of wildlands, open space and outdoor recreation.

A Wilderness Act, establishing a national system of wilderness protection, took another eight years but, in 1958, Congress was ready to create the National Outdoor Recreation Review Commission. A commission report led to the Land and Water Conservation Fund, which established for the first time a continuous source of revenue for the acquisition of federal outdoor recreation lands. The momentum of the incipient wilderness movement of the Fifties gathered strength in the Sixties and led to millions of wilderness acres set aside, including not only forests, streams and rivers, but also wetlands, swamps and pine barrens.

Water Quality Issues

Compared with dam-building under the Bureau of Reclamation, the federal government role in the water pollution field had been minuscule since the turn of the century. A few states had taken the lead in pollution technology development, notably at the Massachusetts Lawrence Experiment Station, and local and state boards of health were set up to regulate water pollution. The federal responsibility, however, was defined by three limited acts: the Rivers and Harbors Act of 1899, forbidding the discharge into waterways of anything hazardous to navigation; the Public Health Service Act of 1912, which authorized investigations of water pollution related to disease and public health; and the Oil Pollution Act of 1924, forbidding oil discharges into coastal waters. None of these laws was extensively utilized for water quality protection, nor were notable efforts made to enforce the laws.

During the 1930s, spurred by continued epidemics caused by known water-borne bacteria, New Dealers attempted to bring water pollution control under federal regulation through public works programs. Many states and cities were granted monies to construct waste treatment plants. This activity laid the groundwork for the Federal Water Pollution Control Act of 1948, legislation designed to expire in five years but later extended until 1956. The legislation stipulated that the primary responsibility for controlling water pollution rested with the states but gave the federal government an advisory and supportive role under the surgeon general of the U.S. Public Health Service. During this period, many civil and sanitary engineers, particularly those who had formed consulting firms (or those who were unemployed), joined forces with doctors, health reformers and conservationists to lobby for water quality protection by means of water treatment plants rather than the older dilution methods.

The federal government's charge was to develop comprehensive programs with the states to reduce pollution in interstate waters, to make loans for treatment plants, and to fund state and interstate water pollution control agencies. The federal public health agency also could take enforcement action against polluters, but only if a polluter in one state threatened the health or welfare of someone in another state and if action was requested by the governor of either state. Such cumbersome action was rarely attempted.

During the 1950s, more people began to notice water pollution from both municipal and industrial sources. Sickening odors and pollution slicks in rivers and streams and fish kills, obviously from industrial sources, forced beaches and recreation areas to close. Thus, there was only scattered opposition in Congress to the 1956 Federal Water Pollution Control Act amendments, and that was regarding the nature and the amount of financial assistance, not whether aid should be given. The Isaac Walton League and other sportsmen's groups kept the pressure on Congress to stop the increasing pollution of rivers that once had provided a rich harvest of fish.

The 1948 legislation was strengthened with more funds for the states, and the laws were made permanent. The approach remained cooperative with the states, but grants instead of loans were allotted for building municipal sewage treatment plants. A grants section, originally part of the 1948 bill, had been deleted because of widespread fear of inflation at the time. In the 1956 law, the Eisenhower administration strongly opposed the 10-year, $500 million grant program and considered a veto; however, Eisenhower's attempt to stop funding of the program failed because Democrats in Congress—overwhelmingly in favor of the program—outnumbered Republicans 2-to-1.

A Quickening Pace: The 1960s

Although the water pollution legislation during the '40s and '50s was a start toward federal cooperation in cleaning up the nation's waters, it hardly scratched the surface of the problem. Democratic President John F. Kennedy wasted no time in 1961 requesting an increase in waste treatment grants. With the strong support of his party, he quickly signed a bill that doubled the previous authorization and expanded the federal jurisdiction over both interstate and navigable waters, including their tributaries. At the same time, the bill enabled the U.S. attorney general to prosecute cases for the secretary of Health, Education and Welfare. Thus, virtually all U.S. waters were brought under the control of the federal government pollution control program, with the power of the attorney general behind it.

The unwillingness of either the federal government or the states to assume responsibility for stringent water quality standards was one reason for only building treatment plants and continuing to research water quality. Very few states developed pollution control programs, and none contained recommendations for enforcement. During the '40s and '50s, only a few pollution abatement cases reached the federal government.

These problems came to public view between 1959 and 1961 because of congressional field hearings and press reports. The Senate Select Committee on National Water Resources in 1959 and 1960 held hearings in 22 states, with dozens of witnesses calling their state's water pollution abatement efforts a dismal failure. These comments were noted in the leading newspapers and amplified by conservation groups and the League of Women Voters.

Widely publicized at the time were: pollution in the Passaic River that killed thousands of fish and threatened drinking water; sewage-contaminated water in Colorado; and an HEW report that warned southwestern Colorado and northwestern New Mexico that their Animas River water contained 40 percent to 160 percent above permissible levels of radioactive content. Futurist Alvin B. Toffler reported these episodes in *Reader's Digest* (March 1960). He concluded, "The time has come to mount an all-out effort to protect our water supply. Every citizen can play a vital part." *U.S. News and World Report* (Feb. 29, 1960) quoted conservationist Bernard Berger, warning that residential and industrial water pollution threatened the nation's future.

Sportsmen complained about rapidly depleting fish stocks in lakes and streams (e.g. Rusty Cowan, "Mystery of the Walleyes and the Water," *Sports Illustrated,* Nov. 6, 1961, among many such articles in most sports magazines). A Rachel Carson article in *Redbook* (August 1961), asked, "How Safe is Your Drinking Water?" Her monumental *The Silent Spring* was published in 1962 and reviewed by well-known naturalist Loren Eiseley in the *Saturday Review* (Sept. 29, 1962). Eiseley called the book a "relentless attack about human carelessness, greed and irresponsibility—an irresponsibility that has let loose upon man and the countryside a flood of dangerous chemicals." Another significant article, "Wastes Spoil Once Pure Sources," appeared in big-circulation *Life* magazine (Dec. 22, 1961). The National Wildlife Federation, the National Audubon Society and the Izaac Walton League mounted campaigns for a strong federal water bill.

The Water Quality Act of 1965

Congress held five public hearings for new water quality amendments, introduced by Sen. Edmund Muskie, beginning in 1963 through February 1965. Muskie proposed that a new division be created inside HEW and made responsible for water quality standards by approving the states' standards. His proposal worried the oil, chemical and pulp and paper industries, all of which said water standards would cost them money. Many state health and water agencies also spoke out against what they considered an infringement of traditional states' rights authority on pollution questions. Industry agreed that because the states were closer to the problem than federal authorities, they could better solve it. Neither states nor industry wanted a damper on inexpensive economic expansion.

Environmental organizations and such public-spirited groups as the League of Women Voters and the National Council of Mayors spoke in favor of the bill, although most wanted a stronger bill. Finally, after two years of inter-house sparring, Congress passed the Water Quality Act of 1965, giving the HEW secretary and his new Federal Water Pollution Control Administration the power to set standards in states that did not file a letter of intent to do so within a year. Grants for waste treatment plants doubled, and a new demonstration program investigated a combined system of storm and sanitary sewers.

The following year a presidential reshuffle sent the new agency to the Department of the Interior, with HEW keeping only health-related issues of water pollution. At earlier hearings and in the press, there had been a great debate over the need for an environmental agency. Industry and state agencies said they had built up good rapport with the Public Health Service and insisted a new agency was not needed. Environmentalists and their allies responded that health personnel were not sensitive to ecological, recreational, and aesthetic concerns and, furthermore, had not proven adequately aggressive in pursuing water quality standards with the states. The concerns of the new environmentalists went beyond efficiency, and emphasized environmental amenities and responsiveness to broader public interests over matters of individual health.

The 1965 act set up for the first time a federal agency with the specific charge of water pollution control. For the first time the federal government proposed to establish and enforce, with the states, water quality standards. The agency's move to the Department of Interior was intended to enable the federal government to carry out the provision of standards more independently. The primary reason President Lyndon Johnson agreed to the transfer of authority was the influence of Stewart Udall, a strong environmentalist and then secretary of the Interior. Of course, the issue was far from settled. Many sportsmen and conservation groups complained that the states continued to drag on major pollution problems.

Many in Congress wanted pollution control responsibility in the hands of regional watershed agencies rather than the states. Muskie fought off these proposals, considering them too radical, but organized a coalition that pushed for more government construction grants.

Congress then passed the 1966 Clean Waters Act, which also amended the 1924 Oil Pollution Act.

Oil Spill Problems

The 1966 law, mainly because of the influence of the oil industry and Rep. James Wright of Texas, redefined the term "discharge" to require that the discharge of oil had to be "grossly negligent or willful" before the government could bring suit against the polluter. Since willful negligence is hard to prove, enforcement against oil polluters became extremely difficult.

During 1967, a number of oil spills received wide publicity. The most notorious was the *Torrey Canyon* spill of 119,000 tons of crude near Great Britain. Also receiving publicity were: 10 miles of the York River in Virginia and several beaches fouled by oil, 30 miles of Cape Cod National Seashore, and a spill of six million gallons of diverse petroleum products near Wake Island in the mid-Pacific.

The largest and most infamous spill occurred in California in late 1969 in the Santa Barbara Channel. As a drillstem was withdrawn from a drill platform six miles off shore, more than 250 million gallons of crude oil escaped, disfiguring a huge section of coastline. More than 800 square miles of ocean were covered with the sticky, black mixture and thousands of sea birds were killed, as were several California gray whales in the middle of their northern migration to Alaska. Once again, thousands protested what they perceived as minimal governmental effort to protect the natural environment.

Finally, in June 1969, the Cuyahoga River near Cleveland, Ohio, burst into flames because of an unidentified oil discharge of thousands of gallons. The stench and filth of the river had long been the butt of local jokes—among them that it should be declared a fire hazard. But the damage the fire caused was no joke and it spurred more people into action. The press began to cover environmental issues with new zeal. Everyone seemed interested in the environment. Environmentalists pointed out that millions of gallons of oil are discharged into U.S. waters every year, with no adequate controls placed on the polluters.

The 1967 oil disasters precipitated a popular mandate for Congress to develop new amendments to cover oil accidents and discharges. But throughout 1968, until adjournment, Congress failed to pass legislation acceptable both to Muskie environmentalists and industry lobbyists. Environmentalists turned up the heat on Congress during 1969, especially after the Santa Barbara blowout and the Cuyahoga River fire.

The new bill covered oil and thermal pollution, acid mine drainage, pollution and pollutants leading to eutrophication. Ship owners were liable for oil spills up to $14 million and, there was no limit on the owner's liability if the spill involved willful negligence or misconduct. Permits were required for any facilities that might pollute waterways, certifying that the facility would not violate water quality standards.

By 1970, after passage of the National Environmental Policy Act and the national celebration of Earth Day, public opinion against pollution, particularly water pollution, had risen to an all-time high. As early as Feb. 10, President Richard Nixon, who had been advised that his chief

Democratic political rival would be environmentalist Sen. Edmund Muskie, recommended to Congress new effluent standards for cities and industries.

Muskie's committee began work on a new bill in early 1971. The new national goals, called "policy" in the Senate bill, were to be that "the discharge of pollutants into the navigable waters be eliminated by 1985." Further, it said: "Wherever attainable, an interim goal of water quality which provides for the protection and propagation of fish, shellfish and wildlife and provides for recreation in and on the water be achieved by 1981."

Besides authorizing more than $24 billion in construction grants over three years, the new bill required a three-fold approach to water quality: "technology-based" standards; "receiving water" standards; and discharge permits for effluents directly discharged into surface waters. The "technology-based" standards was a new legislative approach. Municipal treatment plants had to have secondary treatment facilities built before 1977; industrial sources were required to install the "best practicable technology" (BPT) available, also by 1977, and upgrade them to "best available technology" (BAT) economically achievable by 1983. BPT technology represented the known treatment methods already in use for conventional pollutants; i.e., biochemical oxygen demand (BOD), total suspended solids—non-filterable (TSS), fecal coliform bacteria, pH (acidity or alkalinity). BAT refers to the newer treatment technologies needed to control unconventional toxic pollutants, or more advanced techniques for conventional effluents.

In these sections, the act was "technology-forcing" in that it gradually mandated more and more limited discharge levels and assumed that technology would develop in time to achieve the goal of no discharges by 1985. Adopting a new approach to water cleanup was necessary because of the difficulty in getting the states to develop adequate "receiving water" standards, and especially to enforce them. Environmentalists believed that streams were getting dirtier, not cleaner, under the 1965 legislation. They were convinced that "technology-forcing" standards, with federal oversight and enforcement powers, would push industry to make pollution-control advances faster and more effectively than state-initiated standards based on gradations of cleanliness.

Yet, the states were still required to develop a "water quality standard" for each water body within their boundaries, indicating a limit for each pollutant at "designated water use," e.g., drinking water, fisheries, industrial water supplies. These standards were to go beyond the technological approach of the federal requirements because they considered public health and ecological protection according to "designated water use."

The act required every public and private facility that discharges wastes directly into U.S. waters to have an NPDES (National Pollutant Discharge Elimination Systems) permit, issued through an EPA regional office. Moreover, the act instructed the newly established Environmental Protection Agency to make up a list of "toxic" chemicals and to develop effluent standards for each of the chemicals, allowing an "ample margin of safety." Industrial dischargers were to be allowed one year to come into compliance with the standards, as they were promulgated by the agency. Enforcement for all of the provisions of the bill was local, state and federal in scope, but the EPA had the authority to veto individual permits and the EPA administrator could sue polluters. A provision in the 1970 law allowed citizen suits against violators.

On the day before adjournment, President Nixon announced his veto, which was overridden by a wide majority. Thus did the Federal Water Pollution Control Act, among the most sweeping, innovative environmental legislation ever considered, become enacted into law. The history has been eventful.

More Wilderness Issues

While the League of Women Voters and environmental groups were waging their clean water crusade during the 1960s, much related environmental work also was occurring. The Sierra Club waged campaigns on wilderness issues, and more battles were being fought over urban developments. Events throughout the decade led to the National Environmental Policy Act as well as Earth Day in 1970.

When the Bureau of Reclamation unveiled its Pacific Southwest Water Plan in 1963, at the same time as the Wilderness Act's controversies were beginning to untangle, wilderness advocates were horrified to learn dams were planned for Bridge Canyon and Marble Canyon, both inside the Grand Canyon. Just upstream from the Grand Canyon on the Colorado River, water was beginning to fall in behind the new Glen Canyon Dam, covering a wilderness of breathtaking beauty, all the way to Rainbow Bridge National Monument, which supposedly had been protected under the Colorado River Storage Project Act.

An enraged David Brower, head of the Sierra Club, and a small army of supporters took out full-page ads in newspapers with such headlines as: "Should We Also Flood The Sistine Chapel So Tourists Can Get Nearer The Ceiling?" and "Now Only You Can Save The Grand Canyon From Being Flooded . . . For Profit." This ad concluded, "There is only one simple, incredible issue here. This time it's the Grand Canyon they want to flood. *The Grand Canyon.*"

All the forces of wilderness organizations were mobilized—tens of thousands, perhaps hundreds of thousands of letters of protest, telegrams, phone calls to Washington and bumper stickers. Newspaper and magazine articles and books were published in an overwhelming display of political force. Even ultraconservative Rep. Wayne Aspinall, chairman of the House Interior and Insular Affairs Committee who fought to keep the dams, could not get enough support to stop a 1968 bill that deleted both Grand Canyon dams from the Pacific Southwest Water Plan. The bill went further, prohibiting construction of any dam within the entire Grand Canyon. A few days after that bill passed in October 1968, President Johnson signed a bill establishing the National Wild and Scenic Rivers System.

The National Environmental Policy Act

Not long after Richard Nixon became president in 1969, he reportedly read a poll showing that protection of the environment was the third most-important issue to American voters, behind the Vietnam War and jobs. So he instructed a staff member to prepare an environmental program and in 1970 gave the first of two environmental messages to Congress. Meantime, at the end of 1969, Congress passed the National Environmental Policy Act, which redirected the priorities of the federal government to:

1. Fulfill the responsibilities of each generation as a trustee of the environment for succeeding generations;

2. Assure for all Americans safe, healthful, productive and aesthetically and culturally pleasing surroundings;

3. Attain the widest range of beneficial uses of the environment without degradation, risk to health or safety, or other undesirable and unintended consequences;

4. Preserve important historic, cultural and natural aspects of our national heritage and maintain, wherever possible, an environment that supports diversity and variety of individual choice;

5. Achieve a balance between population and resource use, which will permit high standards of living and a wide sharing of life's amenities;

6. Enhance the quality of renewable resources and approach the maximum attainable recycling of depletable resources.

These generalized aspirations of the landmark law have found their way into many court cases, but the more powerful lever of the law in Section 102(2)(c) mandated environmental impact statements for all federal projects. An environmental review process by government agencies was required to evaluate the impacts of such federal projects as new highways, power plants, coal mines and oil rigs. The U.S. Forest Service and the Army Corps of Engineers were required to hire staff to evaluate environmental impacts of agency projects. Then a number of states passed their own versions of NEPA. Within a few years, the law was used to attempt to stop the Alaskan pipeline and many dams and other development projects.

The Environmental Protection Agency

During Nixon's first year, a blue-ribbon presidential council on governmental reorganization was set up to promote efficiency in federal agencies. The council began its work on natural resource programs in early 1970, and by late spring made its recommendations. Proposals included forming a new agency called the Department of Natural Resources and the Environment, which would deal with natural resources, pollution control, public lands and energy departments and programs. The reorganization touched many agencies, especially the Department of the Interior, and it was expected the new agency would be housed there.

The reorganization plan caused jockeying and politicking because some departments would lose and others would gain influence, but in the end President Nixon created the Environmental Protection Agency as a separate entity. Initially, EPA had divisions of water pollution, air pollution, pesticides, solid wastes and radiation.

Not all of the natural resource or environmental programs were placed in the EPA. Because of the special friendship that Secretary of Commerce Maurice Stans enjoyed with Nixon, several programs were organized into a National Oceanic and Atmospheric Administration in his department. Secretary of Agriculture Clifford Hardin managed to keep the Forest Service in his department. Secretary of the Interior Walter Hickel, who had criticized the Nixon administration for its handling of a war protest at Kent State University, lost the new agency as well as water-pollution control programs.

Given all the political maneuvering at its birth, and that it began its life without the tradition or support of a parent department, it is amazing that EPA was able to survive and be effective. That it grew in strength is a testimony to the ability and charisma of its first hard-working director, William D. Ruckelshaus, a committed staff, the support of powerful members of Congress and a persistently active environmental movement.

Clean Air Legislation

The movement for clean air had been developing momentum at the same time as other environmental activity. But environmental legislation seems to be enacted only as crises occur, and it was difficult to see the effects of invisible toxic pollutants in the air.

For most of the nation's history, polluted air simply seemed to be a necessary inconvenience and a cost of local prosperity. If you were a white-collar worker in Pittsburgh during the 1940s, you simply took an extra shirt with you to work, knowing the one you put on in the morning would be gray by noon. You got used to washing the grime off your face in the morning in the summer because you had to open the window at night when local factories blew out their smokestacks, and coal-burning locomotives passed your neighborhood.

These nuisances were either ignored or addressed in some feeble way by city and county regulations. Chicago and Cincinnati had smoke regulations as early as 1881, and Albany County, New York, wrote a smoke law in 1913. Ohio passed a state law in 1897 to limit smoke emissions from steam boilers. In 1907, the International Association for the Prevention of Smoke, later to become the Air Pollution Control Association (APCA), was established to lobby for smoke-prevention regulations and controls.

New, efficient boiler designs that reduced black smoke and saved money for fuel were developed during the 1940s. The designs were phased into many factories, but because boilers can last for decades and few if any regulations required the switch to newer models, progress was slow. Meantime, the first signs of more toxic air pollution from smog and fog were emerging.

In 1948, a temperature inversion (an unusual meteorological occurrence in which a layer of warmer air overlies a heavier cooler layer that holds down pollution) lasted eight days in the tiny town of Donora, Pennsylvania. Twenty people died and hundreds were hospitalized. Four years later, a widely publicized "killer fog" in London was responsible for about 4,000 deaths. As urbanization crowded more and more people into smaller areas, air circulation decreased, temperatures increased and pollution from the cities could not be easily dispersed by natural processes. The early smog incidents resulted mostly from burning coal in home heaters and in factories.

In 1949, the U.S. Public Health Service reported on the Donora incident, recommending that the federal government research the nature of air pollution. Several congressional resolutions supported the recommendation after the London "fog" episode brought a renewal of the effort. Finally, in 1955, seven years after Donora, a bill was passed authorizing a federal program of research, training and demonstration. The program was renewed in 1959 for four years.

Throughout this period, most legislators and bureaucrats considered air pollution a local problem. Davies (1977, p. 45) quotes an HEW official telling the Senate Public Works Committee that "instances of troublesome interstate air pollution are few in number;" and an internal Bureau of the Budget memorandum that "unlike water pollution, air pollution . . . is essentially a local problem."

A few hard-hit metropolitan regions did act on their own. Los Angeles County, for example, set up an air pollution emergency plan in 1955 with a "first alert" when ozone levels reach .5 parts per million (ppm), and a "second alert" when the level reaches 1.0 ppm. Later the county set up a "forecast system." Also in 1955, the California Legislature created the first of its pollution control districts in the San Francisco Bay Area to monitor stationary sources of air pollution; and in 1961, set up a program to control auto exhaust under the Motor Vehicle Pollution Control Board. A few other cities and states began to act on the air pollution problem, but minimal efforts were made either locally or nationally to work toward a comprehensive program.

However, during the 1960 presidential campaign a number of big-city Democratic legislators reported their constituents' environmental concerns to candidate John F. Kennedy. Then, as president, he called for a federal air pollution control program in 1961 and again in 1962, when a number of air pollution bills were introduced. The president's bill authorized, under the Public Health Service of HEW, more grants for research and financial help to state and local air pollution agencies, for interstate air pollution studies and for enforcement of interstate air pollution along the lines of water pollution laws. President Kennedy was assassinated before his Clean Air Act was passed at the end of 1963.

Sen. Muskie took up the task of further air pollution regulation with hearings around the country during 1964. By this time, most residents of large cities were aware of auto emissions' role in air pollution and clamored for controls; some testimony complained about the burning of garbage and trash as well. Muskie soon introduced a bill defining federal standards and authorized enforcement of auto emissions; the bill also dealt with solid waste disposal.

HEW, having followed the nationwide Muskie hearings, was also ready to present an auto emissions proposal to President Johnson, but Johnson wanted the auto industry to comply voluntarily. HEW relayed the president's objections to the Senate subcommittee considering the bill. The outrage expressed by the country's major newspapers, environmental groups and political organizations caused Johnson to reverse his decision and to support the Muskie bill. In fact, the auto industry wanted federal, not state, standards to incorporate into their auto designs but lobbied for weaker provisions than the original proposals. Soon after the bill was passed in 1965, the secretary of HEW agreed to have the same emission standards that California developed for 1967-model cars applied nationwide, beginning with the 1968 models.

The Air Quality Act of 1967

In 1966, New York City suffered a widely reported temperature inversion for four days. Hundreds of people reported dizziness, nausea and eye irritation; many were hospitalized for respiratory and heart ailments. Eighty people died.

A month later, HEW's third National Conference on Air Pollution met in Washington. Secretary of HEW John Gardner gave the keynote, emphasizing the need for national air quality standards. The agency proposed legislation for regional control agencies as well as national standards. Within another month, in January 1967, President Johnson proposed new legislation that incorporated national standards and regional monitoring of "airsheds" financed by the federal government, along with federal aid for auto inspection and research.

The bill generated heated opposition from industry spokesmen during the hearings on national standards for selected industries, especially when they found out the regional organizations were to develop their own standards. The question of sulfur standards raised the ire of congressmen from coal-producing Eastern states worried that high-sulfur coal would become unsellable, and Johnson's bill was modified considerably.

Sen. Muskie followed the precedent of the 1965 Water Quality Act, which required the states to write letters of intent within 90 days and to establish standards for specific pollutants within another 180 days as applicable in air quality control regions designated by the secretary of HEW. Another lively debate ensued over whether California would be permitted to have more stringent auto emissions standards than federal air quality standards. California legislators and their many supporters won the floor fight, and the Air Quality Act of 1967 was passed. Although the secretary of HEW was given the power to review and modify state standards, the agency was only to look into the desirability of establishing its own national emission standards from all sources of air pollution. The high-sulfur coal states won the first round of many legislative battles, but eventually the argument prevailed that without federally mandated air quality and emission standards, states would lower standards to attract "dirty" industries.

With the states' lack of response on air quality standards, history repeated itself. By the end of 1970, HEW had yet to approve a state implementation plan; indeed, only 21 plans had even been submitted. Public opinion on environmental issues, however, was at an all-time high—with many news stories on oil pollution and polluted cities. *Life* magazine suggested in 1970 that probably by 1980 people in the cities would have to wear gas masks or die because of smog inversions. It was a time of great suspicion of industry in general, and the auto industry in particular. In 1969, the Justice Department began an investigation to determine whether the automobile manufacturers had conspired to prevent an air pollution control device program from being established. The consent decree implied that the big three auto companies (General Motors, Ford, Chrysler) had attempted to do so.

When the 1967 authorizations expired in 1970, environmentalist forces began to gear up to close the loopholes in the new law. President

Nixon had realized the political importance of the issue and wanted to take it from his potential rival for the presidency in 1972, Sen. Muskie. In his major speeches during the year, Nixon sounded like a lifelong environmentalist. He began to assert the need for national emission standards, including for new or hazardous air pollution sources. Earth Day, celebrated in April 1970, added the clout of hundreds of thousands of letters to Washington in favor of stronger environmental regulations.

The 1970 Clean Air Act was similar to the 1967 bill except stronger. Auto emissions were to be cut 90 percent by 1975 compared with 1970 emissions; national air quality standards were to be established; and the states were to have their implementation plans in place by 1975; citizens' suits were permitted in the same manner as in water quality legislation; and appropriations for research and local air quality agencies reached a record high. In general, the 1970 act continued the federal-state partnership idea. The federal government maintained its oversight role and established minimum standards for ambient air quality. The states could supplement the federal regulations with their own rules if they desired. Few foresaw the difficulties to come.

The 1970s

The Seventies brought frustration and dismay not only to environmentalists, policy makers and agency personnel but also to a wide variety of industry and citizen groups. Enforcing the law was extraordinarily difficult because of the complicated history of environmental regulation and the jealous protection of local governing rights. Very often the states, which had the power to enforce the laws, delayed setting up a suitable structure to do so. And because it is so difficult to determine precise standards to protect human health and the environment, the regulations themselves have allowed firms to request delays or challenge the standards. The inflexible time schedule required for industry implementation of rules lent credence to the requests for delays. Economic recessions supported industry claims that the regulations placed undue hardship on the private sector. Public opinion itself became very fickle when Americans were asked to change irresponsible environmental behavior, particularly when it involved the automobile.

The effort to cut auto emissions 90 percent by 1975 well illustrates the difficulties of the decade. The act allowed carmakers to request a one-year delay in implementing emissions standards if they had made "good faith" efforts yet could not develop the necessary pollution control technologies. In 1972 public hearings, the auto companies called catalytic converters ineffective and unsafe if they caught fire. Other witnesses testified they had used converters for thousands of miles safely and effectively. Some witnesses said the devices caused excess gas consumption; others denied it. A few feared a strong regulation would shut down auto production.

According to former Deputy EPA Administrator John Quarles (1976, p. 184), it was David Hawkins, an attorney from the Natural Resources Defense Council, who provided the convincing argument—that for all their protestations the auto companies did not present firm evidence that they could not meet the 1975 deadline. Knowledgeable about recent technological improvements, EPA Administrator William Ruckelshaus denied the applications for the delay.

The automakers then filed suit in the U.S. Court of Appeals to overturn EPA's decision, and early in 1973 the court agreed with the auto companies that economic factors were not given enough weight at the hearing. At new hearings it became clear that the technology was adequate and safe, but it was not certain that the auto firms could gear up adequately on the massive scale necessary. This time Ruckelshaus granted the delay.

Later in 1973, amid war with Israel, Arab nations placed an embargo on oil exports to the United States. Congress passed emergency legislation to cut energy consumption and expand energy supply. Power plants were required to switch from oil to more polluting coal. At the same time, large coal strip-mining operations sprang up in Western states. The Energy Supply and Environmental Coordination Act of 1974 temporarily suspended emission limits of stationary sources, including power plants. Public support of environmental rules began to fade in the wake of the energy crisis, gasoline shortages, high prices and economic recession.

The catalytic converter got another setback in 1975 when a study indicated that the converters could produce potentially dangerous sulfates, which could interact with water vapor in the atmosphere. Congress mandated that final auto pollution standards be reached by the time the 1978 models were marketed. At the same time, the EPA administrator lifted the requirement for the desulfurization of gasoline because of rapidly rising prices and continuing inflation. Critics began to mount a campaign claiming that high prices were the result of pollution control costs.

Then in early 1979 the EPA decreed that the permissible amount of ozone in the air may rise to 0.12 part per million parts of air, up from 0.08 part per million, the earlier standard. EPA Administrator Douglas Costle said the change was "based on a careful evaluation of medical and scientific evidence." Immediately the American Petroleum Institute filed a suit, contending that the rule was more stringent than necessary, and the Environmental Defense Fund and other groups claimed the new standard would seriously affect people's health.

Despite the cooling of environmental enthusiasm during the 1970s, Congress passed 1977 Clean Air Act Amendments, which attempted once again to obtain compliance from polluters. New "non-compliance penalties," equal to the costs of cleanup, were enacted upon those who would not install necessary control equipment. Permit fees were to be charged by the states as well, and state boards were to include a majority of their members from people who represent the public interest, i.e., those who do not derive a significant portion of their income from anyone subject to the permits or enforcement orders. States also could adopt more stringent emission limitations than federal standards required, and especially were guaranteed the right to prevent significant deterioration of state air resources.

In general, the EPA played research, advisory and watchdog roles over the 247 air quality control regions, reviewing state implementation plans, overseeing monitoring and penalizing such stationary sources as power plants and highly polluting industries. At the same time, the agency struggled to get the auto industry to meet national emissions deadlines.

Even during the difficult Seventies, much environmental work was accomplished: inventories of polluting industries, which were monitored and forced to develop pollution control plans by certain deadlines; primary ambient air quality standards to protect human health (sulfur oxides, particulate matter, carbon monoxide, photochemical oxidents, hydrocarbons, nitrogen dioxide) were established as well as secondary ambient standards to protect property and the environment—crops, plants, wildlife, soil, water. Separate standards were set for hazardous air pollutants—asbestos, mercury, vinyl chloride and beryllium and new ones such as benzene during the 1980s.

Clean Water Act of 1977

The Federal Water Pollution Control Act of 1972, retroactively renamed the Clean Water Act, was subject to the same problems of non-compliance, lack of enforcement and delay in meeting deadlines as the Clean Air Act. One difference was that the water quality legislation had been much longer in the making, but intergovernmental cooperation and other factors of environmental legislation made it subject to the same kinds of obstacles as the Clean Air Act.

Another difference in the Clean Water Act was Congress' deliberate effort to require dischargers to limit their pollutants in two steps upgrading pollution control technologies at the designated deadlines of 1977 and 1983. The first water quality standard was to include the *average* of the best existing performance of plants within each category of industry. However, the second standard imposed the best performance level of all dischargers in the industry. The first standard required the EPA administrator to perform a cost-benefit analysis to determine whether the costs of treatment were justified by the quality of effluent control. The second standard did not make this requirement since the goal of the act was to achieve zero pollution discharge by 1983, presumably at any cost. The agency assumed that if some dischargers were polluting at very low levels, the technology exists and others could incorporate it into their operations.

By 1977, at least 16 percent of the major non-municipal dischargers did not meet the first step water quality standard, and about 53 percent of the publicly owned treatment plants failed to meet the deadline. Congress attempted to introduce some flexibility into the deadline structure in its 1977 Amendments to the Clean Water Act.

The 1977 Amendments to the Clean Water Act first links compliance deadlines for publicly owned treatment works into federal funding for secondary treatment facilities; a federal court earlier had maintained that the law held public treatment work deadlines whether or not they received federal funds. The amendments further authorize the EPA administrator to extend the deadline if the discharger has made a good-faith effort to comply with the law; the earlier law stipulated an inflexible deadline and it was upheld by the court. And, finally, in response to court cases brought by U.S. Steel and Republic Steel, the act gave the administrator veto power over state-issued NPDES permits whether or not effluent guidelines formally had been issued. The question was whether industry had to meet congressionally mandated environmental deadlines or could fall back on weaker state standards.

Toxic Pollutants

The most controversial aspect of the 1977 amendments dealt with the mandate EPA was given in 1972 to develop a list of chemicals it considered "toxic," then within six months establish standards for the chemicals. Dischargers of the toxic pollutants were given a year to meet the requirements.

However, the agency was not able to promulgate the list, not only because of the massive proportions of the undertaking but also because the scientific information about the health effects of the chemicals was either unavailable or too complex to translate simply into regulations. Industry and environmental groups provided the EPA with studies that canceled each other out. Realizing it would be impossible to base their rules on "toxicity" to human health, the agency concentrated on the actual discharges of six suspect chemicals.

In 1973 and 1974, the Natural Resources Defense Council sued the EPA administrator four times to force the agency to come up with the list and standards. Finally, in 1975, the cases were consolidated in Judge Thomas Flannery's U.S. District Court, and the EPA offered to settle the suit with the environmental group through a consent decree. The parties in the case negotiated for several months over what constituted a "toxic" pollutant and came up with a list of 65 chemicals, now know as the "priority pollutants," derived from dozens of agency and private sources. The list was not compiled chemical by chemical, based on a consensus of toxic specialists, but was haggled over starting with several hundred and cut down to a number the NRDC felt the EPA could enforce.

At the same time, 21 major industrial categories were selected as "primary industries" to be regulated in intervals until the end of 1979. Since agreement regarding health and aquatic effects had been impossible to reach, the EPA was to concentrate on the "best available" treatment technology for standard-setting, based on availability and cost. Meantime, the EPA would develop a database of information about the priority pollutants, from which numerical, ambient criteria could be derived so that specific standards could be put in place by the states in furure years. The consent decree took EPA off the hook in its inability to develop standards for toxic pollutants, but did not change the way the Clean Water Act was to work.

The Flannery Decree (of the NRDC court case) had been signed by the time the Clean Water Act Amendments were passed in 1977. The best available technology requirements were already in the law, to be enforced for conventional pollutants by 1983. It was generally assumed by the committee that drafted the 1977 amendments that the Flannery Decree would be sufficient to control toxic pollutants as well (cf. Banks, 1984, pp. 39-43).

In 1979, in response to the amendments, court decisions and evolving EPA policy, the EPA recodified the National Pollutant Discharge Elimination System (NPDES) permit system, under which clean-up requirements are given to individual discharge sources through the permits. The purpose of most environmental regulation had been to establish uniform, nationwide requirements for categories of pollutants. Variances were given for special reasons and for special periods of time while dischargers attempted to comply with the regulations.

Under the new NPDES rules, EPA expanded the applicability of a special variance—the "fundamentally different factors" (FDF) variance. This variance authorized the EPA to establish different effluent limits for a particular facility if factors relating to that facility were "fundamentally different" from the factors EPA had considered when developing that industrial category's uniform effluent limit regulations.

The new FDF variance authorization was applied to pretreatment standards for industries that discharged wastes into municipal treatment works, and to the next set of requirements for direct dischargers of toxic pollutants, i.e. those who were to comply with the "best available technology" requirement. What followed was a tie-up of agency personnel on case-by-case determinations of effluent requirements and more serious delays in application of the requirements. Industry again wanted variances for what it considered the economic burdens of the requirements, and began to look to a friendlier federal administration. Their hopes were not long in becoming fulfilled.

The Reagan Administration

After Ronald Reagan was elected president in 1980 and he began to choose his cabinet, a headline in *Science* magazine read, "Environmentalists tremble." They had reason to. The new Secretary of the Interior James Watt immediately disclosed plans to develop the resources of the public lands of the West and the oil offshore. And new EPA Administrator Anne M. Gorsuch (later Burford) proposed a budget about one-fourth the size of the Carter administration's. Over them all, at the center of power at the Office of Management and Budget, David Stockman claimed regulatory oversight and said he would examine the cost-benefit consequences of regulations. In his widely publicized "Dunkirk" planning document for the newly elected president, Stockman lost no time attacking what he called "burdensome" rules on carbon monoxide, industrial boiler emissions, hazardous waste and toxic waste, and especially the Clean Air Act Amendments of 1977, which he characterized as "staggering excess built upon dubious scientific and economic premises." (*Washington Post*, Dec. 14, 1980, C5)

Simultaneously, President Reagan fired the entire 45-member staff of the Council on Environmental Quality, the executive oversight organization created by the National Environmental Policy Act that prepares legislation for the president, to make room for a tiny staff of about a dozen. The president had no plans for environmental legislation beyond minimizing the cost of current legislation. In Reagan's opinion, environmental protection cost too much, and it wasn't his issue.

Gorsuch began her term by dismantling the enforcement division, then announced that the White House wanted a weakened Clean Air Act, including a two-thirds reduction of the program to prevent deterioration of air, a rollback of emission standards for new automobiles and lifting of some deadlines for achieving clean air. Next, the administrator said the EPA would no longer support nationally uniform, technology-forcing controls that amounted to "treatment for the sake of treatment." Decisions were to be based on comparisons of the cost of treatment against cleanup benefits, largely left in the hands of state and local agencies.

In practice, the "best available technologies" Flannery consent decree was tossed aside, for a new pattern that would allow industries to retain their "best practicable" technologies and phase into ambient, geographically limited (on a case-by-case NPDES permit) regulations. In defense of its new policy, the EPA cited an agency-funded study by JRB Associates (McLean, Va. 1981), which found that BPT-level technologies can remove about 70 percent of toxic pollutants from primary industries. At the same time, Gorsuch asked the federal court to let the EPA out of its five-year-old consent decree with the Natural Resources Defense Council on the ground that under its smaller budget it couldn't afford it. Judge Flannery did not accede to the request but an aggressive OMB, a shake-up of agency organization and morale along with politics as usual on Capitol Hill, held up new amendments to the Clean Water Act for more than six years.

The Clean Water Act controversy was an old one. Because local industries and agencies had stalled for a decade, environmentalists remained unconvinced that local "receiving water" standards would clean up the nation's waters. For them it was far better to demand best technological standards (BAT) than leave the matter to local politics and the standards that might not be enforceable. Furthermore, environmentalists wanted standards that would make the water "really" clean, not just adequately clean, i.e., clean enough for people to swim in and for fish to stay free from buildups of toxic pollutants.

Environmental Problems and the Media

During the last years of the Carter administration in the late 1970s, new environmental problems began to surface and absorb the nation's attention. The first national exposure came in the summer of 1978, with heavy media coverage of disturbing health effects of chemicals seeping into homes around the old Love Canal in Niagara Falls, N.Y. Local health officials found higher-than-normal rates of miscarriages, birth defects and liver ailments among the residents. The abandoned, never-completed canal had been used for chemical-waste disposal in the 1940s by Hooker Chemicals & Plastics Corporation, which subsequently gave the filled-in site to the Niagara Falls Board of Education for one dollar. A school was built. Families settled in around it.

In August 1978, the New York health department stated publicly that the lives of Love Canal residents were endangered. President Carter declared a national emergency. The government agreed to buy 240 homes within the "inner ring." By the time President Reagan came into office in 1981, more than $30 million had been spent by the local, state and federal governments on clean-up and relocating residents. Many more worried locals wanted to get out of the area as well, and a national controversy developed over the health studies done on the residents.

This episode was just one of hundreds of public outcries over toxic-waste dumping and groundwater contamination that have remained on newspaper front pages and prime-time television. A number of television documentaries on the environment and health were produced in 1979 with titles that suggest their content: "A Plague on Our Children" (*Nova,* WGBH Boston); "Serpent's Fruits" (WNET NY); "The Politics of Poison" (KRON San Francisco). *Time* (Sept. 22, 1980) presented a lengthy cover story entitled "The Poisoning of America" about the environmental and health effects of omnipresent toxic chemicals.

Most of the media coverage of environmental pollution quoted such scientists as Dr. Samuel Epstein, who wrote *The Politics of Cancer* in 1978 and Harvard biologist Dr. Matthew Meselson, interviewed in "A Plague on Our Children," to point out the connection between cancer and toxic pollutants. The discussion had been alive as early as 1976, when *Newsweek* (Jan. 26, 1976) reviewed research done at HEW and the National Cancer Institute on the causes of cancer that indicated higher rates of cancer occur in petrochemical industrial zones. Another indicator occurred June 22, 1976, when Leslie Stahl stated in a CBS Report Special: "It's now known that increased contamination of our air, water, and food is contributing to our soaring cancer rates." A few years later, even Jane Fonda would say in her *Jane Fonda's Workout Book* (1981, p. 238), "Cancer is a byproduct of the petrochemical age." The idea had become conventional wisdom.

In 1979, 17,000 rusty steel drums were found leaking chemicals in an open field in "the Valley of the Drums," Kentucky, and an EPA survey disclosed hundreds of similar problems around the country. In 1983, the entire town of Times Beach, Missouri, had to be closed and bought out by the EPA for $30 million because dioxin had contaminated a mixture of oil and industrial wastes that were sprayed near the town in the early 1970s. Many other unpaved roads around the country regularly had been sprayed with oils saturated with highly toxic polychlorinated byphenyls (PCBs), toxic metals and sometimes dioxin as a way to dispose of waste oils.

The chemical revolution of the 20th century that introduced so many home and personal conveniences—textiles, drugs, steel, papers, electronic equipment, appliances, colors and cultural artifacts—brought hundreds of different toxic wastes in garbage and hazardous waste dumps, in underground storage drums near neighborhood factories, all located near somebody's back yard. At the 1.2 million gasoline stations occupying every nook and cranny of the country, hundreds of thousands of underground storage containers were rusting and leaking; the tanks have a 15-year life span and 350,000 were projected to be leaking by 1987. Eventually, these toxic chemicals (300 in gasoline) and wastes found their way into groundwater, or were spread or illegally dumped on back roads, or mishandled and some exploded near family homes.

Though factory fires and explosions once were relegated to the back pages of newspapers and left out of TV coverage, the media began to report these events. One such example occurred in July 1980 in northern Meade County, Kentucky, near Louisville. TV audiences around the country watched black clouds of burning vinyl chloride billowing from 10 railroad tank cars. About 10,000 people were evacuated from the area, which was sealed off for days.

Another example indicates how huge numbers of people have been drawn into the problem of dumping of hazardous wastes. By the end of the 1970s, through the persistence of environmental groups, the media and a personal riverboat campaign by folksinger Pete Seeger, the millions of people who live along the Hudson River suddenly became aware that their river, so rich in cultural history and scenic beauty, was dying because of decades of dumping by hundreds of factories and municipalities. What seemed to catalyze action was the discovery that more than 1.5 million pounds of non-biodegradable PCBs were poisoning the fish.

By the early 1980s, dozens of wells throughout California, Arizona and Washington were found to be contaminated with high levels of carbon tetrachloride, trichloroethylene (TCE), both suspected carcinogens, and other chemicals, pesticides and industrial cleaning agents or degreasers. Most of the contaminated wells were near garbage or hazardous waste dumps, abandoned dumps or factories that stored wastes on their own sites.

These problems, plus scandals at the top of the Environmental Protection Agency that eventually caused the administrator to resign, brought public shock over new federal environmental policies that threatened a decade of environmental activity. Environmental organizations suddenly were infused with new members and money to fight the administration.

In June 1981, a Gallup Poll for *Newsweek* concluded: "A large majority of the public believes that government regulation and requirements are worth the extra costs they add to products and services. Three-quarters believe that it is possible to maintain strong economic growth and still maintain high environmental standards." (Cf. R.C. Mitchell in Vig and Kraft 1984, p. 56) A *New York Times/CBS News* poll published Oct. 4, 1981, confirmed that 67 percent of the people polled said they wanted environmental laws maintained even if the economy suffers. A September 1981 Harris Poll said 80 percent of the people opposed relaxing pollution control.

Then in 1982 a Harris survey showed that 95 percent of a national sample considered "disposal of hazardous waste" a "serious problem" and 93 percent thought that "pollution of lakes of lakes and rivers by toxic substances from factories" also constituted a "serious problem." Furthermore, the public was beginning to grasp the underpinnings of the environmental movement, as can be seen in a 1982 *Research and Forecasts for the Continental Group* survey. Seventy percent of the people interviewed said they were hurt by the recession, yet 60 percent believed pollution to be one of the most important problems facing the nation. Eighty-four percent of the sample agreed with the statement, "The balance of nature is very delicate and easily upset by human activities," and 76 percent agreed that "the Earth is like a spaceship with only limited room and resources." (Dunlap 1985) Finally, an *ABC News/Washington Post* poll of April 1983 found again that "Even though the large majority of Americans believe compliance with antipollution laws costs business firms at least a fair amount of money, more than three out of four say those laws are worth the cost." (R.C. Mitchell In Vig and Kraft 1984, p. 56)

Environmental Pressures and Legislation Since World War II

DATE	EVENT/MEDIA COVERAGE	GOVERNMENT ACTIVITY
1948	20 people die in Donora, Pa., from pollution exacerbated by a temperature inversion.	
1952	4,000 die from London pollution's "Killer Fog."	
1955-1959		Federal research program directed toward air pollution is undertaken. Federal agencies perceive air pollution as a local problem.
1960	News reports Passaic River fish kill; Colorado's, New Mexico's Animas River found radioactive.	
1961	Pollution headlined in Sports Illustrated, Redbook and Life Magazine.	President John. F. Kennedy nearly doubles federal funds for waste treatment, expands federal jurisdiction.
1962	Rachel Carson's Silent Spring is published.	
1963	Glen Canyon dam threatens Rainbow Bridge Monument.	
1964	Sierra Club launches campaigns to stop dams planned for the Grand Canyon.	Sen. Edmund Muskie opens air pollution hearings; pushes national auto emission control.
1965		Water Quality Act invests HEW with power to set water standards if states fail to do so.
1966	80 die from pollution-related causes during 4-day inversion in New York City.	Water Pollution Control Administration shifts to Department of Interior; HEW retains health-related issues.
1967	News reports Torrey Canyon, York River, Cape Cod and Wake Island spills.	President Lyndon Johnson proposes federal aid to monitor "airsheds;" industry voices strong opposition.
1968		Wild & Scenic Rivers System created; Grand Canyon protected from all dams.
1969	Santa Barbara oil spill coats 800 miles of ocean. Cuyahoga River erupts in flame. Polls rank voters' environmental concern just behind Vietnam and jobs.	NEPA passes, requiring environmental impact statements for federal projects.
1970	Earth Day celebrated throughout nation.	EPA created in politically charged climate; Ruckelshaus appointed director.
		3 years after 1967 Air Quality Act, no states had approved plans for standards. Clean Air Act sets stronger federal standards, state plans required by 1975.

DATE	EVENT/MEDIA COVERAGE	GOVERNMENT ACTIVITY
1971		Legislators aspire to goal of zero pollutant discharged into navigable waters by 1985.
1972	Catalytic converter controversy and public hearings begin.	Technology-based standards imposed nationally and state goals required for health and ecology.
		EPA develops permit system for toxic chemicals; citizens receive right to sue corporate violators.
1973	Arab oil embargo	Emission limits of stationary sources suspended; power plants required to burn sulfur-rich coal.
1975		Flannery Decree forces EPA to list and regulate toxic pollutants.
1976	*Newsweek* publishes article outlining environmental causes of cancer.	Resource Conservation and Recovery Act (hazardous waste control) passes.
1977	Pete Seeger's Save Hudson River campaign is covered by national media.	1977 Clean Air Act Amendments strengthen enforcement and public involvement.
		Clean Water Act strengthens discharge requirements.
1978	Love Canal exposes health effects of abandoned toxic-waste dumps. Dr. Samuel Epstein writes *The Politics of Cancer.*	
1979	Valley of the Drums, Ky., initiates public discussions of abandoned toxic-waste dumps. Public television airs documentaries on environmental and health effects of toxic chemicals.	
1980	Major chemical explosion from railroad tank cars in Kentucky.	Congress approves Superfund for abandoned toxic-waste site cleanup. President Ronald Reagan appoints James Watt, Anne Gorsuch, and David Stockman.
1981	Polls show a large majority supports strong environmental laws. Water wells in the West found to be highly contaminated with TCE.	
1982		Scandals force EPA administrator Gorsuch to resign.
1983	Times Beach, Mo., abandoned because of dioxin contamination.	
1984	Major industrial accident at Bhopal, India, kills more than 2,000 people.	
1985	Major leak of toxic chemicals at Institute, West Virginia.	

The Resource Conservation and Recovery Act

In 1980, the EPA estimated that more than 70,000 chemicals were being manufactured in the United States, with about 1,000 new ones added every year. About 260 million metric tons of hazardous wastes are generated each year from industries that utilize these chemicals. Most states and cities have had laws regulating waste for decades, and because solid and hazardous waste regulations were in a number of federal laws, even the earliest organization of the EPA included divisions for Hazardous Materials and Waste Management. The Resource Conservation and Recovery Act of 1976 attempted to control the disposal of hazardous waste by establishing a "cradle-to-grave" tracking system from generation to disposal. The EPA was given 18 months to issue regulations on the identification, generation, transportation, storage, treatment and disposal of hazardous waste. The task was monumental, but the agency managed to publish the first set of federal regulations on the generation of hazardous waste in May 1980. In 1982, the EPA published further regulations on the design and operation of hazardous waste land-disposal facilities.

In the meantime, the EPA released a study that estimated that more than 750,000 businesses generated hazardous wastes and 10,000 transporters moved them to 51,000 dump sites—municipal, hazardous, thousands already abandoned—which contained hazardous wastes and represented a threat to the groundwater of nearby residents. Since World War II, because of increased manufacturing of consumer goods, the wastes grew from about 4 million metric tons to about 260 million metric tons a year. Contaminated groundwater was reported from landfills, underground injection wells and surface impoundments of wastes in unlined pits and lagoons.

Soon after Love Canal and related episodes, the EPA developed a plan for a fund to pay for cleaning abandoned waste sites that threatened groundwater. Congress responded by passing the Comprehensive Environmental Response, Compensation, and Liability Act of 1980 (CERCLA), to be commonly known as Superfund, with initial funding of $1.6 billion. For five years, the fund was debated in Congress, at the General Accounting Office and on the state level: How much money is needed? Who is to pay? How should responsibility be divided among joint industry users? In 1985, the Office of Technology Assessment released its "Superfund Strategy" report, which projected cleanup costs of $100 billion to clean only 10,000 of a possible 22,000 sites over a period of 50 years.

To control the problem of leaking landfills in the future, Congress passed a reauthorization of RCRA in 1984, which banned land disposal of certain wastes gradually over a period of five years, in cases in which the wastes could threaten human health and the environment. The EPA was to make such designations by specific dates for specific categories (bulk, noncontainerized liquid hazardous wastes were banned quickly, then dioxins and solvents, and so on). If the EPA did not make a designation by the given dates, the waste would automatically be banned, a provision that came to be known as the "hard hammer" approach, pounding home the importance of action and speed. Another interesting implication of the amendments: The EPA was to base its determination about the safety of land disposal of a specific waste exclusively on the environmental and health impacts, without regard to alternative waste-disposal methods. The assumption was that the requirement will create a market for new technologies, such as recycling or clean incineration, and of course new manufacturing processes that generate less waste.

The Bhopal Tragedy

The modern period of environmental politics began Dec. 3, 1984, when a poison gas methyl isocyanate leaked at the Union Carbide factory in Bhopal, India, killing more than 2,000 people and injuring another 200,000 in the world's worst industrial accident. About 3,000 people a day were treated in 20 medical dispensaries nearby, and billions of dollars of claims have been filed against Union Carbide.

The following year, on Aug. 11, another leak of toxic chemicals occurred at Carbide's plant in Institute, West Virginia, and memories of the Bhopal disaster shook residents there and near many American chemical plants. Soon after, in fall 1985, an EPA draft study reported that in the previous five years almost 7,000 accidents, involving the release of 420 million pounds of toxic chemicals, had occurred in the United States, killing 139 people, injuring 1,478 and leading to the evacuation of 217,000. Then, in April 1986, following a nuclear power plant accident in Chernobyl, experts placed 100,000 Russians at high risk of contracting cancer, and in five European countries high levels of cesium-137 were found in their produce and soils and they will suffer the effects for many years.

By this time most multinational corporations had conducted safety audits on all their plants; nonetheless, insurance rates, soaring since Superfund made many companies potentially liable for hazardous waste contamination and accidents, suddenly became prohibitively expensive for companies generating, storing, hauling or disposing of hazardous materials.

What Does It All Mean?

After two generations of modern environmental regulation, basic questions remain. For example, the nation still lacks an effective, workable definition of hazardous waste to determine what should be landfilled or treated. Further, by any definition, the number of hazardous pollutants in waste, water and air far exceeds the regulators' ability to identify and control them.

It has proven next to impossible to define a "safe" level of exposure, a fact that has tied the hands of legislators and regulators alike. For example, it would take two to four years and cost up to $1 million to test each of the 1,000-plus chemicals introduced into commercial use every year. About 1 percent of all commercial chemicals, 10 percent of the pesticides and about 18 percent of all food additives are now tested each year. At least another 10,000 untested separate chemical entities are in widespread use.

This uncertainty about basic standards allows industry to continue to press to weaken environmental regulations, arguing that many required discharge reductions are not worth the capital and operating costs and, in many cases, could put companies out of business. Industry scientists point out that analytical measurements on which their priority-pollutant standards are based often are incorrect or unreliable. Industry gets its strongest support from state and local governments, which are responsible for enforcing federal laws.

Environmental groups and their supporters, now an unquestionable majority of the country, claim that scientific answers to the questions of toxic risks slowly and surely have been emerging and the conclusions support community experience and environmentalist experience and fears about toxic pollution. Furthermore, they deny that the costs of complying with regulations is excessive, resent industry polluting just to save money and claim the health costs of pollution are far more significant. Each industrial disaster adds to the environmentalists' political, and, therefore, agency, support.

Perhaps the most significant fact of modern environmental history has been the rapid development of political muscle by environmental groups, which have been largely responsible for the laws and regulations. The environmental constituency cannot be ignored in the legislative process. Nonetheless, environmentalists, who have had to fight for everything they've gained, have reason to believe that environmental quality is far from ideal—from the standpoint of any measure they would want to apply.

Whatever position one takes, the regulations are confusing. Federal, state and local authorities often intersect and responsibilities become unclear. Budgets dwindle as work increases and industry fights for time to comply with new regulations.

Because it has been so difficult to scientifically identify the health and environmental risks of air and water toxic pollutants on which to base standards and regulations, the government has attempted to control pollution by requiring better treatment technologies. Wastewater discharges were to have moved from the "best practicable technology" (BPT) to the "best available technology" (BAT) by 1984. Yet there is no list that the average chemical manufacturer, electroplater, textile maker or any other kind of company can check for the BAT, average costs or how effective the equipment is.

Air emissions are subject to the "best available control technology" (BACT), "best available demonstated technology," (BADT) or "reasonably available control technology" (RACT), depending upon whether the emissions come from new or old plants and the quality of the air where the plants are situated. Yet, since early 1979, the EPA has permitted a series of "marketplace" incentives such as the "bubble" concept, which views the entire company rather than individual stacks as a discharger, calculating pollutants from the entire operation; thus, companies can control costs by introducing pollution control at less expensive points.

Another newer mechanism the EPA has offered to industry is "offsets," whereby a new source of pollution can meet its environmental obligations by controlling its own emissions to the lowest achievable level and/or by bargaining with existing firms, which could be paid to reduce their emissions by an amount as least equal to the pollution the new source will add. Companies can control emissions to a greater degree than required and then "bank" the extra for later sale to another company or for their own future use.

Thus, standards have been set by scientific criteria, technological capability and by economic incentives, depending upon the political power at the time standards were developed. Different levels of government have expressed differing levels of interest in implementing pollution-control measures. Industry and government both have been financially hard-pressed to pursue their own goals. And the regulations and deadlines have changed in substance and in form over the years.

Summary

Although modern environmental politics are too complex to make any simple summary, the following points, developed from recent history, can be made:

1. The basic institutions of environmental management come from the legislation and agency regulations at all levels of government, the legislators and courts that define and interpret the terms of the regulations, and the executive branch, which controls budgets and senior personnel. Industry and environmental groups are the primary lobbyists for particular interests, and private consulting firms do a great deal of the technical work generated by the regulations. The media also are extremely important in setting the agenda. Political power still determines how thoroughly the environmental regulations will be implemented and enforced by federal, state and local agencies.

2. Compliance with the basic regulations is elusive not only because it is in the economic interest of industry to delay compliance, especially in times of recession or heavy competition, but also because the goals of clean water and clean air are themselves moving targets. There are about a million stationary sources of pollutants and an incalculable variety of pollutants; each source is unique in its environmental and health impact, as well as in the cost of its clean-up. Great scientific and technical knowledge is required to assess risks of pollutants and for risk management or standard-setting. Because of this uncertainty and countless individual circumstances, environmental legislation is written in what Professors James A. Henderson and Richard N. Pearson (*Land Use & Environment Law Review 1979*) refer to as "aspirational commands," i.e., a command that attempts to induce a party to "do its best" to carry out the spirit of the law. Most industries have proven to be immune to seduction by aspiration. Liability threats, fines and public opinion have been more effective means of bringing industry into compliance.

3. A chasm exists between public worry about the effects of environmental pollution and scientific knowledge of the effects. The data are incomplete, risk estimates are largely a matter of guess-work, and the regulations are hammered out in an emotionally charged climate. The government has not been able to decide how much data are required to set a standard. Industry wants certitude, which does not exist; environmental groups argue the uncertainty should favor safety and attack regulators for delaying implementation; the public wants some moral guarantee that the environment is safe; government budgets are always pinched and the mass media often set the agenda

definitions of the discussion. The most devastating impact of the Reagan administration budget cutting will hit in the next generation because research allocations, except for defense-related research, has been slashed. Although knowledge does not guarantee adequate regulation, scientific clarification can greatly assist the regulatory process.

4. The politics of pollution makes it extremely difficult to set priorities, or to progressively implement a plan based on consensus of what needs to be done in which order. With differing perceptions of need and a limited budget, it's tough to pit environmental concerns with health concerns and come up with a suitable plan. A large constituency has developed to preserve wilderness and national parks, but even the parks have been greatly neglected during the 1980s. During the 1970s, many people, including labor unions, joined the environmental movement because of public health concerns. Priorities must be established within the environmental movement: toxic air emissions, wetlands, parks, world environmental problems, wilderness areas, acid rain, groundwater contamination, wildlife refuges, hazardous waste. EPA priorities often are determined by the most recent environmental disaster. For months after Bhopal the agency was dealing mostly with emergency response problems at petrochemical plants. Agencies such as the Department of the Interior and at the Army Corps of Engineers exist to develop natural resources and their efforts contradict the spirit and letter of environmental regulations.

5. Policy shifts and ideological shifts following elections play a large role in the implementation of regulations. At the EPA, from 1975 to 1985, the workload doubled because of new laws regulating hazardous wastes, pesticides and toxic substances. Yet, after the Reagan administration took office, the operating budget was cut 35 percent, back to 1975 levels. Environmental groups thus resorted to suing the EPA to speed up the standard-setting process, which the understaffed agency believes is impossible because it has not had time to develop adequate data to consider both health effects and costs.

6. The media play a central role in influencing mass audiences, so the interested parties fight for time and space to present their arguments. The media have not been known for their ability to grasp the subtleties of environmental problems.

Thus, the status quo of environmental politics, the mess we're in and trying to pull ourselves out of.

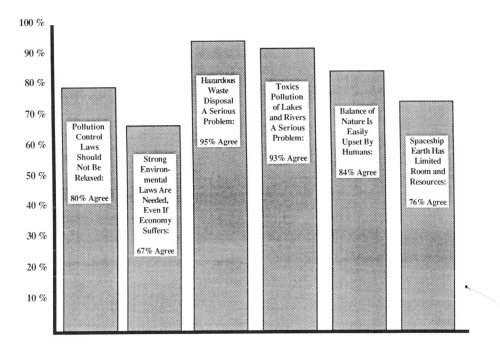

100 %

90 %

80 %

70 %

60 %

50 %

40 %

30 %

20 %

10 %

Pollution
Control
Laws
Should
Not Be
Relaxed:

80% Agree

Strong
Environ-
mental
Laws Are
Needed,
Even If
Economy
Suffers:

67% Agree

Hazardous
Waste
Disposal
A Serious
Problem:

95% Agree

Toxics
Pollution
of Lakes
and Rivers
A Serious
Problem:

93% Agree

Balance of
Nature Is
Easily
Upset By
Humans:

84% Agree

Spaceship
Earth Has
Limited
Room and
Resources:

76% Agree

ATTITUDES ON ENVIRONMENTAL CONCERNS
EARLY 1980S

(Adapted from Dunlap, 1985)

How is it possible that in less than a generation the American public went from indifference and occasional hostility to strong support for environmental concerns? Environmental activists are a major reason, for they have highlighted a never-ending series of public disasters to their fellow Americans by creative publicity and organizing efforts. Recent advances in the scientific ability to measure pollutants to levels of parts per billion and discovery of the cancer-inducing impacts of those minuscule amounts of pollutants are other important factors. Environmental problems now are viewed as influencing us all; the media have dramatized their importance; politicians pass laws; and the public supports even stronger regulations. Unfortunately, it is not enough to demand more legislation. Subsequent chapters illustrate why we need to enforce and implement more effectively the laws we already have.

67

Bibliography

The title of this chapter, "The Politics of Pollution," is taken from the excellent book by the same name by J. Clarence Davies III (Indianapolis: Bobbs-Merrill, 1970), revised with Barbara S. Davies in 1977. The book represented the starting point of this chapter. A critical original source is the U.S Congress, Senate, Committee on Environment and Public Works, *A Legislative History of the Clean Water Act of 1977,* Committee Print 95-14, 95th Congress, 2d Session, October 1978; as well as the committee's *A Legislative History of the Clean Air Act Amendments of 1977,* Committee Print 95-16. Three further sources are also extremely helpful on the history of this legislation: Philip P. Micklin's "Water Quality: A Question of Standards" in *Congress and the Environment,* edited by Richard A. Cooley and Geoffrey Wandesforde-Smith (Seattle: University of Washington Press, 1970); James Banks' "Dumping into Surface Waters: The Making and Demise of Toxic Discharge Regulations" in *Beyond Dumping,* edited by Bruce Piasecki (Westport, Conn.: Greenwood Press, 1984); and Fredric A. Strom, ed., *Land Use & Environment Law Review—1979* (New York: Clark Boardman, 1979), a tome that surveys the environmental legislation of the 1970s. John Quarles, deputy administrator of the EPA during its early years, offers "an insider's view" of the EPA in his lively *Cleaning Up America* (Boston: Houghton Mifflin, 1976). *Environmental Policy in the 1980s: Reagan's New Agenda,* edited by Norman J. Vig and Michael E. Kraft (Washington, D.C.: CQ Press, 1984) illustrates the impact of the Reagan administration on environmental policy. A more specific anthology dealing with the impact of Reagan's order mandating benefit-cost analysis for new environmental regulations is *Environmental Policy Under Reagan's Executive Order: The Role of Benefit-Cost Analysis,* edited by V. Kerry Smith (Chapel Hill: University of North Carolina Press, 1984). Riley Dunlap's "Public Opinion: Behind the Transformation" (*EPA Journal,* Vol. II, July/August 1985) traces the development of public support for environmental pollution control policies from the mid-1960s to the early 1980s by examining surveys from the major opinion research organizations. On the development of environmental consciousness, see Samuel P. Hays, "From Conservation to Environment: Environmental Politics in the U.S. Since World War II," in K. Bailes, ed., cited earlier. J.M. Petulla, *American Environmentalism: Values, Tactics, Priorities* (College Station: Texas A&M University Press, 1980) traces the biocentric, ecologic and economic traditions of thought in American environmentalism in their past and current applications. Roderick Nash's *Wilderness and the American Mind* (New Haven: Yale University Press, 1967) and Donald Worster's *Nature's Economy: The Roots of Ecology* (San Francisco: Sierra Club Books, 1977) contain a detailed history of American environmental thought.

PART II:
In the Trenches

CHAPTER THREE

Industry

"Always remember to stay in the same business your boss is in."

These words were spoken by the supervisor of a young engineer who had decided to apply for an executive position in his firm's environmental compliance division. After detailing the grief the young man would subject himself to from unsympathetic corporate officials as well as persecuting agencies, the supervising engineer reminded him that he'll never make money for the firm in that division. Quite the opposite. The company was paying out millions in environmental costs for past mistakes and present compliance. Furthermore, the young engineer was warned, the environmental job would become a deadend in his career.

The comment echoed one I had heard from David Roderick, chairman of U.S. Steel, in a 1982 documentary film, "The Business of America" (News Reel, San Francisco). He said, "I think that many people don't fully appreciate that the primary role and duty of management really is to make money. And in our case, our primary objective is not to make steel but to make steel profitably."

The notion lies squarely within the American philosophy of private enterprise and rarely is challenged. In fact, it represents the main tenets of utilitarianism's "greatest good for the greatest number" philosophy from which the early conservationists derived their notions of long-term efficiency of natural resource use. The difference is that businessmen and marketplace economists argue that the strength of a nation's economy is measured by the profits garnered by the most efficient firm, unhampered by government regulation. Only with a truly free market will the "greatest good serve the greatest number." Environmental quality is not factored into the free market equation, and the segment of the population not included in the "greatest" number's economic success is factored into the equation as the "lesser" number and its discontents.

The Environmental Manager Study

Yet within management's primary drive to increase profitability by decreasing costs (especially environmental expenses), in a study on environmental management in industry conducted from 1982 to 1985, I found that responses regarding environmental compliance seemed to change fairly quickly. This change was primarily influenced by the same dynamics as have spurred environmental change historically: public events that highlight environmental degradation, heightened by media coverage, pressure from environmental groups, followed by regulations and strong agency enforcement.

The results of my "environmental manager" study are important in this regard because they point up concretely what is going on at the pollution hot spots generated around the country, rather than the generalized environmental statistics from the federal government that tell little about the actual practice of environmental management. Because the data represent industries from many sections of the United States, and the responses from environmental specialists fall into regular patterns, the study presents a reasonably accurate picture of the state of environmental control in the firms of the country. The study also shows how fast events can induce some changes in the practices of industry.

I grouped the respondents into three major categories, based on their level of compliance and corporate interest in environmental affairs: crisis-oriented, cost-oriented and enlightened environmental management. I did not include the 3 percent of the sample that seemed to be avoiding compliance completely. Several other respondents complained that they knew of many firms that were not complying with the regulations, but these data were not included in the final tally.

Crisis-Oriented Environmental Management

The most candid person in this group, an economist responsible for the environmental regulations in a midsized company, expressed this (exteme) viewpoint: "Why the hell should we cooperate with government or anyone else who takes us away from our primary goal (of making money)? Government rules are unrealistic and it is cheaper to hire lawyers to fight the regulations, pay the fines and lobby. It is not in our interest to waste time on paper work and other environmental matters."

Although no other manager was nearly so explicit about this purpose, three or more of the following characteristics applied to 29 percent of the total original sample of firms:

- Employed no full-time trained personnel to sample, monitor and keep environmental or safety records. (This did not apply to firms with fewer than 200 employees.)
- Established no separate environmental unit in the firm.
- Denied breaking air or water standards or fought them when cited by regulatory agencies.
- Bought no new pollution control equipment to comply with recent regulations.
- Developed no environmental policy strategy to comply with laws and regulations.
- Dealt with environmental conflicts from agencies or community on "firefighting" basis rather than by finding out the best ways to comply with the laws.

General Profile

Although firms that fit the "crisis-oriented" description fall into all but the very large firms, the majority of those in my sample are small, with 50 to 1,000 employees. Many of these firms discharge directly into surface waters under permits from the NPDES (National Pollutant Discharge System), specifying quantities and quality of their effluents. The NPDES requires these firms to monitor themselves and tell the appropriate state or federal agency whether or not they are meeting the conditions of their permits. Thus, they are required to sample their own effluents, analyze them (or have them analyzed), and report whether they are meeting the conditions of the permit.

NPDES permits specify which records are required to be available for at least three years, depending on state requirements. These records include sampling data and analysis; original recordings from continuous monitoring instrumentation; instrument calibration and maintenance records; operation and maintenance records; and other reports and data. Violations can and usually do constitute a legal offense.

I asked four of these firms about the data that must be presented to inspectors, and two of the four gave either vague or noncommittal replies. However, one stated baldly that the laboratory that does his firm's sampling, measurements and analysis tells them what they want to hear, and another told me they write with pencils in their notebook records to be checked by the operations manager. Despite strict state and federal regulations on continuous monitoring records, enforcement procedures vary greatly among the states and even among different EPA regions.

One of my four candid subjects, a young manager, told me all of his firm's records are accurate, but apparently no one has bothered to read the data because they show the firm was in violation. This also may be true in several other firms, as the relatively few enforcement officers employed in the agencies can visit only a limited number of sites. When they do, they must be certain before determining that a violation exists. They discuss the situation with plant supervisors before a compliance order is issued. And, finally, if the agency believes that a sanction is in order, they might impose sanctions or file a lawsuit. This process may take years and many polluters are willing to take their chances with the ultimate verdict because they are saving capital and maintenance costs as long as they delay.

Eight companies in this sample had been taken to court for violating water quality standards. Two brought suit against the standards as too stringent, saying the high standards would cause production shutdown and loss of jobs (both lost their legal cases). The firms in this group tended to delay as long as possible and ignore adverse public reaction. Most of the firms had been reasonably successful because state enforcement policies were lax, they had strong local political support or because local officials genuinely feared the standards would put their companies out of business, or simply because agencies or municipal treatment plants lacked environmental concern.

One environmental manager in a firm that discharged wastewater into the municipal sewer system (and therefore was not required to receive an NPDES permit) insisted that his company's waste stream was undetectable in the sewage treatment plant. Another admitted his firm stalled for time by announcing a schedule it did not intend to keep; or by leaving its instruments uncalibrated (even those that are calibrated are permitted to have a wide variance of accuracy—plus or minus 30 percent or 35 percent, which of course can make a lot of difference in the amount of pollution). Most of the industry people in this category were not particularly interested in handling the extra work that environmental regulations caused and put these duties off or ignored them all together.

Case Example

One young manager of an electroplating company, John Q., offered a glimpse of the way companies with a minimalist view of environmental management operate. The difference in his case was that he actually wanted to improve his firm's environmental record but was voted down by senior managers in the firm. The company was family-owned, and he was the son of one of the owners, who did not work at the plant.

There are about 10,000 electroplating firms in the country, many quite large but a great number of "mom-and-pop" operations run out of garages, basements and small factories. The industry is responsible for the protective metal finish on everything from bumpers and refrigerator doors and supersonic jets to hubcaps, nuts and bolts and paper clips. The most commonly used metals for electroplating are chromium and nickel, but also include cadmium, cobalt, gold, silver, platinum and many others.

The metals are coated onto plates by means of electric charges in a simple, sometimes automated, process that requires large amounts of water for baths and rinses. About a billion gallons of toxic metal wastewater a day are dumped into public sewage treatment plants from these plants. Some of the wastes can be treated or they are absorbed into the sewage sludge, but most of the metals—including lead, cadmium, cyanide, chromium—are flushed into the receiving waters, where it is toxic to fish, plants, wildlife and people.

John attempted to talk his uncles into setting up a treatment facility in their medium-size firm, and later even showed them they could save money by putting in an ion transfer system for chromium recovery. He told me: "I had all the facts. We would use about 100 times less water, and save money on chromium. Heck, we could recover just about all of the chromium in our operation (nickel-chrome plating) and have the system paid for in a few years. But they talked to their old cronies (other electroplaters) and decided they (the EPA) were going to back down on the rules."

John took care of the health and safety requirement in the plant as well as environmental regulations, but his primary responsibility was to assist the plant engineer in operations. He was never allowed to talk to the inspectors or agency officials directly. The plant engineer assured the agency officials that they were making plans to set up a pretreatment facility. Because the EPA predicted that about 20 percent of the electroplaters would have to go out of business because of the regulations, they wanted to encourage those who planned to eventually comply.

Nonetheless, the firm never established a policy indicating a plan of compliance and, according to John, never looked into possible treatment methods. "You would think that the water commission people would ask them what kind of a system we were planning to put in," he told me. "I don't think they have any intention of putting any treatment in here. They don't give a damn about it."

I managed to talk to the plant engineer about the system for a few minutes, and he said the company did not want to pick a system until the regulators decided exactly what the standards would be. "Those laws keep changing, and we don't want to get something in here that we'll have to change again in a few years because it doesn't clean good enough. We know some people who put in a system that doesn't work good enough for the water people. We'll wait and see," he told me.

As a matter of fact, the senior manager had some reason for caution. According to the National Commission on Water Quality *Staff Report,* published in March 1976 (p. II-68), some of the technologies suggested by the EPA to meet best available technology requirements actually did not meet water quality standards for some pollutants. Electroplating standards had not been set by the time this report came out but the anomaly was well-known throughout industrial circles, and gave managers reason to continue some degree of recalcitrance.

I asked six inspectors of firms that discharge their wastewater into publicly owned treatment plants (POTWs) whether they believed, based on their experience, that most small companies (often working in basements or garages) emptying into the communities' sewers were in compliance with state or federal water standards. After being assured they were simply offering an opinion, three of the six said they thought no more than half of these companies were in compliance. Two believed that about a third were not complying; and one guessed that about a quarter were not in compliance.

In this group of inspectors were two who worked at POTWs, two at consulting firms hired to run the plants, and two from agencies. Three came from large metropolitan districts, three from smaller communities. All thought the major problem of enforcement was lack of personnel, but those from larger districts considered their enforcement program adequate. One of the inspectors from a community of about 100,000 people explained his gloomy assessment this way: "I have about 10 jobs at the plant and am the only person assigned to do inspections. I don't have the time to nose around the industrial district or the older side of town where a lot of little shops are probably set up. Our monitoring system is hit and miss. I'm probably missing at least half of the shops that we're supposed to regulate and I think that our situation is normal around the country."

Three Years Later

Five of the eight in this category contacted in 1985 reported significant changes had been made in the level of compliance since 1982, which here means that their firms would now be reported as "cost-oriented." Corporate officers had become more concerned with possible liability, and a number of state regulatory agencies had become more aggressive in their enforcement practices, according to respondents.

Cost-Oriented Environmental Management

The major difference between this category and the above is that environmental regulations have been officially accepted as a cost of doing business, and efforts made to comply with them as efficiently as possible (if not enthusiastically). As one manager put it, "Just because we are keeping the regulations, it doesn't mean that we agree with them or like it." Yet those in this group, both large and small companies, seemed to handle environmental regulations with some consistency, though a few of the younger technicians complained that managers wanted to do their jobs as quickly as possible without concern for accuracy or standards. The characteristics listed below apply to 58 percent of the original sample:

- Established company policy, separate unit and procedures for environmental compliance.
- Full-time personnel with some training for environmental compliance work.
- Negotiation (sometimes protracted) with agencies over disagreements regarding standards and regulations rather than conflict.
- Capital outlay for pollution control equipment.
- Occasional resource recovery of wastes (by giving them to a solvent recycler) or other cost-cutting recycling.

General Profile

Most companies in this group are larger, in the 5,000-employee range, though at least a quarter are under 1,000. Also significant is that they were visible, known to enforcement agencies as well as environmental groups, which viewed them with suspicion. Finally, a number of the supervisory managers in this group had been responsible for meeting regulatory requirements for a number of years, in most cases since the 1970s.

This latter fact is important because they had seen a great deal of confusion in implementing the regulations. In the case of water pollution, their "effluent limitation guidelines" had not been published by the EPA until years after the 1972 amendments were passed, and those were challenged in court by most large industrial groups; in many cases the courts remanded effluent limitations to the EPA for revision. Typically, these managers did not act until the suits were settled. (Many were settled by the end of the 1970s, but at that time a new Republican administration was in power and that portended less enforcement to plant managers.)

None of the 10 respondents who questioned the standards had heard of the Flannery decree that mandated best available technology regardless of standards. But they had experienced years of delays in getting permits out to the 60,000 industrial and municipal sources. Many did receive permits and were able to discharge pollutants, but never came into compliance with the best practicable or best available technology requirements because of instabilities in the regulatory process.

Thus, on the one hand, the managers I talked to in this category were visible and had to do something about their environmental problems;

and, on the other hand, they had gone through a few economic recessions and wanted to delay as long as they could. As much for public relations as any other reason, the companies in this group stayed in at least nominal compliance with environmental regulations ("nominal" if court cases had not been settled). Some had obtained variances or delayed their compliance schedules.

At least a third of the group complained that enforcement is uneven and sporadic and said they did not want to spend a lot for pollution control equipment if their competitors were not also required to do so. And if they did invest a great deal in a specific technology, they insisted on getting assurances that they would not be required to upgrade soon. This group was the most vocal about their competitors, who were dumping illegally and gaining an advantage from poor enforcement of toxic waste laws.

By 1985, more than a third of the managers in this group who could recycle wastes were doing so. Most were sending organic solvents to processor-recyclers for purification and reuse. One was recycling spent etching and pickling solutions. A large chemical plant recycled the calcium fluoride hazardous waste into fluorine-based chemicals needed to produce gases for refrigerators and air-conditioners. The common denominator in these innovations is that it saves money to recycle. As long as it was cheaper to send the wastes to landfills, the managers used the cheaper option. Even after it became clear that resource recovery saves money, a number of managers decided not to use the option, perhaps because it required some time to evaluate the possibilities. Many managers prefer to stick to the ways that are least bothersome and with which they are most familiar.

Case Example

A large semiconductor plant made it through the 1970s without an environmental division, with the work being done by its health and safety division, consultants or the facilities division. The firm did not respond to my original questionnaire in 1982 shortly after it had organized a separate environmental division, but the following year I was put in touch with a new environmental manager. The company had become the object of a major environmental lawsuit and began to give environmental concerns high priority.

My contact at the company, Russ T., was initially hired as an environmental engineer to bring the company into compliance with the regulations. Within two years, he was promoted to corporate environmental manager with two engineers under him who supervised six technicians hired to keep records, handle permits and monitor and package wastes. Much hazardous waste is generated at large semiconductor plants because the chips must be continuously cleaned (after being sliced and etched) by organic solvents and deionized water through several phases. The etching is done with strong acids, which create another hazardous waste. As these chemicals are used, volatile organic compound gaseous emissions escape and a hazardous waste-water stream is generated as well.

When Russ took on the job, the attitude of the company and especially the production manager was that environmental matters were a "nuisance and interfered with manufacturing and production." Russ found that even though the company was in great difficulty with state and federal enforcement officers as well as the local community, he received little cooperation from the people in his own firm. After working night and day for about a half year to do his job ("spinning my wheels"), he decided to go to the president of the firm and ask for more corporate support.

He soon received a policy letter from the president, describing specific responsibilities and authority, including the mandate to develop a cost-effective program of environmental management. He also received more staff support and was told to report directly to the vice president of Facilities. The production manager was instructed to develop environmental goals, which were to be evaluated regularly.

The production manager's attitude gradually changed from hostility ("which made my life miserable," said Russ) to respect, as he saw that Russ was loyal to the company and wanted to save it money, by using resource recovery techniques (primarily of solvents, sent to a recovery firm) and some minor process changes that cut down on waste. Russ also proposed that they recycle fluorides by precipitation through calcium hydroxide, then reprocessing the precipitate into hydrofluoric acid (used for etching), but the scheme was turned down as too costly.

After the heat was off from the lawsuit and agencies, the company laid off half of its environmental staff personnel. The two engineer supervisors were transferred to production positions and two technicians were laid off. Russ went back to 12-hour days while other engineers "had to think of things to do in the afternoon," according to Russ.

After three years, Russ left for a position in environmental management in another firm. The following are excerpts from a phone conversation I had with him in 1985:

> I think I was able to accomplish a lot at _____ because I showed them that you can keep the law at far less expense than they wanted to believe. But I had too many problems with most of the managers and engineers. I had to check and recheck air emissions forms that they made out because their calculations were wrong every time. At first I thought they were changing figures deliberately, but many times they were cheating the company. They just didn't give a damn about this part of their job and slopped through it. But my biggest problem was that after three years, when there was a little recession in the industry, the first thing the company did was lay off half of the environmental staff. They actually wanted to go back to two people, me and one technician. The work is not considered important there and there is an uneven distribution of the work load that shows how much value is given to the work.

Another young environmental manager told me, "The only potential this job has is the potential for more work." Although the firms in this group usually had some kind of environmental policy stated in writing, their day-to-day practice illustrated that few employees tended to spend more time on the job than they absolutely had to. They seemed to look on the environmental division as a necessary but unfortunate cost of doing business, one that should be examined for surplus personnel (to be laid off) before any other section when company cuts were called for. *if cut were to be made*

Three Years Later

Again, phone interviews with 22 original respondents in 1985 indicated some progress in this category. Six companies have developed more sophisticated, "enlightened" environmental management practices, such as recycling hazardous waste or environmental audits as described below, and four added more pollution abatement technology, with 12 firms remaining substantially the same in their practices.

Enlightened Environmental Management

The most forward-looking firms have established strong corporate support for an aggressive "enlightened" environmental management policy that goes beyond mere regulatory compliance to long-range environmental planning. Environmental affairs are often integrated into company health and safety programs, with the entire division accepted within the firm as a critical part of the whole. Environmental planning is viewed as important to protect the firm from damaging liability claims in the long-range scheme of business; therefore, the company views the work as going beyond a short-term cost orientation. As one environmental manager told me: "We see ourselves as a good neighbor to the people in this community, and do the things for the community a good neighbor will do. Anyway, in the long run it's in our own interest, to keep us from lawsuits and generate some good will." Although only 9 percent of my original sample fit into this category, my 1985 sample showed an increase from firms in the "cost-oriented" group. The characteristics are:

- Complete support of chief executive officer or president and corporate attorneys.
- Strong environmental management division under a major corporate officer, who demands the same high-quality environmental work as any other division.
- Trained environmental personnel, with advancement given those who seek further education and training.
- State-of-the-art pollution control equipment.
- Sophisticated environmental monitoring, surveillance and record-keeping system, usually by computer.
- Periodic environmental audits with reports to corporate headquarters.
- Cooperation between environmental and production staffs.
- On-going research to determine cost-effective methods of better environmental quality and resource recovery (including energy).
- Generally good relations with agency officials and community groups.

General Profile

Because there was so much publicity about large corporations that were strengthening their environmental affairs divisions and introducing far-reaching resource-recovery systems, I assumed that most of the firms in the "enlightened" category would be very large (10,000 to 50,000 employees) and highly capitalized. It seemed to make sense that companies that generated a great deal of income, especially those in the public eye, would be most willing to spend it on environmentally sound policies.

Yet, I found no clear connection between size and environmental management practices. To learn whether the high-profile firms fit into the "enlightened" group, I interviewed people in three of five large corporations that had been touting their environmental programs and read data on the other two. Only two of the five would make the "enlightened" group, one because much public information is available about their environmental program (I had no personal contact with this firm). The others had strong public relations programs, but that did not alter an essentially short-term cost orientation. The past environmental record of two of these firms had created such adverse publicity that they attempted to overcompensate with announcements that had little to do with day-to-day healthy environmental management. And in the general survey itself, only about half of the "enlightened" category (six of 11 firms) in the original sample had more than 10,000 employees.

In fact, firms with the most forward-looking environmental programs practice modern management techniques; they are known as good places to work, and are viewed as "good neighbors" by the communities in which they are established. The majority of those on my list have been established since 1964, a few in the 1970s, and come from all sizes. Their managers understand the importance of a good work environment, good public relations and relations with government personnel, and the need to minimize civil and criminal liability potential.

Most of all they see that long-range planning and spending money in the short term can save millions more in liability and other costs in the long term. Environmental departments furthermore are looked upon as "profit improvement centers" that try to find ways to avoid generating pollutants. This attitude is different from (short-term) cost-oriented managers, who look only at the quarterly or yearly balance sheets.

Another difference between this group and the two mentioned above is their attitude toward independent environmental audits, which assess degree and quality of compliance and safety. Many less forward-looking firms are avoiding independent audits because of what might be found and worry that the information could be used against them. It's the same reason they avoid computerized systems that track potential compliance problems. Of course, companies that do audits must first decide they will do something about any problems found. Furthermore, it is possible attorney/client privilege could legally protect firms worried about audit information being used against them, even though a company would be required to submit corrected monitoring reports if any had been inaccurately filed in the past.

The organization of environmental divisions within firms of this group is diverse, with very large firms placing primary environmental responsibility at the corporate level over smaller environmental divisions in each facility; and companies with only one or two plants placing environmental responsibility on a high-level executive with corporate leverage. Computer systems have been installed to track chemicals, compliance records and waste streams. Expert personnel tend to be well-paid and happy in their jobs. Corporate commitment extends to meticulous work habits in environmental divisions, and when such work turns out to be incomplete or faulty, all levels on the environmental team are held accountable.

The firms in this group have not only elaborate policies and procedures covering all possible regulations, laws and potential liabilities, but also a multilevel compliance reporting structure to the head of the firm and annual environmental reports indicating expenditures. All environmental division activities are available for inspection. Finally, all had established on-going training programs for their workers, covering such details as handling chemicals and products safely and emergency response procedures.

Case Example

One respondent in this "enlightened" category was the supervisor of seven environmental specialists at a refinery. The specialists performed many tasks, from escorting air agency personnel during inspections, to handling company air and water compliance and permits, reports, hazardous waste disposal permits, preparing monitoring charts and even attending corporate environmental compliance meetings.

Until 1978, the refinery staff consisted of only two technicians who worked with the operations manager. But related companies within this very large corporation had been in compliance trouble, so the chief executive officer and board of directors decided to form an environmental division at corporate headquarters to improve their environmental policies and phase in new technologies, systems and staff over a designated period of time.

First, the new corporate group hired an outside consulting firm to prepare a report from which the group would begin its task. The manager said he believed the experience and leadership of another petroleum company also guided his firm. The audit showed, among other problems, poorly trained workers, badly functioning pollution-control equipment and no emergency response planning.

This case example was not chosen because most of the approximately 175 refineries in the United States represent enlightened environmental management. In most cases they do not, although petroleum refining is very profitable. Most refineries still discharge great amounts of hazardous substances into waterways. Petroleum companies blame their poor environmental records on the complex chemistry of oil refining, which is polluting and very expensive to clean up. Hydrocarbons in the crude have to be separated into select groupings or fractions, which are converted into marketable products. When the impurities of sulfur, nitrogen and trace metals are removed, these, along with hundreds of pounds of fugitive oil and grease, leave the refinery as air or water pollutants.

All stages of the refinery process represent pollution problems: mixing of crude with water in a desalter; distillation of light and heavy hydrocarbons; cracking or breaking large hydrocarbon molecules into smaller ones through heat, pressure and a catalyst in a fluid catalytic cracker (FCC); often solvents are used to remove impurities from the product. The major air pollutants in the catalytic cracking process are sulfur oxides and hydrocarbon gases, but large amounts of nitrogen oxides, carbon monoxide and particulates also represent big problems. For example, the strong oxidizing power of nitrogen dioxide not only promotes nitrates and nitric acid, but it also helps form sulfates and sulfuric acid in acid precipitation problems and is a great contributor to local smog. It is extremely difficult and expensive to control nitrogen oxides. It is also expensive to treat highly polluted wastewater from distillation, desalting and other refinery processes.

This refinery's operations manager, quality control superintendent and environmental manager all approached the cleanup by examining each stage of the process, taking care of the inexpensive means first, and gradually introducing more cost-effective technologies. For example, they first tightened methods of storage and handling to minimize spills and, at the same time, controlled evaporation losses with a vapor recovery system and eventually floating roof storage tanks, which inhibit the formation of a vapor layer. One by one, they examined the rest of their pollution-control technologies, such as hydroprocessing (desulfurizing), cyclones and electrostatic precipitators for particulate removal. Steam stripping of sulfur-bearing wastewater, other water treatment processes, and an incinerator for heavy solids and sludges also were examined systematically for which would give the most environmental value for their money.

The corporate team and groups at each facility were given the mandate to not only bring the company into compliance but also save money for the firm by avoiding potential liability problems and finding efficient technologies to meet environmental goals. They also were to plan for probable future requirements, such as standards for toxic air pollutants and acid precipitation legislation (e.g., more efficient new boilers). Each facility was to handle its own environmental program, sending all independent audits, compliance reports (now computerized) and regular planning reports to the corporate environmental office. The planning document defines goals and objectives and lists proposed actions and costs along with a timetable for accomplishing goals. After almost four years, the program has resolved old compliance problems, increased employee safety, facilitated the permitting process for new corporate activities, reduced and lessened potential liability for the company. The results also exemplify what constitutes enlightened environmental management.

Corporate Culture and Environmental Access

Throughout the research project, it proved extremely difficult to get information, even information that presented the company in a positive light, that might add to our picture of environmental management in industry. During the 1983 interview phase, when I was able to identify managers willing to discuss problems of environmental management, I asked these specialists whether it was because most people in industry did not trust academics to keep quiet about the proprietary aspects of their businesses. The most graphic and succinct reply came from a friendly corporate lawyer. The young woman looked me straight in the eye and said:

> *I trust you personally but I'm really surprised at your naivete. I have no idea where this information will end up, nor do I know how valuable it is to our competitors and the government. Don't you understand that we have to be defensive about our image? Any lawyer working for industry . . . acts the same; they take the narrowest view of what they let out to the public. Anything can come back to haunt them.*

Most of the managers answered in ways that were difficult to classify, but I was able to group their responses into the following categories in the order of importance as presented by the respondents:

1. Outsiders are adversaries, regardless of their motives. Since the legal departments have the most influence in large firms, it is understandable that their adversary persona should establish the rules of the corporate culture. The attitude could also be derived from the perceived need to maximize profits and the assumption that environmentally related activities are seen as a potential threat to economic security. Minimally, the response is that time is money and the firm cannot afford to spend time on non-profit-oriented work. In any case, I noted strong corporate paranoia in many of the responding firms, an attitude consistent with the historical account presented in Part I.

2. Risk of bad press. The following two comments summarize the feelings of the group:

> *We are scared to death that the community or the media will find something wrong in our operation and publicize it.*

> *Every industrial business protects its image as much as its line of profits. We know that bureaucrats on all levels of government have leaked embarrassing information to the press. We have to cover our flanks.*

Here a structural connection is drawn between public image and profits, which may in fact depend on the public image of the firm.

3. Couldn't care less. Many industrial managers on all levels manifested some annoyance with my persistence. For example, "This is not my affair. Go to our legal department or public relations. I'm here to move our products, not to answer questions about environmental affairs."

"This is not my job" is a comment I heard many times by managers who view environmental rules as so many bothersome flies to be shooed away. Yet all production or facilities managers are very much involved with waste streams and transport of materials as well as other pollution-control matters.

4. Knowledge is power. This refers not only to the fact that information can be used against industry—thus the protective stance vis a vis government agencies and the media—it is also true that the information is complex and can be unwittingly misinterpreted. So, understandably, even those who are willing to offer information want to know how it will be used and why. Obviously, the company wants to protect itself against misuse of its resources.

This is important because many firms (though certainly not yet the majority) are more open and cooperative with regulators and the community. Usually, the firm's position first is formulated by the president or chief executive officer who establishes rewards and punishments around the value of cooperation and openness. As Laura Nash, a Harvard Business School professor, put it: "Every company has values that are expressed through the corporate culture. Those values come down from the chief executive. And it is in shaping that culture, in deciding what the company is about, that ethical behavior will or will not be built in. . . . Business ethics is largely a question of corporate character." (*New York Times,* Dec. 11, 1983, 4 F)

Environmental Specialists

I developed two indices based on interviews with 92 environmental specialists in industry; one measured profit- or business-orientation, and the other measured environmental-orientation. I rated interviews on the basis of interest in environmental activities as well as specific answers given to questions relating to problems complying with the regulations. Ten was rated as highest in either category, and those working in firms with "enlightened" environmental management tended to receive high rankings in both profit-orientation and environmental-orientation.

I was especially interested to see how age, years with the firm, position in the firm and type of education and experience correlated with environmental- or profit-orientation. I found that older respondents in a supervisory role in management were more likely to identify with profit-oriented goals rather than environmentally oriented goals. Other variables that related to profit-orientation were the number of years put into the firm and training in business, engineering or law. Thus all but one of the supervisors who had been with the firm more than 10 years and had undergraduate training in business administration, engineering or law received a 10 on the profit-oriented scale. These seven managers (four business backgrounds, two engineers, one lawyer) had environmental rankings of between 1 and 9, with the mean registering at 4.

Middle-level managers, 24 of them, also received very high profit-oriented rankings, from 7 to 10. The majority of this group had an engineering background and all had been in the firm more than five years. The group's environmental-orientation ranged from 1 to 10, with the mean at 5. Since this group complained more about environmental regulations than any other, their mean ranking is higher than I had expected, but in most cases they took care of environmental regulations according to their perception of company policy.

The major complaint of these managers was that they could not figure out the regulations and did not trust anyone from the regulatory agencies to give them an answer sympathetic to the problems of their firm. One engineer complained, "Every time I call the state agency I get a new story. The company is waiting until those guys decide what they want." He went on to say that he talked the plant manager into getting a consulting firm to recommend a good pretreatment wastewater system for their operation. The company agreed to spend a large amount of money on a study that eventually proved useless. The engineer

TRENDS IN INDUSTRIAL COMMITMENT

1982-1983

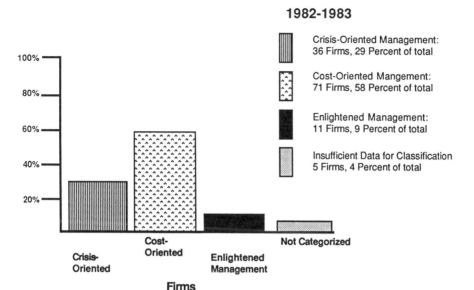

Crisis-Oriented Management:
36 Firms, 29 Percent of total

Cost-Oriented Mangement:
71 Firms, 58 Percent of total

Enlightened Management:
11 Firms, 9 Percent of total

Insufficient Data for Classification
5 Firms, 4 Percent of total

32 Firms Revisited - 1985

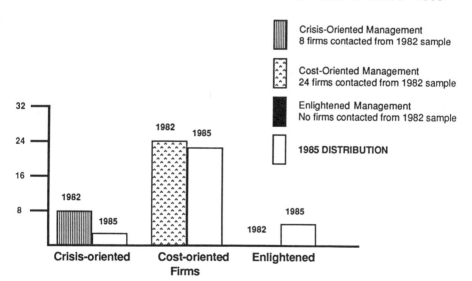

Crisis-Oriented Management
8 firms contacted from 1982 sample

Cost-Oriented Management
24 firms contacted from 1982 sample

Enlightened Management
No firms contacted from 1982 sample

1985 DISTRIBUTION

The chart shows the percentage of firms in each type of management firm (crisis-oriented, cost-oriented, and enlightened) for the 1982-1983 and 1985 studies.

questioned the consultants' basic knowledge of the firm's production process, so the study was scrapped and the engineer looked bad. "After that experience," he concluded, "I kept my mouth shut about environmental rules."

Virtually all of the environmental specialists with strong profit-orientation mentioned the cost of compliance—the cost of control equipment and also the cost of maintenance and new personnel—as excessive. Most genuinely worried about the impact environmental regulations were having on profitability, and many comments dealt with competitors in the United States and abroad that were cutting corners on the regulations. "We have to pass our costs on to the consumer," one manager told me, "and they won't keep paying higher prices forever."

Other concerns mentioned more than five times were the inconsistency in the interpretation and enforcement of the laws and in the expanding scope of the regulations. Speaking about how it was impossible to keep new standards, one said, "We don't want to keep going to court, but they (the government agencies) don't give us any choice." The managers also spoke of the inordinate time that compliance work takes; all groups apparently work overtime, for regular tasks as well as for corporate, agency and community meetings. Seventy-seven of 92 in this sample said their workload had substantially increased in the previous two years.

One manager who had to work with the firm's community relations department said, "Our company is in an industrial area, but just because we are bigger than the others, we get blamed for everything. I have to spend a lot of time proving we weren't the polluter. I wish the air agency would help us but they know less than the people in the community."

When an environmental problem threatens to embarrass a company, the environmental staff is under the gun to do something fast. They deal with the regulators, placate the public, explain to their supervisors, and are overburdened with paper work through it all. In their spare time they write contingency plans for potential problems such as spills and gas releases. Not surprisingly, overwork is almost universally cited as a major problem.

Younger Employees

Most of the interviews, almost 60, were with people with fewer than six years at their firm. In general, younger employees, in age and in years with the firm, tend to rank higher in environmental orientation. At the same time, the younger environmental specialists more often have educational backgrounds in the life sciences and political science, 38, than in business and engineering, 17. The younger specialists who are engineers tend to rank much higher in profit orientation and much lower on environmental orientation than those trained in the life sciences. But the longer many of those trained in biology or environmental science stay with the firm, the more their rankings converge with other employees of the firm. The environmental-orientation mean for the entire group is 7; profit orientation is 5. Eight people scored 10 in environmental orientation.

Many of the comments of younger employees reflect the same concerns as their seniors: excessive workload, regulatory inconsistency, interactions with agency personnel, environmental groups and the community. At the same time a great number of the group, 17 (all non-business and non-engineers), complained about lack of company support, supervisors who neither cared about nor understood the dimensions of the environmental problems in the companies, changing job descriptions (except the standard mandate that regulators are to be kept at bay).

Here are two quotations that reflect the concerns of this segment of environmental specialists:

When I came here I thought I was going to help set up an environmental department and work on a program to solve the company's environmental problems. I do everything from taking samples to filling out waste manifests, but nobody's interested in going to the real problems at the production end. They just want the EPA off their backs, not long-term solutions.

And a second comment from a young woman:

I worked hard to develop skills in water pollution management and felt fortunate to get this job in industry. I don't think many people here, even in the lab, care much about improving the environment. My bosses think that everybody outside the company is the enemy, especially the inspectors and the regulators. Environmentalists are all considered kooks. . . .

Some of what the engineers say is true. The people at the agencies don't care about how much pollution control is going to cost us; if we go out of business, tough. But I know that we can get a good environmental program going around here with any kind of long-term commitment. . . . We can do a lot better than we're doing now. Heck, we can recycle a lot of these wastes and save some money. But for them, (the treatment technology) costs too much money. . . . I'm trying to find a job with a consulting firm. They don't have to be embarrassed about working for the environment.

The disillusionment reflected in the last comments stems from several sources: both of the specialists were out of college for less than a year, and not long before had spent their summers doing ecological field studies. Neither was prepared for the shock of factory life, much less a corporate environment where their environmental commitments were neither shared nor appreciated.

Although 17 of a total of 92 specialists were clearly unhappy about their firms' attitudes and management practices, the majority believed that their companies were slowly coming around. The 1985 interviews confirmed that such was the case, even though those from the group of 17 still had some conflicts with supervisory engineers or profit-oriented business managers.

Conclusions

1. The strongest conclusion of the study is that the most important indicator of a strong, enlightened environmental management program at any firm is the position of the president or chief executive officer and

their attorneys. If that position is committed to environmental compliance and long-term planning to minimize problems of risk and liability, everything else falls into place: a clearly articulated policy, adequate budgets, training programs, augmented environmental divisions, goal-oriented programs, cooperation from plant managers, environmental audits, resource recovery. I found that if the attitude at the top was neutral or negative, the environmental sections tended to muddle along without a plan, "putting out fires," in a state of disorganization, do shoddy work and suffer morale problems.

The effectiveness of environmental management in industry seems to depend, first of all, on pressures outside industry. Yet within each firm a distinctive "corporate culture" determines the quality of the company's response to these pressures. The most influential person in the organization in shaping environmental policy tends to be the president or CEO, the chief executive officer, followed very closely by the senior attorneys, since they are in a position to inform the board about the hazards of legal liability or bad press. Next, the environmental management team will in large measure establish its own standards in the department, depending on the age, commitments, training and competence of the personnel. Finally, the quality of environmental management in industry in large measure depends on the quality of the laws that regulate it: whether or not they are clear, specific, enforceable, equitable to all firms engaged in competition for the same markets, and based on a rationale that can be accepted by the majority of companies.

An early hypothesis of the study was that environmental divisions were less effective when placed within production divisions, since the latter were primarily profit-oriented and gave environmental work low priority as well as a minimum amount of money for compliance. Although I interviewed no one in a separate high-level environmental organizational slot, I believed that only a high-level executive and a separate budget could provide the group with the independence needed to handle compliance and planning adequately.

In fact, I found environmental sections organized in many different divisions: facilities, production, engineering, legal affairs, health and safety, public affairs, personnel, quality control and others. The quality of the work seemed to have little connection with the organization, though it was more convenient to have the environmental group close to the pollution control equipment, i.e., in the factory. Each company seems to have worked out its own convenient organizational chart (often combining with health and safety or industrial hygiene), that fits the personnel and products of the firm. No matter how awkward or smooth the fit, compliance and enlightened practices depended on the CEO, and how much money the firm was willing to commit in the short term to solve potential problems in the long term.

In a report from the Center for Environmental Assurance at Arthur D. Little Co., Cambridge, Massachusetts, the staff found six characteristics performed by the "cutting-edge" companies in environmental management: 1) long-range planning horizons; 2) planning for risk as well as compliance; 3) a clear and direct linkage between the environmental, safety and health planning process and the CEO; 4) strong interaction between corporate and division staffs; 5) a formal channel through

HOW MUCH ARE FUTURE BENEFITS WORTH?

CRISIS-ORIENTED MANAGEMENT:

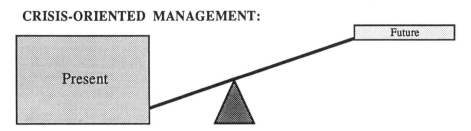

The primary future benefit to be gained from compliance with environmental regulations is the ability to stay in business. Future economic benefits are highly discounted compared to present costs.

COST-ORIENTED MANAGEMENT:

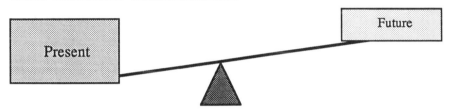

Includes a willingness to incur costs for future economic benefits when benefits can be clearly defined and guaranteed. Future economic benefits are included in the company's long-range planning.

ENLIGHTENED MANAGEMENT:

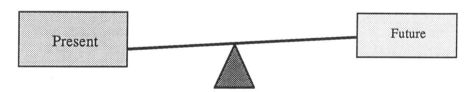

Demonstrates a willingness to include non-quantifiable future benefits in the company's long-range planning. Future values are discounted, but benefits such as corporate image and preparing for future environmental standards are included in the calculation.

> *The essential core of enlightened environmental mangement is represented by a willingness to invest in the future, to calculate material and non-material benefits into the firm's long-range plan. To the extent that a company works for short-term gains, the firm is viewed as crisis- or cost-oriented.*

which the corporate environmental group contributes to the strategic planning process; 6) driving forces that extend beyond compliance to social responsibility, preventive environmental policy, and a recognition that economic benefits can be realized. None of these characteristics can be realized without strong support from top management.

2. The two factors that most commonly influence the development of an enlightened environmental management policy are economic: 1) the recognition that corporate responsibility for the environment can affect both short- and long-term profits, e.g., because of toxic tort claims making the firm liable for accidents, health damage, chemical spills, discharges and emissions; and 2) the understanding that costs for environmental responsibility can be minimized, perhaps even some profit can be realized, if quality and cost control mechanisms are established.

In mid-1985, two events had an especially sobering effect on companies whose environmental and health policies historically had been considered inconsequential aspects of company policy. The Manville Corporation settled for $2.5 billion for the expected 60,000 health claims from damage caused by asbestos it manufactured. And the murder conviction of officials of a Chicago photo lab in the death of an immigrant worker precipitated a spate of district attorney investigations of industrial deaths and illnesses as well as corporate negligence in regard to environmental toxic discharges. These developments indicated that corporate officials can be jailed when official neglect can be proved.

Regarding minimizing of environmental costs, Frank B. Friedman (1985) says that sound environmental management can become a "profit center" under a systems approach to cost reduction:

> One of the first steps involves inventorying of emissions from all media. In essence, you need to know what is out there if you are developing a systems approach to the reduction of environmental costs . . . the most cost-effective program is in the waste reduction area. The broad and long-term liability for waste disposal alone argues for the inventorying of wastes and for close attention to actual waste reduction. The increasing costs of disposal and the variety of taxes on wastes, present and pending, make this program imperative. . . .
>
> In efforts to reduce personnel, care must be taken to avoid hasty cuts which are not well thought out. In some instances, it may be desirable simply to change the personnel mix. For example, as new Clean Water Act discharge permits are issued, which may control more pollutants at lower levels, including a wide variety of toxic pollutants, the first inclination might be to hire more chemists to do the analytical work. However, the best approach may be to review not just permits, but the entire manufacturing process, to determine if changes may be desirable. Process changes previously considered and rejected for lack of cost-effectiveness perhaps should be reconsidered in light of the continued regulatory climate and increased costs in the toxics area. . . .

The most-publicized example of cost-cutting through good environmental management is 3M Company's "Pollution Prevention Pays" program. Begun worldwide in 1975, it rewarded employees to find ways to reduce environmental control and pollution costs. About 600 projects incorporated into the program have saved the company more than $100 million within 10 years and eliminated 900 million gallons of wastewater, 125,000 tons of air pollutants and 12,000 tons of sludge.

The Pollution Probe Foundation (1982) and INFORM (1985) published a compilation of industrial waste reduction and recycling techniques that show how dozens of hazardous wastes have been turned into useful products and at the same time saved on disposal costs as well as the land, water or air the wastes would have polluted. In the last several years, a spate of newspaper and journal articles have appeared showing how many companies are saving money on resource recovery programs. Because of skyrocketing disposal costs and insurance costs and potential liability claims, old recovery methods have suddenly become economical.

3. Historical events and legislative history have become layered onto contemporary business practices. Conflicts with agencies and outside groups establish the pattern of relationships for managers in the firms. Scientific understanding and technological control equipment are channeled into whatever fits company policy, rather than what might be better environmental practice. Environmental managers either are not interested in cheaper innovative control technologies or are so beleaguered and overworked by in-house politics or agency bureaucratic inconsistencies that they lose whatever interest they might have had in saving the company money or lowering pollution effluents. It is easier to recommend an engineering consulting firm to solve the company's problems, usually at very great expense.

4. But, although it appears there are enough external economic pressures to bring most companies to the conclusion that good environmental practice has become very good business, many firms are toughing it out with enforcement agencies. They continue to believe that regulations are unfair, inequitable, unrealistic and may force them out of business. David Roderick's comment at the beginning of this chapter remains the norm and must be figured into any environmental calculus.

Many pockets of "enlightened" environmental management exist around the country, certainly more than when I began the study in 1982. Yet it is equally certain that large numbers of firms, large and small, have managed to delay the implementation of environmental regulation, either because of weak state standards or variances, poor agency enforcement or illegal activities (sewer dumping or unlicensed waste haulers). Better environmental management, therefore, is closely connected to the quality and effectiveness of work in federal, state and local agencies, continued pressure by environmental groups, higher professional standards in the growing corps of environmental specialists and, perhaps most basic of all, sets of standards that all groups recognize as necessary and enforceable.

Bibliography

The first reports of the research described in this chapter were published in *Environment* magazine in an opinion column entitled "Environmental Management." The articles appeared in October and November/December 1983, and January/February, April and July 1984 and one in *The Environmental Professional,* Winter 1985. A notable series of articles in *The Environmental Forum* on contemporary practice in environmental management was written by Frank B. Friedman, July 1983, May 1984 and February 1985. Another good article on the subject, by Raymond W. Kane, came out in the journal, October 1982. The Center for Environmental Assurance at Arthur D. Little Inc., Cambridge, Mass., has published two short reports on effective environmental assurance management, i.e., minimizing environmental risks, both in 1981; and an "Annotated Bibliography on Environmental Management" (1985), prepared for the Environmental Protection Agency. *The Choices of Power* by Marc J. Roberts and Jeremy S. Bluhm (Cambridge, Mass.: Harvard University Press, 1981) use organizational behavior analysis to show how six utilities handled increasing environmental demands. The Conference Board (845 Third Ave., N.Y. 10022) published two reports on the way corporations have organized themselves for environmental compliance, one in 1970 (Report No. 507), and another by Leonard Lund in 1974 (Report No. 618). Monica E. Campbell and William M. Glenn compiled the industrial waste reduction and recycling methodologies in their *Profit from Pollution Prevention* (Pollution Probe Foundation, 12 Madison Ave., Toronto, Ontario, Canada M5R 2S1, 1982). A more recent survey of industrial waste reduction practices is *Cutting Chemical Wastes* (1985) by D.J. Sarokin, W.R. Muir, C.G. Miller and S.R. Sperber, a publication of INFORM, a public interest research group in New York City.

CHAPTER FOUR

Government Agencies

"We're doing as much as we can get away with"

This comment was part of a response to a questionnaire statement that during the 1980s more industrial firms seemed to be complying with environmental regulations. I wanted to know whether this associate director of a state health department, which took care of hazardous waste regulations, agreed or not. His complete response touched on many key issues that confront regulatory agencies:

It might be true, then again it might not be true. One thing that is certain in this state, probably in every state, that industry wants to get away with as much as it can. If there is a way to delay, they will delay. If they can get away with dumping illegally, a lot of them will do it. If they can keep the rules cheaper, most of them will. . . .

Heck, everybody acts this way. We all want to cut our costs, make an extra buck. I've met very few people in industry who are crazy about the environment. For them it's just a pain, an expensive pain, so they do what they can to get out of the rules. . . .

We're the same way around here. We not only have to put up with companies that are trying to get out of the rules but also with a lot of politicians and some agency dead wood, too. Politicians don't help much. They pass laws, then don't give us money to enforce them. If we don't enforce the laws, let me tell you that nobody will keep them out of the kindness of their heart to the ecology. . . .

So we act the same way. We don't have enough inspectors, and we can't follow up on every complaint that comes in, so we zero in on the ones that look worst. We double- and triple-check companies that we think are dumping illegally. Industry gets away with whatever it can, and we're doing whatever we can get away with to enforce the law.

The comment touches on several points that made me as confused about the operation of agencies as I was about the environmental departments in industry. Sometimes government agencies were effective in their efforts to implement environmental policy; very often they were not. On the one hand, the agency this manager represented realized it was not getting the resources necessary to do its job well, so it pulled together and did the best it could on enforcement matters. At the same time, my respondent frankly stated that the agency had a number of employees who did not help the rest of them in this effort and that the political forces were difficult to cope with. Furthermore, he admitted, they usually did not stringently enforce policies, certainly not to the extent the guidelines call for. "Why not?" I asked. "Politics," he replied.

Politics and Enforcement Actions

Strict enforcement is the key to compliance for firms that are concerned only with short-term costs. After Louisiana Gov. Edwin W. Edwards won election in 1983, *Chemical Week,* an industry news magazine, reported:

> *Edwards' victory was greeted with resounding approval by Louisiana's chemical manufacturers, who expect him to throttle back on the outgoing administration's drive for environmental control and cleanup. "Edwards knows that if the chemical industry doesn't have to spend a lot of money on environmental matters, we can use that money to create jobs," says Frederick Loy, executive director of the Louisiana Chemical Association.* (Nov. 2, 1983—a time when many large corporations were beginning to worry about lawsuits and liability problems.)

The second well-known example relating to the political influence in the enforcement of environmental regulations is one that sent Rita Lavelle, former EPA assistant administrator for Solid Waste and Emergency Response, to jail for six months. The Reagan administration EPA appointee sent a memorandum to the agency's general counsel for prosecuting companies that dumped hazardous waste illegally, and in it she chastised the lawyer for "alienating . . . the primary constituency of this administration, big business."

Thus it was not surprising that, when asked about obstacles to environmental compliance, 73 percent of my sample of government agency personnel listed "political" problems. Respondents were made up of all levels of federal, state and local agency staff, and they provided a variety of examples of political interference. Along with political problems, I have grouped nearly all of the remaining comments by agency personnel into two further categories: implementation and procedural difficulties, and bureaucratic inertia.

Political Impacts on Agencies

The tradition of political appointees to senior positions in all levels of government stems from the U.S. Constitution itself, which allows the president to nominate and, with the advice and consent of the Senate, appoint officers of the United States and further permits Congress to delegate the appointment of lower-level staff to the president, the courts or to the heads of departments without the consent of Congress.

Thousands of such appointees serve in federal, state and local governments; some are expected to carry out a particular mandate of the party and/or are subject to much political pressure to do so, others are not. It depends on the issue, the party and the time (e.g., election period). Politicians, as do most in industry, often think in short-term modalities; they want special immediate advantages because of their position.

On the other hand, most staff of environmental agencies (and other agencies as well) reach their positions through competitive civil service examinations, regardless of political affiliation. Government staff, in most state and local agencies, are protected by procedures based on a merit system developed by the U.S. Civil Service Commission. Senior staff with many years in an agency have an advantage over new political appointees by knowing networks in other agencies, political power-brokers, as well as influential industry contacts. Some use this information to put themselves in a strong position with a new appointee.

The majority of environmental agency staff, almost two-thirds of the sample, complained about political interference in their work, especially cutting budgets or not budgeting enough to carry out mandates of the law, as well as blatant political moves to subvert the agency's work. Even in state or local governments where environmental problems, such as toxic waste or polluted lakes and streams, had been popular issues, legislators often passed laws but didn't authorize enough money to carry out the laws' intent. Agency personnel, not environmental groups, are the first to understand the implications of the allocation process.

Other methods, such as reorganization, are commonly used by political appointees for political purposes. One respondent recalled mid-1981 when EPA Administrator Anne Gorsuch Burford dropped the unit responsible for enforcing federal anti-pollution laws. Burford claimed she simply was developing more efficient management by decentralizing enforcement into the four operating divisions of air, water, solid wastes and toxic substances. The actual impact, according to the respondent, was to make it more difficult to cite violators; local units concentrate on technical advising, not enforcement.

Other comments, representing 8 percent of the total sample, indi-cated that, particularly in small agencies, political appointees reorganize the department and make themselves direct supervisors of inspectors. Thus, the director has responsibility to follow up on complaints, negotiate with noncomplying companies, or redirect the budgets to projects less controversial than enforcement. These administrators do not seem inclined to compromise on their fixed position, whether personally or party-inspired.

Some respondents commented on traditional antagonisms between states and the federal government, particularly over allocation of federal funds. Many states resent federal intrusion and, particularly if they are required to put the heat on influential and financially supportive industries, prefer to let the feds handle enforcement. There are so many political ways to block action—by using procedures and "going by the book" to underbudgeting—that cleanup always takes years longer than expected. I received 34 examples of political interference into agency work, all perceived as negative influences.

At times it happens that day-to-day environmental policy is developed by old-hand agency personnel themselves, often in an alliance with industry specialists. In one state, with understaffed, poorly paid, part-time legislators, a number of state engineers met with counterparts in industry to work out standards and procedures. As a younger agency staff member, non-engineer, put it:

"The whole thing was incredible. One day we don't have any on-site/off-site criteria (for hazardous waste generators), and these guys meet with their buddies (engineers in the chemical industry) down the road; and the next day, there they (the criteria) are—all neat and tied up in a package." The federal RCRA requirements on many issues are minimal, so it is possible for states to impose a wide variety of rules on industry. The minimal option, based on "economic" and engineering feasibility, tends to be chosen in his state, according to the respondent.

Case Example

The Environmental Department of a large Sun Belt state was organized in the 1970s along the lines of the sections of the EPA. Although the amount of work in the department is huge—permitting, inspecting, enforcement of air, water, solid and hazardous waste—fewer than 70 employees handle it all. The reason lies in the tiny budget allocated by the Legislature; although many additional funds are provided by the EPA, it's not nearly enough to manage the work of the agency.

Industry in the state generates more than 800,000 metric tons of hazardous waste, which must be tracked from generation to disposal, and several thousand hazardous waste and other pollution-generating firms must be permitted and inspected. Because of the small number of agency personnel, most companies are inspected by the state about every two and a half years, though the EPA has stepped into this breach from time to time when it has received a significant number of complaints from environmental groups.

The Legislature has passed environmental laws that measure up to minimal standards, somewhat stricter when the demands of an active environmental community have had to be accommodated. Yet, for at least 10 years, the Legislature has grossly underfunded the environmental agency, assuming that the level of compliance is acceptable and there is no need to increase funding or staff.

Environmental problems in the state have gradually intensified because of increases in population, especially around three metropolitan areas, new business and industrial activity and traffic problems. More than three dozen documented hazardous waste dumps are contaminating local water supplies, and negligible state funds, at the time of the interviews, were unavailable to begin a cleanup. Significant air- and water-pollution problems plague the state.

The director of the state agency, a political appointee, shows little interest in environmental problems, according to respondents in the state. The chief administrator is a career bureaucrat, who reflects the will of the Legislature and the conservative director and rarely asks for more funds or staff and never makes difficult decisions. Most agency personnel accept the situation, either because they agree with the mild policies or because they prefer not to increase their workloads or because they think nothing can be done to change the way the agency operates.

Three department agency staff members believe the primary cause of the deteriorating environment in their state lies with the Legislature, which neither funds the agency properly nor wants to create a "bad business climate" by strictly enforcing regulations. Although no one has actively held them back from doing their jobs, state personnel rarely cite violators, and enforcing only with small fines clearly signals that the agency is not serious about enforcement. The following are comments by the three agency staff:

The big problem here is that we don't know who is violating the law and who isn't. The state is big and there are thousands of potential polluters out there. Our supervisors even try to pinch pennies by allocating gas money to the inspectors.

It will take us 10 to 15 years to license all the toxic waste generators and handlers in the state, and that is no exaggeration. There are illegal waste dumps all over the place. Practically none of our direct dischargers (of industry or municipal treatment plants) is monitored on a regular basis.

What bothers me is that no one even pushes the Legislature for more money or more staff. They say we'll just have to get along with what we have. Well, to get by we'd need at least three times as much money and staff. We're not getting by, and that's a fact.

Several of the problems listed as "political" referred to problems with leadership, perceived inequity of workload and inequitable treatment of other personnel or conflicts of value, as well as outside political interference. Most respondents understand that politics plays the major role in how the agency functions, in terms of budget allocation, leadership, and interplay among political appointees and career staff.

Yet, only when clear agency goals are set up and means to achieve the goals agreed upon, in the framework of political conflicts, can the work of environmental management in agencies begin. The work environment within many agencies explains why enforcement practices vary widely, and enforcement actions often fall short of regulatory guidelines.

Implementation and Regulatory Procedures

About 30 percent of the sample indicated difficulties in trying to implement the regulations by simply persuading companies not in compliance to take substantial steps toward compliance. Trying to persuade firms to comply with pollution-control regulations voluntarily often proves to be a problematic tactic, especially if standards are challenged in court and resolution of the case is not imminent. Standards change or, more often, are challenged, then change. Companies are given temporary permits justifying noncompliance for a period of time, and hold them indefinitely. Meantime, agency personnel suggest methods of compliance, usually to no avail.

Sometimes local agencies sympathize, aid and abet their local firms in this purpose; this is possible because most federal environmental laws delegate regulatory powers to the states, which then pass them along to local or regional bodies. If a complaint about local delays in enforcing the law reaches a federal office, it takes some time to respond, and when it does the EPA may find the firm is "making an effort" to solve the pollution problem. Environmental laws generally prescribe that controls be fashioned to meet the circumstances of the offender and equities of the situation, i.e. whether they threaten jobs or bankruptcies.

Agencies know they cannot watch all potential violators closely or regularly, and that it doesn't do much good to threaten court action, particularly when industry financial resources exceed the agencies'. Very often, the agencies depend on engineers from industry for technical information; therefore, they spend a great deal of time trying to work with the plant manager. More recently, the EPA and some state agencies have tended to spend most of their resources on highly visible, larger firms, taking them to court, hoping to set examples with large fines and occasional imprisonments. It's not clear how effective this strategy has been, but most smaller companies now realize that environmental agencies have been loathe to take actions that would put them out of business, send their officers to jail, or even fine them heavily. This realization makes it difficult for federal technical personnel to work out a compliance program and timetable with a company that is inspected by local agencies that often are in no hurry to prosecute.

Rule-Making and Other Complications

Prior to such compliance negotiations, however, agencies are involved in complicated tasks, the most time-consuming of which is rule-making. The process occurs both on the federal and the state levels, since states can establish their own standards as long as they meet minimal federal standards. The EPA has five steps in its rule-making process: initial review, working party review, steering committee review, external review and administrator decision. The process involves everything from scientific data and alternatives analysis to environmental, health, economic and energy impact analysis. Everyone gets into the act on the federal level: the Office of Management and Budget, which attempts to substitute less costly alternatives; regulated firms and trade groups, which always have their own science advisers to debate health and environmental costs; congressional committees, other affected agencies, and of course the public and environmental organizations that have an interest in the rules. Public hearings are held throughout the country. It takes at least four years for each rule to get by these hurdles. While the EPA is trying to develop a consensus among affected interests, not much is happening in the trenches, except a little jawboning by agency staff.

The complexity of rule-making is one reason it took four years to implement the first rules of the Resource Conservation and Recovery Act (RCRA). Before the states started to define and implement their own rules, the EPA had to identify hazardous wastes; establish a manifest system for tracking the wastes from generation to transporter to disposal facility; set federal minimum standards for hazardous waste disposal, enforced through permits for disposal facilities. As we shall see in the final chapter, few people along the way understood the basis of the research, which dictated the level of the standards, criteria, rules. Furthermore, although all interested parties are brought into the rule-making somewhere in the process, the context remains a conflict from beginning to end. The context for the rules is not established cooperatively from the beginning by concerned interest groups.

States that wanted more protection held their own rule-making process, and went through the same agonizing appraisal the EPA staff suffered. But a great many states did nothing until they received federal funds, for which they were not eligible until they submitted an implementation plan. A few states did nothing because they were not willing to commit money and agency resources to establish programs that were especially unpopular with the industrial community, which was not even interested in the scientific basis for the standards. It is not difficult to understand why agency personnel on both the state and federal levels were frustrated for many years after the passage of RCRA. In the perception of the public, which heard weekly horror stories about Love Canal and dozens of local toxic waste dumps, the villain of the story was the EPA or the state regulatory agency.

But the public usually was not organized, and when environmental groups publicly attacked state agencies, conservative administrators passed the blame to the EPA, citing its slowness in making rules. At the same time, industry complained to legislators about the inadequacy of the scientific basis of the rules or standards. Thus, corporations tended to appeal to the courts, whose criteria mainly refer to questions of fairness, consistency and reasonableness. Environmental questions and equity to groups most sensitive to toxic materials very often end up in the court battles by contending interest groups. The process is messy and agencies fall between environmental groups and industry. It is not a comfortable position in which one can happily dream about free-flowing streams and mountain valleys. Therefore, the respondents who commented about difficulties in the regulations spoke about the tradition of voluntary compliance in their agencies as well as the problems associated with rule-making.

Case Example

The respondent in this case is a young man in a state water department who performs field inspections for violations of the Clean Water Act, checking for unauthorized discharges of wastes to waters, either surface or groundwater. He also reviews permit applications, wastewater permits and waste disposal permits, as well as investigates complaints about leaking underground tanks. Furthermore, he is responsible for enforcement procedures, such as cleanup and abatement orders and cease-and-desist orders.

Though there are thousands of on-site and off-site industrial waste facilities, municipal waste sites, and oil and gas drilling operations in the state, fewer than 70 personnel handle all the permitting and monitoring activity. A state this size would be expected to have at least 250 agency personnel.

The state agency has been unwilling to go beyond the minimal EPA rules for hazardous waste disposal, particularly specific land-use rules for disposal of oil drilling wastes or criteria for siting waste disposal landfills because of a long-standing controversy over their own hazardous waste legislation. The agency announced to its critics that it planned to hold public hearings on the rules, but never followed through, later claiming it could not afford to take time away from more pressing work.

Neither has the agency taken anyone to court, or sent cases to local district attorneys, for major or minor violations of the regulations. Staff believe that if they can eventually achieve voluntary compliance to their satisfaction, they will save time and money. Other state agencies have maintained the same position. Where cleanup of dump sites is involved, they also feel they can save court costs and have the site cleaned up sooner.

Because the state never wrote its own regulations on oil- and gas-drilling wastes, which are exempt from RCRA rules, a number of groundwater aquifers and wells have been contaminated by wastes from drilling muds and brine, carrying high salt concentrations, toxic metals and organic chemicals. The 66,000 drilling wastes in the country are customarily placed in pits or ponds or injected deep into the ground, or, in the case of brine, discharged directly into rivers and streams. The state and the EPA have been hesitant about using authority from the Clean Water Act to take steps toward proper disposal of these wastes.

One of the people in the middle of these controversies is the respondent who provided information in this case example. Here is how he described the problem:

> At the moment we are in a serious situation in this state. We know about over 100 cases of noncompliance (of hazardous waste rules) out there right now, and we still think that they're going to run right out and clean up their dumps by themselves. We haven't pushed any of these guys. They just laugh at me when I go out and tell them they've got to do something about their problem soon. When my boss goes with me, they sit down and have a cup of coffee and talk about good old times. I've written reports about these fellows for three years now, and no one's done anything.
>
> Then when I go back to my office I have some environmentalists waiting for me with another 20 or 30 names and they ask me if we did anything about the other names they gave me. Then they start shouting at me as though I'm covering up something. They're generally OK, though. They know I'm on their side, but the department is just dragging its feet.
>
> What I wish we could do around here is tighten up some rules on landfills and injection wells. I know darn well that stuff (hazardous waste) is going to end up in our groundwater. Sure as shootin' it will.

As reasonable as the voluntary compliance policy seems, the procedure does not offer a strong incentive for companies not in compliance to change their mode of operations. They have no reason to do anything but "talk about good old times."

Bureaucratic Inertia

About 25 percent of the total sample complained of problems within their agencies, in most cases about supervisors who care more about their own careers or their own biases than about doing the agency's work. Their responses often were a mixture of professional, ideological and personal opinion.

For example, in six cases the respondents, all among lower-level agency personnel, described supervisors who either acted very slowly or not at all in regard to compliance cases. In the majority of these cases, these midlevel supervisors appeared to be carrying out the policies of senior managers or directors. Junior personnel wanted their superiors to act aggressively on environmental issues, and midlevel managers wanted to protect their positions. It seemed to me that at least in some of these cases, the managers would have acted aggressively in a progressive political climate, just as they had learned how to act conservatively in a conservative political environment.

In five other cases, differences existed in professional approaches, specifically between senior engineers and environmental scientists or biologists. Currently, engineers occupy the majority of senior positions in environmental agencies, even health departments where engineers head toxic-waste divisions. Their training encourages the assumption that most technical problems can be solved economically simply by applying tested engineering principles. Therefore, engineers tend to utilize standard designs off the shelf and traditional methods of disposal, such as large wastewater treatment plants, deep-well injection systems or liners in land disposal sites. Many environmental scientists tend to look more to alternative technologies or recycling and eschew solutions that do not lessen long-term environmental and health risks. The young biologist quoted above opposed the solutions (deep-well injection and land disposal) agreed upon by agency engineers because he was convinced that these solutions represent long-term danger of ground-water contamination.

A final group of sporadic comments complained about bureaucratic work habits in agencies as being nonproductive at best and parasitic at worst, particularly in locations where a great deal of work needed to be done.

Case Example

An environmental scientist in a municipal division of a state water commission was assigned to investigate pollution violations of a suburb of a metropolitan area. One older section of the town had not been connected to a main sewer line because it was separated from it by a small lake and several miles, so each property owner installed his or her own septic system.

The inspector found widespread and serious pollution problems, including the direct discharge of sewage into a river that a few miles downstream was used for recreation and fishing and for drinking water 12 miles away. The city was in direct violation of several sections of the Clean Water Act.

The city had three options: build a sewer line to the wastewater treatment plant of a nearby city (closer than its own line, which could not handle the additional sewage); build a new treatment plant for that section of the city; or develop a local communal treatment system with subsurface disposal of treatment system effluent, an alternative that has been successfully utilized in other parts of the country.

In the first case, the neighboring plant would be obliged to add facilities to handle the increased effluent because it already was in violation for unsuitable treatment. A new treatment plant for the suburb would be extremely costly to construct and maintain.

The inspector recommended the alternative system as long as several safety controls could be provided, particularly land available with soils suitable for the subsurface disposal of treatment system effluent. He talked the city into commissioning a study to present a detailed engineering proposal. The study showed that each house would install a new septic tank/pump chambers, where solids would settle or be screened out; effluent would receive a second subsurface sand filter treatment off the chambers, and be pumped to a final soil absorption system in a lot outside town that would act as a leachfield. By the final phase, the effluent would lack significant contaminants and odor.

The proposal was rejected by senior engineers in the department as an untested solution. This is how the inspector expressed his disappointment:

> I worked for over a year on all aspects of the proposal and was excited about it because it could have acted as a model for the many small towns around the state that simply can't afford big treatment plants. Even with federal money, these towns don't have the funds to keep them going, or get trained people to run them.
>
> The engineers here don't want to take a chance on anything except what they know, and that is the standard design they studied in engineering school. For them it's either Metcalf & Eddy (basic wastewater treatment engineering design textbook) or nothing. They don't care about small-scale technology or about solving problems for little communities. All my work down the tubes.

From this environmentalist's perspective, it is important to find alternatives for the hundreds of small communities in the country, which are still not in compliance with the Clean Water Act because of difficulties getting funds for water treatment. Construction costs for treatment plants went up about 60 percent between 1972 (Clean Water Act) and 1983. In many cases, according to a 1981 EPA report that reviewed the federal sewage treatment construction grant program, there are dozens of inadequately constructed and poorly maintained plants whose construction was a very poor investment. The report cited grantees who did not have the technical expertise to manage their projects properly, and plants that did not fit the community in which they were built. A large portion of the report highlighted deficiencies in design, plans and specifications. The 1982 reauthorization bill specifically recommends nontraditional means to handle sewage problems.

Agencies with NEPA Requirements

Because the National Environmental Policy Act requires that the environmental impacts of major federal actions be carefully evaluated before the projects are permitted to proceed, most federal agencies dealing with land and water, such as the Forest Service, the Park Service, the Bureau of Reclamation and the Army Corps of Engineers, have hired their own environmental analysts to review their major projects. Eleven environmental analysts from these agencies as well as two from local environmental review boards responded to my questionnaire, and I interviewed five of them. It also should be noted that about half of the states have their own versions of NEPA, many of them much stronger. California, for example, requires environmental impact reports for private development projects (exempted in NEPA), before local governments can issue building permits.

There was an uncommon level of agreement among the analysts about the problems, obstacles and possibilities of NEPA, so it is possible to summarize their comments as one response. For example, they all agreed that the intent of the environmental review process usually is not fulfilled and few agency policies have been significantly changed because of it, for reasons beyond overwork and budgetary limitations. They also agreed that the law and the process it established has significantly affected project planning and increased sensitivity to environmental issues. The very least that can be said for the law is that plans for a great number of highways, dams, airports, coal mines, oil drilling and buildings have been postponed and in a few cases stopped. And in many instances the projects had to undergo modifications in design, relocation and other changes to mitigate undesirable environmental effects.

Many of the respondents have begun to view their role as educational, alerting old-guard agency bureaucrats and the public to potential conflicts over upcoming projects. Although the findings of the review process need only be considered, not necessarily acted on, environmental groups can take legal action to stop projects in which agencies appear not to have acted on information in the review document, particularly if the agency decision seems "arbitrary and capricious," or if the document or the agency does not consider alternatives the environmental group can present. Significantly, most of the respondents also said they believed project modifications would not occur if this legal action were not a threat to agency bureaucrats. In the case of NEPA, the citizen's "agency" remains the courts.

Respondents believe the review process has introduced a new kind of holistic, interdisciplinary analysis (though three thought the analysis is usually poorly done) that forces project developers to consider a wide array of impacts and interrelationships between the built and the natural environment. These are the kinds of questions that come up in public hearings and in court so that all parties involved in a project must consider them, even if it causes grief and delays for the project managers.

Serge Taylor (1984) studied the way the U.S. Forest Service and the Army Corps of Engineers were affected by NEPA between 1972-78 and concluded that the law has begun to refashion some of our administrative and political institutions, for reasons already stated and some of his own. He says the review process has introduced analytical competition between old-guard bureaucrats and the younger environmental analysts hired to draw up the reports for agency projects. Taylor believes the EIS science model or strategy of reform adds new kinds of information to the knowledge the agency has accumulated over time, and the agencies are now in the position of advancing a new kind of institutional knowledge through analytical competition, the type that exists in the scientific community.

Taylor also uncovered similar difficulties among his respondents as I did in this study. He became aware of the plight of the environmental scientist who often is viewed as the enemy because he or she represents a threat to the agency's projects—and next year's budget.

One of my respondents summarized his position in a sometimes alien agency environment in this way:

> Sometimes I don't feel exactly loved around here. For one thing, any engineer who works on a project thinks of it like his baby, and cannot stand the idea that there might be anything wrong with it. They seem to be unable to cope with the notion that they're not thought of as the salvation of this country, or that there is another way to look at a problem.
>
> We have the most trouble with them when we look at alternatives to the project. This is the most important part of the report anyway, not the other 10,000 pages. I usually have to watch it if I mention something that one of the environmental organizations said at a public meeting. They're not supposed to be experts but they're much better than anyone around here when it comes to looking at alternatives. The rest of them (engineers and project managers) have a hard time thinking beyond costs and benefits, and a pretty narrow range of benefits at that.
>
> Our EISes rarely are considered seriously. I often wonder if it's worth it to me to stay around here much longer. We don't get our budget to stop building dams, or to stop dredging up the rivers. . . .
>
> We are getting some new environmental work in the agency monitoring water projects. This looks more interesting than compiling a lot of facts into a report that doesn't seem to make much difference.

Like analysts in federal agencies, the respondents in state and local agencies came from a variety of disciplinary backgrounds: environmental science, biology, forestry, planning, political science, public administration, engineering and liberal arts. Though there appeared to be a difference in approach and opinion between engineers and non-engineers, and between younger and older agency personnel, the rest of the differences in comment and opinion seemed to depend on career goals, commitments and even personality traits.

Agency Culture and Personnel

Environmental work in industry and in agencies represents obviously different goals and subcultures. Their personnel reflect those differences dramatically. For example, everyone working in a business or corporation knows that if they do not make money, they won't be in business. This "bottom line" consideration tempers even the most enthusiastic environmental manager, junior or senior, and provides a commonality between them and the rest of the firm, even those working on the production line.

Although agencies have goals as do other organizations, and their personnel have specific duties, other factors such as personal priorities, career goals, constituencies (if middle- or upper-level manager), personalities and commitments seem to play a larger role than agency goals in the day-to-day implementation of policy. At the same time, traditions and procedures in public agencies control the personnel in a way that shapes the way they do business.

I have grouped respondents and their colleagues (described by respondents) into three types, depending on the way they have acted in implementing environmental policy in their agencies: Risk-averse conservatives, pragmatist conservatives and ideologically committed. It is possible to exhibit combinations of two or even three of the types, but usually one predominates.

Risk-averse conservatives are the people a number of the respondents complained about because of their tendency to delay compliance procedures, resist new methods of problem-solving, or take any action at all. They generally are long-time agency personnel with much seniority who have developed slow, methodical work habits that have proven effective at evaluation time. They are risk-averse in the sense that they avoid conflicts. ("He is only interested in one thing," said one respondent. "He just wants to keep his flank covered.") Their techniques deal with "going by the book," documenting all their activities for the record (protecting their flanks), and avoiding any change (or challenge) in his or her day-to-day work patterns. They are the last to jump in the pool.

Pragmatist conservatives could also be called careerists, as that is the motivating force in their activities. This type was identified as also taking a conservative approach to implementing environmental policy, but the reason appeared to be that their own superiors wanted them to act that way. In a different political climate with more aggressive superiors they might have acted more aggressively, particularly if it seemed such action would gain them favorable notice. However, in most instances, pragmatists are also risk-averse because risks imply the possibility of failure, the most-feared outcome for career-oriented people. It is better to act too slowly than too fast, for fear of making the wrong career move. ("Don't be the first or the last to jump into the pool," as the old saw goes.) Until they are certain of the correct move, they will set up a committee or hide behind procedures, which is why they tend to be poorly regarded by environmentalist-oriented agency personnel. Some in this group intend to gain enough experience to move to the private sector and do not want to develop a bad reputation in industrial circles. The majority of agency personnel seem to fit into the two types of conservative groupings: they have found out it doesn't pay to alienate supervisors by moving on an issue too quickly, to become too visible in their work, or to go too far beyond what is written in one's job description.

Ideologically committed personnel refers not only to the environmentally committed, who comprised about half of the respondents, but also to ideologically conservative directors, political appointees of the Reagan administration or conservative governors. Of course, many ideological conservatives are not political appointees. Ideologies also can be developed through one's education. Engineering solutions, for example, tend to be conservative and establishment-oriented since by definition they must be cost-effective and efficient according to a very narrow calculus. Life scientists and environmentalists do not place such a high value on the economic, particularly a short-term economic, analysis. As previously noted, an engineering/non-engineering struggle emerged in the comments of a number of environmentally oriented

GOAL DEFINITION IN INDUSTRY AND GOVERNMENT

PERSONAL ADVANCEMENT

INCREASE CORPORATE PROFITS

DEVELOP CORPORATE IMAGE

GENERATE CUSTOMER SATISFACTION

PROVIDE PRODUCTS AND SERVICES

DEFINE NICHE IN MARKETPLACE

STAFF PERCEIVES PERSONAL ADVANCEMENT IS LINKED TO ACHIEVING THE CORPORATE MISSION.

WHICH PATH LEADS TO PERSONAL ADVANCEMENT?

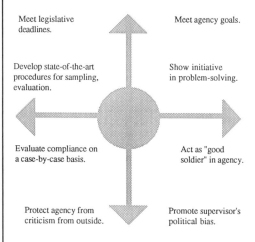

Pursue vigorous enforcement.

Meet legislative deadlines.

Meet agency goals.

Develop state-of-the-art procedures for sampling, evaluation.

Show initiative in problem-solving.

Evaluate compliance on a case-by-case basis.

Act as "good soldier" in agency.

Protect agency from criticism from outside.

Promote supervisor's political bias.

Give industry the benefit of the doubt.

PERSONAL ADVANCEMENT MAY BE LINKED TO ONE OR MORE CHANGING, INCOMPATIBLE GOALS ACTIVE IN THE AGENCY.

The path to career success is clearly defined to employees in industry, and environmental professionals can advance insofar as the environmental program is integrated into the long-term goals of the firm. In government agencies, political factors can play an important role, causing careers to shift with the political winds. Professional standards do not necessarily determine career advancement in either sector.

respondents. Many respondents were ideologically committed to environmental change, very competent and hard-working. They admitted that, in their haste to correct environmental problems, they often made mistakes, but could not understand why so many of their colleagues never wanted to utilize their positions to full advantage and be aggressive in implementing the regulations.

Another difference between agency personnel was between older and younger staff, though the typological differences described above seemed more operant. That is, many young people are risk-averse because they place their careers above personal ideologies. But in general the questionnaires and interviews indicated that younger personnel are more environmentally committed than older personnel, who may have been transferred to the agency from another department. Agency "personality" differs greatly, and it is difficult to generalize or predict effectiveness from location, age of personnel, or disciplinary backgrounds. Older personnel usually can accomplish far more than younger employees because they know the ropes and how to use their power.

Conclusions

Since environmental legislation has grown steadily over the past generation, the demands it has placed on federal, state and local agencies have been unprecedented, particularly in light of continual budget-cutting on all levels of government. The most an adequate budget can do, however, is provide the precondition of an effective agency; a strong legislative mandate to enforce the law also must be present. Other problems are bound up with the regulations, institutions and personnel, along with the conflicts that come with strong ideologies and political power. It is also clear that many agencies have not been able to organize themselves to do their work effectively. Many agency offices lacked an organized routine, perhaps because of ineffective leadership or the overwhelming workload, probably both.

Quality of agency staff is critically important in their training, commitment and even energy level. Most agencies have reported a steady drift of their environmental specialists to the private sector, sometimes because of morale problems, more often because of higher pay. Because the agency tasks are difficult, top-quality leadership is essential to define and clarify goals and to attract an excellent staff and cheer it to worthwhile accomplishments.

Whenever I interviewed at a federal or state agency with good morale and at least moderate success, the head of the agency or office was an excellent manager, highly competent, sensitive to staff needs, fair in distributing work assignments. The effectiveness of the office is lessened by weak or poor leadership. As in industry, these managers have great control over behavior and morale of their workers. This conclusion, although not an unusual finding, remains the most critical because top public administrators are usually political appointees.

In general, in the agencies, I found large numbers of good-willed, hard-working people who have to cope with myriad obstacles to enforce the law and perform their duties effectively. Very often this group has not grasped the technical requirements of the field: risk assessment, the sophistication of analytical instrumentation and pollution-control technologies, much less the production processes. On a higher level, enforcement of environmental regulations generally has not yet become a government priority despite public and environmentalist pressure. Thus have environmental groups grown and become increasingly effective in the task of environmental protection. It also is more apparent that the training for environmental professionals in all sectors of public activity must become more demanding.

Bibliography

The Politics of Pollution by J. Clarence and Barbara Davies (1977), cited at the end of Chapter Three, again provides a very useful appraisal of federal, state and local government implementation of environmental legislation. Guy Benveniste's *Regulation & Planning: The Case of Environmental Politics* (San Francisco: Boyd & Fraser, 1981) is an excellent presentation of "the way government bodies interact with the private sector," using environmental regulations as grist for his mill. Three more books further show how environmental regulations have been implemented in the past generation: *The Politics of Hazardous Waste Management,* edited by James P. Lester and Ann O'M. Bowman (Durham, N.C.: Duke University Press, 1983); *Environmental Policy Implementation,* edited by Dean E. Mann (Lexington, Mass.: Lexington Books, 1982); and Elizabeth Haskell and Victoria Price, *State Environmental Management* (New York: Praeger, 1973). The book cited in the text on "the environmental impact statement strategy of administrative reform" is Serge Taylor, *Making Bureaucracies Think* (Stanford, Calif.: Stanford University Press, 1984).

CHAPTER FIVE

Environmental Groups

"We can't let up for a second."

This statement in 1982 was part of an exhortation by a young woman to members of a San Francisco neighborhood group attempting to get the Regional Air Quality Control Board to close down a nearby specialty steel plant. Her words capture the mood of many contemporary environmental groups: intensity, doggedness, commitment, suspicious of industry and doubtful about the usefulness of government. Often disappointed by agencies, they have learned to put their own kind of pressure on industry and politicians. They have been able to elect their own candidates, press for better enforcement, wage campaigns against polluters, rewrite environmental laws, go to court and influence the media to present their views.

Yet it is difficult to generalize about voluntary citizens groups. Some are national and large, such as the Sierra Club and the National Audubon Society; some are ad hoc, organized for a short time for a specific purpose, as was the Love Canal group and the group the woman quoted above belonged to. Some are old and conservative, such as the National Wildlife Federation, with millions of members and supporters; the majority have come into existence since 1970 and are much smaller. Many focus on the natural environment, ecology and natural history issues. Some, such as the Izaac Walton League, are linked to sportsmen's or hunting and fishing groups. Still others direct their energies toward such issues as nuclear power, e.g. Friends of the Earth. More recent groups have focused on issues of human health and cancer.

There are hundreds of these groups, and all share a concern for the natural environment, ecological issues and/or human health deterioration because of environmental pollution. They are comprised of people who do not believe government agencies, legislators and, most of all, private industry, will act positively to solve environmental problems unless they are pressured into it—by citizens or the courts. They lobby lawmakers, petition them to act, accuse and harass agencies they believe are sloughing off their duty, picket and boycott private industry, educate the public and utilize the mass media.

A few national groups, including the Environmental Defense Fund and the Natural Resources Defense Council, founded in 1967 and 1970, respectively, were organized to take legal action in court to defend environmental positions. Using the courts has been an effective tool for all environmental groups because the courts traditionally have been less open to manipulation by politicians and private industry, and because public trials have generated much-needed publicity for the environmentalist cause.

These groups constitute the third force, along with industry and the agencies, in U.S. environmental management. The environmental movement has greatly influenced public policy, federal and state legislation, and implementation of environmental rules throughout the nation. While industry has developed large and effective teams of lobbyists that pressure EPA with their own scientific data supporting lenient standards and enforcement, the environmental community has sent its experts to testify at public hearings.

Through court cases, environmental groups undoubtedly have extended the reach of some legislation, broadening the interpretation of the scope of environmental impact statements as prescribed by the National Environmental Policy Act. Environmental organizations have stopped or delayed huge construction projects, redirected agency enforcement efforts, forced multinational corporations to comply with pollution abatement regulations, and pushed legislators into action. Very often groups have joined together in alliances for lawsuits or particular campaigns, such as the Clean Air Coalition, the Energy Coalition, the Alaska Coalition and others on the national or local level, for legislation to protect the wilderness, wild rivers, drinking water, laboratory animals, whales, and so on.

Most significant about environmental groups is that less than a generation ago they were dismissed as unimportant, many were considered strange and effete, nor were they so successful or effective in their work. This chapter examines models of environmental groups and reasons for their unanticipated effectiveness.

Four Models

The first and most traditional model emphasizes environmental education and policy formation on a national scale; the second includes those that primarily undertake local grass-roots political work; the third model is derived from public interest/activist groups; the fourth is the environmental law or litigation model, which has characterized the EDF and NRDC and sections of other environmental organizations.

National Education Organizations

Myriad groups have been created to establish a national constituency for environmental concerns, mainly through education. Besides such well-known, established conservation groups as the Sierra Club, National Audubon Society, Wilderness Society and National Wildlife Federation—all of which use education and legislation to protect and conserve natural resources—hundreds of more specialized groups work in similar ways, through publications and membership networking designed to influence legislation. These groups want to gain millions of supporters, then use this constituency to get enacted laws favoring conservation and environmental protection.

National organizations, particularly the older groups, exist not only to educate the public about general environmental issues, but also specific conservation problems concerning wilderness and animal and plant

110

species: birds, wildfowl, wild horses, whooping cranes, wetlands, wild rivers, laboratory animals, deserts, sport fishing, stripers, oceans, trout, beavers, trumpeter swans, dunes, tall grass prairies, safari animals, pacific seabirds, redwoods, rare trees, cetacean species, and dozens more. There are numerous groups organized for each of these and other species. Furthermore, there are groups whose special interest focuses on air and water quality, toxic waste, energy, land use and environmental health concerns. They all have their own education programs. The groups solicit membership nationwide, publish newsletters and books, sponsor conferences, circulate petitions and attempt to influence the passage of legislation.

Depending on size, the organizations have a staff, paid or unpaid, office and a mailing address. Most larger organizations have a small paid staff, a core of volunteers who work on the publications, projects and research, and a large membership that supports the organization's work with contributions. Until the mid-1970s, national organizations relied on local chapters for new members, but since then have devoted a greater percentage of their income to direct mail campaigns. They have shared membership lists, spreading the word of their work while they campaign for members and funds. Although the groups attempt to influence legislation, they usually do no official lobbying, as that would affect their tax-exempt status.

Tax-Deductible Contributions

Lobbying is non-tax-deductible political activity, according to a U.S. Supreme Court decision in 1954. Since much of the work of environmental groups deals with legislative efforts, some environmentalists have established a special organization to lobby in Washington, the Citizens Committee on Natural Resources. With a special lobbying organization, the groups have been able to concentrate on education, citizens' petitions and letters to their local members of Congress—as well as retain their tax-exempt status. Besides its membership club, the Sierra Club has established a special tax-exempt foundation to finance educational and scientific projects and publications, as well as a tax-exempt legal defense fund to support environmental lawsuits.

In 1970, the Internal Revenue Service ruled that the then-newly established National Resources Defense Council could not have tax-exempt status if it planned litigation, which was and is the purpose of the organization. At the time, the IRS indicated it was reviewing the tax-exempt status of other environmental organizations. In its letter to NRDC, the IRS claimed: "Litigation is a coercive activity, like boycotts, picketing, demonstrations, and disruptive protests and therefore should not be considered charitable."

The IRS action provoked a national outcry of protest, including from the influential Sen. Sam J. Ervin, Jr., William Ruckelshaus, Russell Train, Ralph Nader and editorials in the press throughout the country. The IRS backed down, issuing new guidelines allowing litigation by tax-exempt environmental groups if done in the public interest. This ruling did not include the Sierra Club, the Citizens Committee on Natural Resources or Friends of the Earth, which publicizes its lobbying efforts. It did include the traditional conservation groups, which concentrate on education and letter-writing but often join other groups in lawsuits to protect resources or stop pollution.

The following describe the work of some of the better-known national environmental groups, listed in the National Wildlife Federation's *1985 Conservation Directory*. The descriptions are edited from their own materials.

National Wildlife Federation

This non-profit conservation organization is dedicated to educating the public about the need for wise use, proper management and conservation of the natural resources upon which all life depends: air, water, soils, minerals, forests, plant life and wildlife. It distributes numerous periodicals and other educational materials, sponsors outdoor education programs in conservation and litigates environmental disputes in an effort to conserve natural resources and wildlife. Organized: 1936. Publications: *International Wildlife, National Wildlife*—unusually beautiful magazines that are unique recruiting devices—as well as a conservation report on Congress, conservation stamps, albums, an annual conservation directory, conservation education pamphlets, catalogues, and more.

Sierra Club

This well-known membership group was founded in 1892 by John Muir to:

- Protect and conserve the natural resources of the Sierra Nevada mountains, the United States and the world;
- Undertake and publish educational studies concerning all aspects of the environment and the natural ecosystems of the world;
- Preserve and restore the quality of that environment and the integrity of these ecosystems.

With 50 chapters coast to coast, the club's non-profit program includes work on legislation, litigation, public information, wilderness outings, white-water trips, skiing, mountaineering, knapsacking, films, exhibits, conferences, 14 huts and lodges, a library, and publishing. Publications: *Sierra* as well as reports on environmental news and local chapter monthly bulletins, and a line of Sierra Club Books.

National Audubon Society

Founded in 1905, Audubon Society is among the oldest of the conservation organizations in North America. Its purposes are to:

- Promote the conservation of wildlife and the natural environment;
- Educate citizens about their relationship with, and their place within, the natural environment as an ecological system;
- Publications: *Audubon, Audubon Leader, American Birds.*

Wilderness Society

This national conservation organization was created to secure preservation of wilderness, educate the public about the value of wilderness and how it may be best used and preserved in the public interest, to encourage scientific studies of wilderness, and to mobilize cooperation in resisting its invasion. Organized: 1935. Publications: *The Living Wilderness, Wilderness Report.*

Grass-Roots Groups

People who remain in small, voluntary, local environmental groups over a long period of time are likely to also belong to some large national group such as the Sierra Club, working on local issues through a local chapter. These local offices are divided into committees that focus on specific concerns such as toxic waste, development or land use, wilderness, water and air quality. In regions with active local chapters, the committees are continuously busy.

Other kinds of ad hoc grass-roots groups also draw on local populations for limited periods because of environmental problems that arouse people normally less committed to environmental causes; for example, in 1977, when a few people living at Love Canal, N.Y., were alarmed that chemicals from a toxic dump site were seeping into their basements. Most residents of the neighborhood initially were unconcerned. Later, a state health officer declared the "inner ring" of the neighborhood, the section nearest an abandoned chemical dump site, to be a health hazard, particularly for young children and pregnant women, and the neighborhood quickly formed a Love Canal Homeowners Association to lobby for government funds to move all endangered families to safe environments.

The leader of the homeowners group, Lois Gibbs, did her own survey of health problems of residents of the outer ring and found a high incidence of disease and miscarriages. During the next two years, the neighborhood became progressively radicalized as members of the group attended public meetings, confronted state officials, circulated petitions, sent delegations to Washington, D.C., picketed and blocked trucks going in and out of the dump site where remedial work was going on. A few of the activists were jailed. The media, local and nationwide, became heavily involved in the story. Eventually, in 1980, state and federal funds were made available to buy all the homes in the neighborhood after appearances by the governor and President Jimmy Carter.

Since then, dozens of groups around the country have been formed to pressure the government to act faster to clean up abandoned toxic dumps, particularly where drinking water wells have been contaminated. Lois Gibbs founded the Citizens' Clearinghouse for Hazardous Wastes (CCHW), which sponsors national conventions on toxic wastes for grass-roots groups. This tradition of citizen action has become familiar since the civil rights activism of the 1960s. Odom Fanning collected more than 100 such earlier cases in a random search for his book, *Citizen Action.*

It is instructive to examine the examples Fanning cites because his success stories illustrate a great variety of individual and collective motivations. Fanning's first story is about Verna Mize's one-woman campaign to stop Reserve Mining Company from daily dumping 67,000 tons of iron mine taconite tailings into Late Superior. She wrote thousands of letters, circulated petitions, did research, testified at public hearings, publicized her findings, talked to dozens of public officials and legislators, rallied local groups, and picketed government offices. Shortly after EPA was organized in 1971, Administrator William Ruckelshaus asked the Justice Department to sue the company. In August 1974, seven years after Mize started her campaign, the company accepted the court judgment.

Other examples in the book show how local recycling and other ecology groups were established; how highways were stopped (in Cedar Rapids, Iowa, one road would have removed 660 homes, displaced 2,340 people and destroyed landmarks); how wilderness areas were preserved and developments in wild land stopped or modified; and how one group, the Monroe County Conservation Council, even developed the capability to do monitoring and testing of air and water pollution. In a more recent book, *Restoring the Earth* (1985), John Berger provides examples of individuals who organized groups to solve a variety of serious environmental problems.

Every region and municipality has its own groups: Boy Scouts, Girl Scouts, the League of Women Voters, even some labor unions concerned about health problems in factories. There always seems to be an organized group to which a concerned citizen can turn if a serious environmental problem emerges. The result is that an astonishing mix of young and old, educated and working-class, are turning to their own devices to make government more responsive and industry more responsible.

Public Interest Research/Activist Groups

A particular type of activist group grew out of civil rights and consumer groups and from the tradition of Ralph Nader's public interest work. Nader's 1965 book, *Unsafe at Any Speed,* develops a powerful engineering design argument for his conclusion that the automakers were more interested in making money than safe cars. His book underlines the point that it is automotive design, not human error, that is primarily responsible for automobile deaths, and he argues that the car manufacturers should be liable for these deaths.

General Motors hired a detective to dig into Nader's background and monitor his movements, presumably trying to find something that would undermine Nader's reputation. The dectective was unable to smear Nader, but was caught trying to do so, and Nader sued GM for invasion of privacy. The company settled out of court for $425,000; a third of the award went for legal fees, and the rest went toward establishing several public interest groups.

The original "Nader's Raiders" groups worked out of the Center for Study of Responsive Law, and two of the original task forces worked on air and water pollution, publishing their studies as *Vanishing Air* (1970) and *Water Wasteland* (1971). These books and other Center publications were widely reviewed and read; more important, they were used by legislators to develop regulatory policy. *Vanishing Air* accused Sen. Edmund Muskie of subverting a strong air pollution bill in 1967 when he insisted that regional air boards establish their own standards rather than have the federal government issue stronger regulations for the entire country. The book also suggested that Muskie was interested in pollution control only for its political value. The Center's books were reminiscent of Nader's own demanding yet acutely informed syle with little regard for personalities. The books attacked corporate heads with the same relentless persistence that the Raiders accused their profit-hungry corporations.

The Washington Center also focused on air and water pollution agencies, occupational health and safety, and transportation safety, as well as dozens more issues that affect consumers (especially meat and poultry inspection laws), resource issues (especially the Bureau of Reclamation's record of damming Western rivers and the Forest Service's clearcutting practices), and environmental matters (pesticide registration and pesticide licensing programs).

Colleges and universities in more than half the states have established Public Interest Research Groups to follow the Nader model of activism: research, more research, then action, mainly by intense publicity of research findings, then lobbying for regulatory or legislative reform or filing lawsuits. Nader was especially effective in using the media to publicize his findings, comments, causes by sending out regular press releases and leaking his letters to high government officials to the press, even before the officials themselves received them. Often lawsuits were filed against government agencies and industry to force what Nader considered to be more responsible behavior. His most recent activity is directed against the insurance industry over rapid rate increases for all its customers.

Among the first Raider teams sent out of Washington was a pair of lawyers who traveled to Anmoore, West Virginia, to investigate Union Carbide's ferroalloy and graphite manufacturing plant. *Vanishing Air* had described the plant's impact on surrounding vegetation, killing plant life for miles around and coating the town with black debris. The town was poor, receiving only about $9,000 in taxes from Union Carbide. It had one paved main street; the others, running up and down steep hills, were dirt, which became mud during the winter. Sewage ran in open ditches beside the dirt streets, and bags of garbage in the ditches diverted the sewage down the ruts in the muddy streets. Sickness was endemic to the townspeople.

With the help of a local couple who had read *Vanishing Air* and wrote to the Center for support, the team and a young lawyer from the Appalachian Research and Defense Fund got about 50 people to sue Union Carbide for smoke abatement and asked for $100,000 in punitive damages. Meantime, the mayor used a state law to get a tax increase from the company.

Next, reporters from the *New York Times, Newsweek* and the *Wall Street Journal* descended on Anmoore and took its case to a national audience. A *Times* story told about the statue outside the local Catholic church that had been eaten away by pollution, until it was replaced by a new one protected inside a glass case. The story of the pollution at Anmoore was covered by local and national radio and TV. Even *Business Week* published an article about Carbide's pollution problems. All of this publicity stirred action in Washington. After some initial resistance, Carbide agreed to an order by EPA Administrator William Ruckelshaus to clean up its pollution on a tight schedule.

Citizens for a Better Environment

Many of the traditional environmental groups, particularly their local chapters, have adopted the Nader method of research, publicize, lobby, sue, along with his style of aggressive activism. One of the best known of the public interest research/activist environmental organizations, outside of groups on university campuses, is Citzens for a Better Environment (CBE). Founded in Chicago in 1971, within a decade it had spread to four other states. CBE's core staff is made up of scientists, attorneys and investigators who dog agencies and private industry on pollution problems. Teams of canvassers go door to door to explain CBE's programs and educate, collecting hundreds of thousands of dollars to finance the independent local offices, which publish regular reports of their work.

One study the San Francisco group published revealed that each year 24 sewage treatment plants discharge more than 350,000 pounds of toxic metals and more than 9 million pounds of oil and grease into San Francisco Bay, and that hundreds of industrial direct dischargers into the bay regularly exceed the limits of their water permits. To dramatize the pollution of one refinery, CBE filled a kiddie pool full of its toxic effluent and placed it in front of the Regional Water Quality Control Board's office. Television cameras picked up the story and a few months later, the water board made stronger pollution abatement demands for "best available technology" in its reply to the refinery's application for a new permit.

Although most of CBE's activities nationwide in the 1980s have dealt with hazardous waste and groundwater contamination, it has continued the strong air quality program begun in Chicago in its early days. The group reviews and challenges air quality permits issued by regional air boards. When new facilities have not filed environmental impact reports, CBE demands them. Since many abuses have been reported regarding use of the "bubble policy" and air pollution credits, CBE has monitored these applications as well.

The Illinois CBE group convinced its pollution control board to restrict industry's use of emission reduction credits from the shutdown of facilities. Some companies wanted to claim the credits when they shut down their facilities even though the closure occurred because the plants were not economically viable, not because they were bought by other firms that needed the credits to expand. CBE's proposal, eventually accepted by the board, was that emission reduction credits for shutdowns be granted only if a facility is closed prematurely—before the end of its useful life—and only if it closes specifically to make its emissions available for credit. In all, the CBE groups around the country have been involved in thousands of cases of urban pollution, playing the role of researcher and watchdog to be reckoned with.

Environmental Law Groups

Most national environmental organizations have units devoted to suing the government for allowing harm to the environment or to enforce standards and regulations. Since EPA publishes its standards openly, environmental groups can act as affected citizens to see to it that industry adheres to the federal standards. Before the early 1970s

116

when the Clean Air and Clean Water acts were passed, state and local authorities determined their own standards and it was difficult to sue offending parties. But when federal standards were established, citizen-suit clauses in the acts gave individuals and groups legal standing to sue.

A few well-known court cases in the 1970s paved the way for citizen suits beyond the Clean Air and Clean Water acts. The first was the 1965 case of *Scenic Hudson Preservation Conf. v. Federal Power Commission.* The Federal Power Commission had approved the construction of a reservoir and pumping station on the Hudson River at Storm King. At the time, any "aggrieved party" was permitted to seek judicial review of FPC decisions. Several conservation groups appealed the decision, claiming the reservoir would destroy the region's aesthetic appeal. The groups were granted standing as "an aggrieved party" because the court ruled that it is possible to be affected by something other than economic loss, previously the only basis for standing. This decision led to citizen-suit clauses in later environmental legislation.

In the 1972 Supreme Court case of *Sierra Club v. Morton* (the Mineral King case), the court amplified the lower court's decision by stating: "Aesthetic and environmental well-being, like economic well-being, are important ingredients of the quality of life in our society and the fact that particular environmental interests are shared by the many rather than the few does not make them less deserving of legal protection through the legal process."

Perhaps the most interesting of the legal standing cases was the one that established that any citizen can bring suit if all citizens are affected by potential harm. In 1973, in *Scrap v. United States,* the first National Environmental Policy Act case was heard by the Supreme Court. A group of George Washington University law students and others opposed the Interstate Commerce Commission's (ICC) approval of a railroad freight rate increase primarily because no environmental impact statement had been filed. The plaintiffs argued that a rate increase would decrease the value of recycled materials, thus causing more litter and waste in the area. The ICC answered that the alleged harm was too vague and unsubstantiated, and therefore the plaintiffs should not be granted standing in the case. The court ruled in favor of the plaintiffs, noting that the case affected anyone who viewed the country's scenic resources and breathed its air.

Other court cases within a few years of the passage of NEPA attacked government agencies on a broad range of projects: highway and airport construction; Corps of Engineers water projects such as dredging, channeling rivers and streams; nuclear power projects; even federally funded housing projects. In one 1971 suit, *Calvert Cliffs Coordinating Committee v. Atomic Energy Commission,* the court contended for the first time that NEPA required that environmental costs and benefits be measured equally with economic costs and benefits; i.e., that the environmental impact had to be considered as seriously as economic benefits: "NEPA requires that agencies consider the environmental impact of their actions 'to the fullest extent possible.' . . . Compliance to the fullest possible extent would seem to demand that environmental issues be considered at every important stage in the decision-making process concerning a particular action." Thus, at the very beginning of the law's history, the courts made it clear they would consider all implications of the act.

By the 1980s, environmental organizations had brought hundreds of citizen lawsuits against government and industry, often simply by obtaining a company's own records of compliance or noncompliance with air and water regulations. If researchers find that the companies have not been complying with regulations, particularly where federal or state agencies have not enforced them, they take this information to their attorneys to file lawsuits. In the early 1980s, environmental law groups won more than 100 court-approved settlements and collected penalties for local public uses without the cases even coming to trial.

Besides suits to stop the government from acting exclusively in behalf of economic development to the detriment of the environment, or against industry for noncompliance with regulations, another type of environmental lawsuit has developed in the 1980s that has greatly influenced the way industry now conducts its environmental affairs. Through cases called toxic torts, citizens are making huge damage claims from industries for personal injuries when it is established that those industries have been responsible for adverse health effects, such as an injury inflicted on an individual by a hazardous or toxic substance. Personal injury damage claims are similar and most common in automobile accidents.

The most notorious case came from the Bhopal, India, disaster and the billions of dollars of claims made against Union Carbide. In the United States, hundreds of thousands of workers were exposed to the mineral asbestos, and tens of thousands came down with asbestosis and cancer: 16,500 private liability lawsuits were filed against Manville Corp., which took shelter from litigation by filing for Chapter III bankruptcy. Dozens of claims have been made against other corporations whose underground dump sites have contaminated drinking water wells. One of the first big cases was tried in Massachusetts where eight families sued W.R. Grace's Cryovac division, Beatrice Foods and other companies for dumping toxic chemicals known to cause cancer near their Woburn, Massachusetts, drinking water wells. Each of the families has a member with leukemia or who has died from that cancer. W.R. Grace Co. settled out of court in 1986, without admitting guilt.

In the Woburn and other cases, it is still difficult to prove a definite correlation in all cases between chemical exposure and cancer, which has a long latency period, but toxic tort lawyers are arguing for corporate liability because adverse impact was immediate, though it might not be apparent for 20 years or more. They also claim that even if other factors contributed to the cancer, such as smoking or other chemicals, under the theory of joint and several liability, any one of several contributors to a harm can be held fully liable for the harm. Under this theory, a few states have passed laws called "deep pockets" laws making those industries or government bodies that can pay damages in toxic tort and other liability cases fully liable to pay the claims when other parties are unable to pay, even if the parties that can pay have been responsible for only a small percentage of the damage. What often has happened, as in the case of groundwater contamination from the underground storage of several electronics manufacturers in Santa Clara County, California, is that ad hoc environmental groups are formed to demand cleanup efforts and file toxic tort lawsuits.

By the mid-1980s, environmental groups were forcing huge fines against polluters by going to court. The Sierra Club filed a Clean Water Act suit against a Maryland paper reprocessing firm, which was required to pay $1 million for violating water pollution regulations. In 1986, environmental groups forced a $1.3 million fine against a meat processor in a decision that, for the first time, the violator was held liable for past violations of its NPDES permit. This case will be a powerful deterrent for water pollution violators to settle their differences with environmental agencies quickly, if the agency is willing to pressure these firms. If not, environmental groups will undoubtedly sue both the agency and the firm.

The fines are beginning to wake up corporate violators. In Los Angeles, the U.S. attorney's office has filed a suit against Chevron for penalties that could total $8.8 million. And Phelps Dodge was fined $1 million in Arizona for water quality violations. State and local district attorney's offices in New Jersey, New York and California have dozens of cases pending involving millions of dollars.

The NRDC and EDF

Virtually all environmental organizations are somehow involved in the formation of environmental policy and filing of lawsuits, but two groups have distinguished themselves in this work: the Natural Resources Defense Council (NRDC) and the Environmental Defense Fund (EDF). Both built their reputations by winning lawsuits against government agencies and industry. They forced agencies to write or rewrite regulations, or write standards that had been postponed. Both groups also have sued companies to clean up water pollution and to come into compliance with environmental regulations.

The NRDC was primarily responsible for the lawsuits that resulted in the 1976 Flannery Decree that forced EPA to set a timetable for developing standards for 65 toxic chemicals and to require industry to install the "best available control technology" for toxic wastes. It also won a similar lawsuit in 1982 that required EPA to enforce industrial "pretreatment" regulations on discharges that go to municipal sewage plants. The groups have been monitoring EPA's "bubble policy" that allows companies to view their pollution as one integral outlet and selectively control sources. In two cases, NRDC, EDF and CBE won against steel companies that had proposed under the "bubble policy" to pave dirt roads to control dust rather than putting in their own pollution-abatement equipment.

NRDC and EDF have worked for acid rain controls by suing large private utilities to clean up sulfur dioxide emissions; under a settlement with the Tennessee Valley Authority the power plants reduced their sulfur dioxide emissions by more than a million tons a year. They also have challenged utilities to develop energy conservation plans rather than build new nuclear or coal power plants. In fact, lawyers and scientists in both groups agree they spend more time doing research and jawboning with agencies and industry over writing and the interpretation of regulations than filing lawsuits.

In the early 1970s, EDF convinced some electric utilities to use off-peak pricing mechanisms, as are used by telephone companies, to even out electrical demand and avoid the need to build new power plants. EDF constructed a computer model that could be used to study the comprehensive economic possibilities of a large power system and leases it to power companies for conservation and cogeneration studies. The group also has made suggestions for water conservation in California that preclude the need to build a multibillion-dollar canal to ship water from the north to the south, a project that would damage San Francisco Bay and the Delta.

Both organizations hire roughly equal numbers of scientists and lawyers, who work together building legal cases and developing strategies for sound environmental policies that can be realistically implemented. They testify at hearings, help write regulations and keep the pressure on industry and environmental agencies. The *Wall Street Journal* (Jan. 13, 1986, p. 48) made a comment about the NRDC that could be applied to several environmental groups: They have "grown to be a kind of shadow EPA. (They have) influenced laws on air pollution, water pollution, toxics, drinking water, pesticides, nuclear wastes, strip-mine reclamation, land use, energy conservation and much more. It's hard to find a major environmental law (they) haven't helped shape within Congress, the courts and federal agencies. And often, the influence is profound."

Public Opinion

The key to the environmental movement's success has been its ability to influence and direct public opinion toward its goals. According to the Opinion Research Poll (Princeton, N.J.), in 1965, only 13 percent of Americans considered water pollution a "very serious problem." Ten percent believed air pollution was very serious. By 1970, the percentages had shot up to 38 percent and 35 percent, respectively.

By 1981, a Harris poll indicated that 80 percent of Americans did not want pollution control regulations weakened. A CBS News/*New York Times* Poll during the same year asked participants to respond to the following statements and say which "comes closer to your own feelings."

- *We need to relax our environmental laws in order to achieve economic growth; or*
- *We need to maintain present environmental laws in order to preserve the environment for future generations.*

The results: 67 percent wanted to maintain existing laws; only 21 percent wanted to relax them, with the rest volunteering no opinion on the statements. A 1985 Harris poll repeated the 1981 finding that a little over 80 percent wanted to maintain the current environmental standards. Water and air pollution were objectively much worse in 1965 when 10 percent to 13 percent of the population worried about pollution problems, but a strong consensus has developed since that time. Lou Harris said of the results of his poll:

> *In the environmental area, the dynamic of change in recent years has always been in one direction: the American people get*

tough and tougher and more adamant and more shocked about the state of environmental cleanup. And they are literally furious that there has been so much perceived foot-dragging on the part of those with the power to get things done. Thus, the majorities in any sound poll conducted on this subject are simply huge and staggering.

Much of the change in public opinion is the result of the work of environmental groups. Success or failure of a movement always depends on the strength of public opinion for or against it. And the public's understanding and perception of environmental problems has come almost exclusively through the media, mostly directed by environmentalists. The vast majority of the population has not seen gross examples of water pollution firsthand, does not regularly fish or recreate where pollution might cause some consternation. Even air pollution, which is more widely dispersed and annoying in large cities, causes only a small percentage of the population physical distress; rooms filled with cigarette smoke are far more irritating.

In 1921, Walter Lippmann wrote his extraordinary book, *Public Opinion,* which provides a perceptive understanding of how public opinion develops. He notes that it takes time to inform, persuade and convince a large number of people scattered around the country. The media—print, radio and now especially television—make it easier, but it still takes time. Using the media makes the opinion devastating in its impact when three conditions are fulfilled: 1) a "casual fact" will be cited or shown, then 2) it will be absorbed by the "creative imagination" of readers, listeners, viewers, and 3) if there is a "will to believe" the event or fact, out of these three elements a "violent instinctive response" can emerge.

The purpose of environmental groups is to take their story to the larger population, and they have been reasonably effective in presenting their case. A tradition of environmental thought has emerged in the past century: writings that have extolled the glories of nature, more recent writings that have stressed the importance of not disrupting the processes of nature; and there have been traditional writings, from religious sources and natural resource conservationists, that we should not waste environmental resources. This literature gradually has made an impact on public opinion and carried over into attitudes about pollution control.

The seed has been sown in American culture for decades. Yet not until the majority of people have felt that "violent instinctive response," where events have caused deeper concerns about the health of their families, has environmental awareness reached so many contemporary citizens. The majority of environmental stories in the media since the late 1970s also relate to health concerns: groundwater contamination, toxic pollutants in water and the air, hazardous waste disposal, drinking water contamination. Americans traditionally have distrusted government and industry, so their "creative imagination" and "will to believe" tend to lead to the instinctive response of fear when they learn about Love Canal, Bhopal and hundreds of other events near and far. There may not be conclusive evidence that such fear is warranted, but still the event builds a community of attitudes in growing numbers of people.

The Love Canal story was instructive in this context. Not only were there dozens of national news stories on network TV on the problems of the community, but in 1982 an effective TV drama depicting the story of "Lois Gibbs and the Love Canal" was presented. During the early 1980s there were several other dramatic stories on the evil effects of toxic dumping. On the popular *Lou Grant* TV series (journalist's adventures), an illegal dumper caused serious health damage to innocent people, and on *Quincy* (the coroner), the county pathologist battled the government and a large corporation after he discovered that a community had been contaminated by toxic wastes. In early 1987, illegal dumping of toxic waste was the theme of a convincing drama in the *Cagney and Lacey* series. The program was notable because it presented reasons for uneven enforcement of hazardous waste laws to a mass audience: low fines in most states; high-level managers' efforts to distance themselves from illegal activities; the practice of compliance with the law part of the time to deceive enforcers; low funding and staffing of enforcement agencies.

It should be no surprise, in pollster Lou Harris' words, that "the American people get tough and tougher and more adamant and more shocked about the state of environmental cleanup." The media have been playing a greater role in shaping the country's environmental awareness and practice.

Effectiveness of Environmental Groups

There have been several reasons for the successes of environmental groups during the last generation.

1. Mobilization of public opinion, not only because more people are aware that increasing urbanization and industrialization have caused more serious, apparent environmental problems, but also because these problems have been linked to cancer and other health problems. Environment and health are now commonly and perceptibly associated with one another. Although there have been more public hearings in Washington regarding acid rain than any other environmental issue in the last six years, little has been done about the problem, and one reason (besides the lack of political and scientific consensus) is that acid rain has not been linked with a human health problem. Coke and Pepsi, for example, are far more acidic than acid rain water. People are not personally touched by knowledge that higher acidity from acid precipitation makes drinking water more "aggressive" in its capacity to carry toxic substances, like copper and lead out of household water pipes. This latter issue is difficult to dramatize.

2. Environmental groups have become better trained scientifically and in the law. Since the mid-1970s, hundreds of full-time employees— scientists, lawyers, economists, public policy experts and others—now work for environmental groups. These experts not only train their own members, they also exert great influence on public policy by filing lawsuits, testifying at hearings and lobbying. In 1985, *Environmental Forum* magazine asked 80 top Washington policy-making officials which environmental or industry lobbying groups they found to be "most influential, most effective, most respected and credible in helping

establish meaningful environmental management programs at the federal level." The highest-ranked organization was the Natural Resources Defense Council, followed by the National Wildlife Federation, Conservation Foundation, Environmental Defense Fund, National Audubon Society, League of Women Voters, National Forest Products Association (industry group), American Petroleum Institute (industry group), Sierra Club. The ranking indicates that environmental groups have developed a sophistication that now matches or betters industry, no small achievement to be sure. No longer can it be assumed in courts of law or public hearings that the industry expert has deeper or wider scientific understanding than experts from environmental groups.

3. The management of environmental groups also has improved. Not only have their direct mail appeals succeeded in lining up millions of members and supporters, but they also have learned to cooperate in major programs and legislative efforts. The major organizations have compiled computerized lists of members and activists in each congressional district so they can contact these members when crucial legislation comes before Congress. Huge mailings can be mobilized very quickly. In 1985, the heads of the 10 largest environmental organizations published a major policy document, *An Environmental Agenda for the Future*. Industry has long utilized stockholders' lists and other purchased lists to influence policy in Washington, and trade groups cooperate to lobby Congress. Furthermore, the latest efforts of some of the larger environmental groups include a willingness to compromise with industry over the development of regulations, and this newer posture has convinced many resistant members of Congress that environmental protection is good politics.

4. Other institutional changes in the past generation also have strengthened the power of environmental groups. It has been very important for environmental groups to gain "standing" in the courts to fight their battles in that neutral arena. New models of public interest activism, and litigation and bargaining with industry and agencies have brought stronger tactics during the past generation. Better-educated and more affluent people, especially in the middle classes which have tended to support and contribute to environmental causes, undoubtedly have helped to accelerate environmental awareness. Events, the disasters, found people ready to believe the worst could happen to them as well.

Thus, most activities of environmental groups in the 1980s can initiate the drama that inevitably draws reporters and television cameras. Over the past generation, the media have presented enough images of industry-caused disasters to create strong public opinion supporting environmental groups. Americans give millions of dollars to these groups each year and are asking them to keep the pressure on industry and government. Members of environmental groups, in turn, knowing that success is not automatic, have enough experience to realize they "can't let up for a second."

Yet, the intense commitment, the distrust of industry and government, the unwillingness to compromise their values, the social need to press immediately for "all or nothing at all"—these qualities of the majority of environmental groups ultimately may lead to perennially unsatisfactory solutions. If environmental progress during the past generation has proved elusive, one reason is the polarization that has resulted from isolating those in all sectors of society committed to environmental change. Perhaps we should change our approach from the bottom up.

Bibliography

Most of the materials in this chapter come from the environmental groups themselves. Odom Fanning's *Citizen Action* (New York: Harper & Row, 1975), in the "Man and His Environment" series, is an excellent survey of environmental groups of all kinds, including case examples and all the ways a person can get involved in voluntary environmental activities. Another book that shows the power of individuals who made a difference by organizing others into ad hoc environmental groups is John J. Berger's *Restoring the Earth* (New York: Knopf, 1985). *Citizen Nader* by Charles McCarry (New York: Saturday Review Press, 1972) provides an informative background on the work of Ralph Nader personally and the groups he inspired. Two of the research projects of early Nader groups referred to in the text are John C. Esposito, *Vanishing Air* (New York: Grossman, 1970) and David Zwick with Marcy Benstock, *Water Wasteland* (New York: Grossman, 1971). The Love Canal story and other hazardous-waste incidents are included in Michael Brown's *Laying Waste* (New York: Washington Square Books, 1981). In *Environmentalists: Vanguard for a New Society* (SUNY Press: Albany, 1984), Lester W. Milbrath has described the emergence of a new world view or paradigm, based on environmentalist, non-material values of a non-exploitative view of resources and species and a preference for avoiding risk and advocating social change. Walter Lippman's excellent *Public Opinion* (New York: Macmillan, 1921) remains convincing after 65 years.

124

PART III:
Root Problems

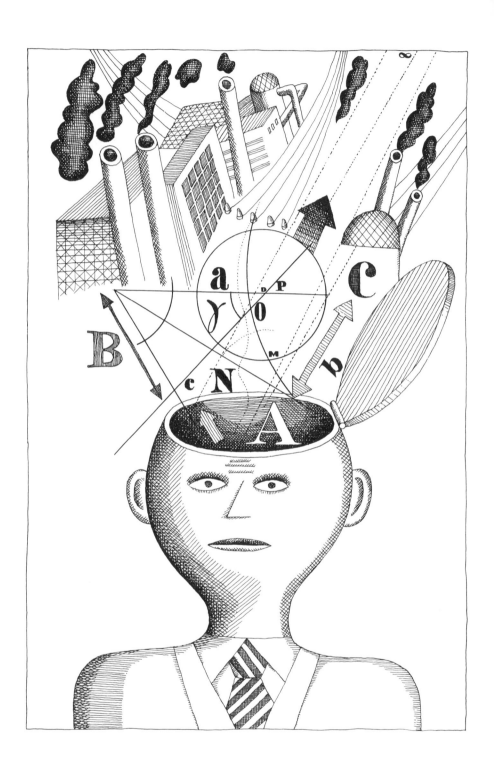

CHAPTER SIX

Professional Standards

M ost Americans assume that when environmental problems loom large, and after political struggle, laws are passed and problems resolved. Of course, such a course of environmental protection does not occur. Even when political and bureaucratic institutions are established and functioning well, it can be years before the laws take hold in cities and towns throughout the country. When the institutions involved in environmental management are adversaries and work at cross purposes, progress in all aspects of environmental protection will be slow or nonexistent. What environmental management needs most are institutions able to integrate the legitimate concerns of each of the broad interest groups involved in the process.

This section identifies two such institutions: the professional sector, where those who work as environmental specialists tackle the day-to-day problems of environmental management in industry, agencies and even environmental groups; and the role of the federal government in carrying out basic and applied research in the process of establishing standards, criteria and rules.

We have seen that several obstacles have recurred in different guises to hinder progress toward environmental protection goals in the United States. The first set of problems developed over several generations as compromises were hammered out among special interest groups and appeared in the laws and regulations themselves: unrealistic timetables, undeveloped technologies that were expected to curb pollution, the influence of powerful lobbies that blurred the intent of the regulations, aspirational commands in the wording that dulled strong enforcement, the impact of court battles and a cumbersome regulatory apparatus burdened with overlapping jurisdictions and political jockeying that has precluded the possibility of setting priorities. The evolution of events has balanced the political scale, at least on the national level, so that environmental concerns have emerged as a major political reality. Yet even with a broad constituency, it is difficult for federal agencies to establish priorities because of budget problems, an outmoded division of agency responsibilities and controversial methods of risk management. These structural problems will be considered in Chapter Eight, where I show that environmental agencies, particularly in their research and rule-making divisions, must be organized in a way that will maximize participation by scientists and citizens with divergent viewpoints of the interest groups from the beginning of the rule-making process. The current system of participation at varying stages heightens the adversary nature of the process.

A second set of recurring root problems relates to environmental specialists. The data and comments of environmental specialists reveal an emerging profession that embraces workers with few similarities. The group is divided by training, disciplines, backgrounds, interests, commitments, historical development, identities and group standards. These disparities have had a profound impact on their job performance. One significant conclusion of this study is that the weakness of the profession has contributed greatly to the problems of environmental protection. Unless this basic problem of work force is addressed, it will be difficult to implement changes to solve other structural problems such as organization, regulations, standard-setting and political-infighting.

Because their positions have been defined by the work place or subculture of industry and agencies, the quality of their professional standards also has been determined by what is expected of environmental personnel in each work situation. The field has no specific identity or professional image, models of excellence for practitioners to imitate, nor has any curriculum been established as the best route to an environmental management position. Professional goals have not been agreed upon, nor have ethical codes been established. It is not even clear which groups should be included in the field.

There are obvious differences in function among industry and agency environmental personnel and professional staff members of large environmental groups. Yet all these environmental specialists look at the same data with similar methods, are concerned with the same problems and regulations, study the same research reports and theoretically are interested in good results. The industry people assume they are hired to cut the best deal they can for their firm (regardless of the merits of the case); agency personnel are blown by the political winds; and environmentalist staff are out to make the strongest case they can for the strongest regulations possible. The result has been regulatory gridlock.

Those in industry desiring genuine environmental progress often consider themselves "closet" environmentalists because of these traditional adversary relationships. These crypto-environmentalists often are embarrassed by what they consider unwarranted demands and claims of the environmentalists. Indeed, because environmental groups seem to have a monopoly on what constitutes an "authentic" environmental commitment, those whose feelings are more restrained cannot identify with many in the environmentalist community.

What about the professional staff of environmental groups? Should any professional distinction be made between these scientists, researchers or environmental lawyers and their counterparts in industry and agencies? Should their training or even their commitments be determined by the position they occupy or by broader performance standards and ethical responsibilities? Since society has entrusted the day-to-day work of environmental management to all specialists in the field, not just those in government, a social expectation has developed that performance and ethical standards will be applied throughout the profession.

Performance standards are assumed not only for the established professions, but also for most occupations. Workers in every field strive to develop their skills above a given standard and are rewarded by their peers and community for their excellence. In traditional professions many conventions and institutions exist to inspire their members to excellence. Entrants to these fields learn the standards; furthermore, they have accepted professional roles long before they apply for their first jobs. This striving for excellence does not seem to apply to environmental managers as a professional group, according to my survey and interviews, for the reasons previously specified and because they have no societal identity as environmental specialists, nor have they accepted a role that characterizes the field.

Whether or not we consider environmental management a profession—it undoubtedly is not one in the classic tradition of doctors and lawyers practicing their "professions" independently—societal demands for environmental protection have increased dramatically during the last generation, and those working in the field must master a great deal of scientific and practical information to perform what amounts to a public work. Society's expectation that industry and government provide a healthy and aesthetically pleasing environment have produced a massive code of regulations that have been incorporated into the law, literature and culture of the country. The educational system from preschool to post-doctoral research is now imbued with abundant curricular activity—from natural history to new pollution-efficient industrial designs. These cultural and historical expectations presume an educated group of people who work for the public good, and in large measure shape the expectations and demands placed upon environmental professionals. Indeed, standards are already assumed to have been acquired by the profession, mainly through the country's sophisticated educational system.

Environmental Management History

Environmental managers and ancillary specialists are responsible for managing land, water resources, the air environment, and solid or hazardous wastes under the administrative mandates of federal, state and local regulations. Though recent environmental legislation has fragmented the work and greatly increased the work force in the field, resource managers have been identified as environmental specialists for about a century. Steeped in the European tradition of forest management practices and having learned the utilitarian perspectives of the English radical philosophers in America, Carl Schurz was appointed secretary of the Interior in 1877. He emphasized in one of his annual reports that forests should be managed for long-term public use. This period was noteworthy for reformers' efforts to control the chaotic plunder of American forests by the early timber industry.

The movement found its exemplary advocate in Bernhard Fernow, a German-trained professional who managed reserves for the Division of Forestry from 1886 to 1898. By the end of Gifford Pinchot's tenure at the U.S. Forest Service in the first generation of the 20th century, techniques and institutions of forest management had been created to assure the most efficient use of our nation's resources. The concept of long-term, sustained yield and use subsequently came to be applied to water, wildlife, land use and other aspects of the natural environment. The U.S. Forest Service personnel charged to fill that mandate have long had a code of procedures, practices, ethics and standards, and industrial forest managers have since claimed a similar code of professional standards.

The sanitary movement, described in Chapter One, took longer to get organized, primarily because the "garbage problem," "foul smells," and smoke and water pollution were considered local problems not requiring national legislation. Its origins sprang from England and Germany, where people in cities needed protection from serious health problems earlier than in the United States. In 1842, Edwin Chadwick had already proposed to remove water wastes from London by a sewerage system, and later, in the 1870s, sewage treatment and water filtration systems were developed in that city. At the same time, knowledge in the biological sciences helped to locate the sources of disease, which could be fought by methods of health science and sanitary engineering.

By the turn of the century, hundreds of men calling themselves sanitary or civil ("public works") engineers were building sewerage systems and new water supplies for the growing U.S. cities. They also were advising cities about health problems from polluted water sources. At that time, they organized themselves into municipal engineering societies and sought to rise above political rivalries in order to solve local public works and sanitation problems. Many joined other engineering organizations in the Progressive movement, which looked to engineers to apply their skills in the common effort to rationalize all spheres of society for the public good.

By World War II, sanitary engineering was thoroughly engaged in the construction of wastewaster treatment plants throughout the country, and this work multiplied with increasing federal grants. Also by this time, the field was well-integrated into the engineering profession as a whole, adopting its educational program, values and goals. Unlike the forest managers, whose goals were identified as long-term (economic) management of the country's resources, a public service ideal, engineers customarily were employed by industry to develop efficient technologies to make and save money. They spearheaded the U.S. industrial revolution and have been entrusted the task of keeping America in the forefront of the industrial world, by making money for industry through better designs for new products in the expanding marketplace.

By the 1960s, engineers (even the Army Corps of Engineers) and resource managers were identified as the people who handled environmental problems. With the passage of the National Environmental Policy Act and the demand, through environmental impact statements, to "attain the widest range of beneficial uses of the environment without degradation, risk to health or safety, or other undesirable and unintended consequences," another wrinkle was pressed into the story. A new industry was created to write environmental impact statements and satisfy the demands of the law. Thus, hundreds of new environmental consultant firms sprang up to help developers, cities and any other body that might impact the environment. This law, along with corresponding state acts, created a billion-dollar industry almost overnight.

The first companies called on to write the reports for government agencies were those new firms and some older engineering and architectural ones with established ties to industry—particularly utility, gas and oil companies as well as developers. Some engineering firms, which had evolved large staffs to build sewage treatment plants because of the federal funds, expanded into the EIS business, though most were slow to do so. They had plenty of government business already without taking on an unknown headache.

The new companies started with biologists, meteorologists, geologists, even social scientists such as archeologists and economists because the statements were to include elements from the geological, biological and social sciences as well as air and water quality issues. Engineers were not in great demand in the beginning because the intent of NEPA referred more to land use than pollution control in industry. As these companies sought to find a suitable method to present the dozens of possible environmental impacts of a project, the emerging popularity of the science of ecology, the study of interrelationships in the natural environment, was called upon. In the vast majority of the EIS work, however, contractors simply covered all the items demanded: impact on wildlife, plant species, pollution generated, historical or archeological significance. Very often, one person handled the bid for the project and supervised it as each section was subcontracted to individual specialists. In the early 1970s, government agencies were either transferring resource managers to do EIS work or hiring new coordinators. For a few years the environmental field was a booming industry.

The Clean Air and Clean Water acts also demanded additional personnel in industry and the agencies, as well as private consultants. New laws covering occupational health and safety and solid and hazardous wastes were passed by federal, state and local governments. Many states require health reviews that focus on the potential impacts of toxic chemicals, handling problems, fugitive emissions and catastrophic events. Permitting for new construction required by all levels of government has become so complicated that specialists need months of lead time to begin the planning process. People with diverse backgrounds, especially in the sciences and engineering, have been hired to perform these tasks.

Consider the broad demands and amount of expertise required by the Clean Water Act's National Pollutant Discharge Elimination Systems (NPDES). Well over 64,000 permits have been issued. All the firms that discharge into surface waters have special permits and must be monitored regularly to determine compliance. Environmental managers in industry need to know effective and cost-effective sampling and monitoring methods and keep up on pollution control, recycling and source reduction technologies. State and federal agencies must have staff at least as competent in monitoring as their industry colleagues.

One respondent of the study reported that his solvent-recycling firm regularly diluted over half of the dirty solvents with water when air inspectors came to check so that the emissions would come in under the standards. His firm's emission numbers undoubtedly differ greatly from similar operations, but in over 10 years of inspections none of the inspectors has bothered to inquire about the discrepancy. Although budget and personnel cuts have seriously affected the agencies' ability to enforce regulations, the personnel employed as enforcement officers need the technical competence and diligence to stop such offenders from blatant violations.

Yet it is understandable that many agency personnel are out of touch with the realities of the field. Environmental specialists are expected to be experts in dozens of disciplines and impacts, from land use and hazardous waste management to occupational health and safety and toxicology. And billions of dollars are involved. The work demanded by the 1980 Superfund law, the cleanup of toxic waste dump sites, is gargantuan. The Office of Technology Assessment estimates it could cost up to $100 billion over 50 years to clean up only 10,000 of 22,000 possible sites that threaten groundwater. This work demands hundreds of hours at each dump site, on the part of agencies, industry and their consulting firms. It would require about 2 million full-time jobs for the task to be accomplished as described by OTA. This monumental task is to be done by a group of people expected to take on new duties and perform them efficiently, effectively and ethically.

Environmental Professionals

The environmental field is expanding, even without the huge influx of toxic dump cleanup money from government and industry, mainly because new laws are being passed to cover each new potential threat to human health and the natural environment. The traditional resource management fields of agriculture, soil conservation, forestry, wildlife conservation and fisheries and recreation continue. The new fields require specialists in air and water quality, industrial hygiene, and especially all aspects of hazardous waste management. Toxicologists and epidemiologists are needed to do research on toxic effects of past and future chemical products.

The environmental field is deeply fragmented; indeed, it is scarcely recognized as a separate field of study. The respondents to the questionnaires of the study described in Part II represented about two dozen undergraduate majors or specialties: mostly in biology, but also different kinds of engineering and business, chemistry and physics, political science and law, industrial hygiene and environmental studies, English and other language specialties and liberal arts, sociology, economics and other social sciences, public administration, nursing, and a few more. Several specialists did not have a college degree.

Eighty-seven percent of the total study sample answered the question, "Have you been trained mostly on the job, or through a particular curriculum?" with "Mostly on the job" and a brief explanation. Even a majority of chemists were provided with quite a bit of on-the-job training in EPA methods of analyzing samples and new instrumentation. The majority of people in the sample had little knowledge of the work when they entered or were transferred into it from other sections of an organization (by private firms or agencies that were reorganizing to cut costs). One can understand why the latter group (transfers), which represented about 15 percent of the original sample, do not tend to be enthusiastic about a complex and demanding job. They didn't ask to be in it.

The diverse academic backgrounds of those in the field contributes to the fragmentation because people tend to favor or emphasize the work they do best and minimize knowledge or methods with which they are unfamiliar. For example, engineering is now generally considered a favored background for environmental positions in agencies as well as industry and consulting firms. The basic engineering curriculum focuses on mathematics, the physical sciences and the engineering sciences. The method of engineering is quantitative problem-solving, with the result that the graduate will have solved thousands of specific mathematically oriented problems by the end of college. This leaves little time for the humanities, the social sciences or even the physical and life sciences, all of which enable a person to understand the complexities of environmental problems. On the basis of undergraduate education and experience, engineering has few advantages over other disciplines and many disadvantages in positions that require the habit of synthesizing large amounts of information from various disciplines.

Sometimes in the environmental field what is needed most is someone with the expertise to solve a great variety of pollution-control design problems using traditional quantitative methods and new technologies, where engineering skills are critical. Other disciplines that focus on general, vague goals simply cannot be applied to most specific problems. The humanities and social sciences do afford the skills that enable someone to utilize a diversity of information from many fields in broader analysis. Both types of training and analysis are needed, but fragmentation in the field has bred intolerance among disciplinary interests and personality types.

The main stumbling block with most on-the-job training in any field is the perspective the context provides. It would be difficult to learn about techniques or regulations from industry or agency personnel or environmentalist specialists without seeing the field mostly from the perspective of the subculture teaching the subject matter. Regulations in environmental management will largely be annoying to industry; a matter of politics, agency policy, or simple compliance to agency personnel; and an inadequate solution to most environmentalists. Yet society expects environmental specialists and the lawmakers to look out for its larger interests. The question addressed below concerns the need to create a professional corps of environmental specialists whose training, goals and commitments could satisfy the demands of the public interest, cutting across special interests of industry, agencies and even the professional staffs of environmental groups.

Professional Roles

The roles we play in our lives constitute our public identity. Environmental specialists and managers do not hold a common conception of their professional roles or responsibilities nor does society provide them a clearly defined identity. Rather, their identity is determined by each person's specific job, academic discipline, ideologies and subculture—

this is a basic conclusion of the study described in Part II and confirmed by other literature in the social sciences (Cf. Emmett 1966; Perrucci and Gerstl 1969; Kaufman 1967). Unless environmental specialists gain some kind of common identity and sense of their role in society, fragmentation will remain in the profession and an obstacle to effective environmental management.

In *Professional Ethics,* a book that analyzes the meaning of professional responsibilities and ethics, mostly in the context of the ministry, Karen Lebacqz (1985, p. 45) lists four factors that largely determine professional roles and behavior: goals, images, models and professional training. These factors will be examined and applied to environmental professionals in a way that might help determine whether an identity among environmental specialists is possible, thereby establishing the foundation for standards in the emerging profession.

Goals of Environmental Specialists

The goals of any professional group help determine its standards, responsibilities and behavior. Physicians, for example, all subscribe to the Hippocratic oath, which provides an identity for doctors and places demands on their professional behavior. To know how a professional should act, one should know the basic purpose of the profession. In the case of the environmental specialist, the work-setting of the professional (in industry, agencies, environmental groups) has defined the goals of environmental management in the past, and these goals have been contradictory.

Resource or forest managers have less difficulty understanding their goals. Their title itself connotes some kind of enlightened economic use of natural resources. Resource agencies have developed lengthy procedures and regulations manuals that are specific about their intent. Thus, in his basic survey, *The Forest Ranger* (1967), Herbert Kaufman writes: "The federal lands of our nation are too extensive and too important for us to tolerate administration or management at less than the full economic potential." (p.v) Resource specialists assume that wise economic use of forests and other natural resources will also establish wise conservation policy. Yet environmentalists often clash with the Forest Service for neglecting long-term impacts of clear-cutting timber because of overriding economic aims. Wilderness advocates have attempted to stop the Forest Service from putting in logging roads for the same reason. Because large timber corporations and the Forest Service have essentially the same goals, forestry schools at U.S. universities train students for both industry and agency service.

Environmentalists have come into conflict with other sections of the U.S. Department of Agriculture (the Forest Service is a section within USDA) for similar reasons. The department was established to increase crop production and otherwise assist farmers. Conventional wisdom in the department has dictated more and more assistance to large corporate farms for economies of scale and the utilization of artificial fertilizers, pesticides and monoculture. The move to corporate farms has led to progressive soil erosion, water waste and water pollution, again provoking reactions from the environmentalist community. Although the department professes conservation goals and heavily supports its

Soil Conservation Service, environmental goals are subordinate to larger economic goals.

The history of engineering provides another good study of the conflict over goals in a profession. From the beginning of engineering in the United States more than 200 years ago, entrepreneurial goals have dictated the engineers' aims as well. And engineers have largely identified themselves with business organizations. David Noble (1977, p. 34) quotes a well-known engineering dean of the 1930s: "Whatever the numerator is in an engineering equation, the denominator is always a dollar mark."

During the Progressive Era, however, many engineers struggled to develop their own "engineering progressivism" to apply engineering rules of rationality to all spheres of society. In a well-known study on the history of American engineering, Edwin T. Layton (1971, pp. 53-74) shows that one group of engineers wanted to become independent architects of the new society, separate from the interests of industry. A different, more traditional group, agreed with the principles of "engineering progressivism" but believed it was foolish and naive to separate the profession from the goals and protection of the industrial sector. The professional struggle between the two groups lasted until World War II. After the war only a remnant of the "independent" group remained, and today is scattered around the many engineering professional groups (civil, mechanical, electrical and others). This history indicates several goals can coexist, but in the case of engineering the majority of the profession accepted the traditional position of engineers working within the business environment.

Confusion or political manipulation of goals can be disastrous, as Alston Chase (1986) illustrates in his well-documented study of the National Park Service's long-term management of Yellowstone National Park. Because the Park Service administration has shifted philosophically— influenced by hunters, tourist-determined budgets, environmentalists, the latest fads in wildlife management and other political vagaries— dozens of species of Yellowstone's wildlife have been decimated or driven to near-extinction. And as the goals of its administration settled primarily on an enforcement mode of controlling people rather than on a natural history or education mode, the naturalists' viewpoint of ecosystem management has been subordinate to what amounts to a law-enforcement mentality of people management. Meantime, grizzly and black bears, beavers, wolves, mountain lions, bobcats, coyotes, bighorn sheep, moose, antelope, mule and white-tailed deer and other species have disappeared or are disappearing from the "protected" borders of the park. This extraordinary book forcefully pounds home the importance of continually clarifying goals and means in every profession.

Environmental Goals and Work

The broad goal of environmental specialists is environmental protection. Environmental specialists in industry do a great deal of regulatory paper work, monitoring, laboratory sampling, air sampling in the plant smokestacks, industrial hygiene and safety, community work, jawboning with senior corporate officers as well as enforcement personnel. In agencies, the work includes permitting, inspections and enforcement units, sometimes with laboratory sections and a variety of planning tasks.

The specific goals relate to "what and how much now and in the future"; "what can be done given the present knowledge and economic limitations?"; "what needs to be done and how soon?" and other practical issues. As was evident in Part II, environmental laws are not always hard-and-fast rules that have to be applied immediately. New scientific information and technological breakthroughs, changing political winds and public demands all make a difference to the manager whose charge it is to negotiate the optimum position both for his or her firm and for an improved standard of environmental quality.

Why shouldn't environmental managers in industry be exclusively concerned with the desires of their employers rather than some abstract environmental good? An example will provide one of many reasons. An environmental manager told me that one big problem he had with agencies was the difficulty in planning huge capital outlays for pollution-control equipment. So he wrote a memo to the plant managers telling them that though the company had a special permit for discharges above the standard, there was no way to know whether the government—federal or state—would refuse to renew it. Therefore, he set up a 10-year environmental management plan, for which he got plant and agency approval, that provided the company with a longer time-frame to pay for the capital equipment than might have been allowed under sudden political pressures. He also phased out old, ineffective treatment processes.

Technical Negotiation

The term I use to describe the work of environmental management is "technical negotiation." The profession assumes a grasp of technical knowledge of production processes, engineering, science, law and economics, and the ability to work with teams of experts. The designation of "technical negotiator" includes much more than the traditional connotations of a person who clarifies issues and brings together conflicting parties. The term goes beyond what has been referred to as environmental mediation, i.e, someone who hammers out agreements among conflicting parties in an environmental dispute. Environmental mediators assume conflicts and attempt to facilitate compromises among adversaries.

Since environmental problems are extremely complex and in industry and agencies usually handled by management teams rather than individuals, the environmental professional needs a personal repository of expert knowledge to explain the consequences of the firm's or agency's options. Thus, a technical negotiator must be able to make specific recommendations to both the company management team and to local, state, and federal regulators. The environmental manager's experience and knowledge can help resolve a dispute or work out a corporate policy, but does not replace the contending parties' decisions. The environmental manager does not necessarily resolve conflict, but rather knows enough to recognize technical difficulties and pose solutions. Environmental managers must evaluate the reports of specialists so they can make informed judgments on cost-effective pollution control strategies that also comply with environmental regulations.

Environmental professionals should be able to do technical negotiation. They need a broad background in the liberal arts and sciences, as well as solid engineering skills. The worker in industry should be able to look beyond the immediate goals of production and profit, to long-term goals of the firm that merge the intent of environmental regulation with its own enlightened interest. Agency personnel should be able to overcome political obstacles and bureaucratic myopia or inertia, and move beyond deficiencies and irrationalities in the regulations. Environmental groups need a more realistic approach and a less strident message, something beyond the "good guys/bad guys" mentality that polarizes people of good will.

The environmental manager in industry will not take on the role as the regulator's alter ego in the plant but does have to see to it that the regulations are met and the company's long-term survival is assured by solid management and planning practices. Environmental specialists in agencies can have their sights lowered by the multiplicity of political angles and bureaucratic infighting that threaten any objective analysis. Environmentalists need to practice looking at the problem from other people's points of view, without giving up their genuine ideals and hopes for a better environment. In reality, there are many points of practical agreement between conflicting parties.

The goal of the environmental professional needs to focus on the work of a technical negotiator, defined by Walter Lippmann (1955, p. 43) as a "rational" person, "one who decides where he will strike a balance between what he desires and what can be done. . . . In the real world there are always equations which have to be adjusted between the possible and the desired." Idealized environmental protection is always qualified by what can be done, what is possible. Such a goal presents a standard worthy of any profession.

Images

As Karen Lebacqz (1985, pp. 47-48) puts it: "In addition to the aims of a role, we acquire images of what it means to hold that role well. . . . Most professionals have an ideal image of themselves as selfless, dedicated, tireless, competent, humble, and a host of other role-related virtues. Such images are upheld as well by society and are sometimes perpetuated within the professional group."

Role images often cut a romantic figure. Forest rangers are depicted on horseback perched on the top of a forested mountain surveying the valleys below, or fighting fires that threaten to destroy our natural heritage. Their history is filled with dozens of role models who pioneered the work of forest conservation, fought off the robber-baron forest plunderers, and saved our natural resources. The contemporary forest professional is trained to continue this important work.

Engineers also have longstanding positive images of their profession, generally considered to be inventive, creative, men of genius, the people who have made America great. (Few women entered the profession until quite recently, and are still relatively rare in the field.) The overriding image of the engineer is someone who can create as well as get down and make things work. Engineers are pictured working on huge computers or industrial apparatus, beside space capsules, or draped over complicated machinery. The word "engineer" comes from the French *ingenieur*, the word from which "genius" is derived. Engineering genius has always referred to the ability to use technical knowledge to create new and better machines making better products. Edwin Layton (1971, p. 57) describes the engineering self-image during the Progressive Era:

> By 1920, the philosophy of professionalism had become something of an obsession with engineers. Three themes served at once to express and to encourage this new ideology. In speeches delivered in the period 1895 to 1920 before major engineering societies, presidents and others in the vanguard of professionalism portrayed the engineer in glowing terms. They saw him as the agent of all technological change, and hence as a vital force for human progress and enlightenment. Secondly, such men drew an image of the engineer as a logical thinker free of bias and thus suited for the role of social leader and arbiter between classes. Finally, these speeches indicated that the engineer had a special social responsibility to protect progress and to insure that technological change led to human benefit.

Virtually all established professionals connote their own images—doctors, scientists, teachers, clergymen, lawyers—as do other occupations like politicians and businessmen. One problem with the role of the environmental professional is that no overarching image yet exists with it. Those who work in business are expected to affirm the industry position; agency personnel are assumed to be bureaucrats; environmental activists are expected to exaggerate. The field has no image that adequately projects the work.

Of course, environmentalists have many role models and heroes: John Muir fighting the despoilers of Yosemite; Rachel Carson taking on the makers of pesticides and their allies; Aldo Leopold and his plea for an environmental ethic in *Sand County Almanac*. In the study from which this book is derived, it was apparent which of the professionals were carried in their work by the image of one or many environmental role models. These images informed their commitment and infused them with special energy. They also acted as stereotypes among their fellow workers.

All positive role images convey the sense of commitment that Muir, Carson, Leopold and others demonstrated in their lives. It is also significant that they projected professional virtues—"selfless, dedicated, tireless, competent"—that actually are needed by a successful environmental specialist, or technical negotiator. They need to keep their ideals while they settle for practical solutions; to use shrewdness in their bargaining without becoming cynical; stay loyal to their employers but within the context of societal environmental protection goals. Unfortunately, most chemists and engineers have difficulty with unalloyed standard images of environmental heroes.

Professional images often gather their power from the general culture. Some parallels in classical and modern literature have been applied to the environmental world view, as that of a "steward of the Earth." The Bible praises the steward, the manager of a large household, as a "trusty and sensible person," able to take care of the needs of each in the household while managing resources wisely. The word steward in the Bible is translated from *oekonomos,* manager or municipal officer, the Greek word from which "economy" is also derived. Much modern environmental literature says we should be "stewards" of the gifts of the natural environment, preserving it for future generations. The image is one of "trusty and sensible people" watching out for the needs of the natural environment. The steward as someone who can be trusted is an image that scientists and engineers can identify with.

The image of the new environmental steward contains elements of many figures past and present: of committed environmentalists (without whom little work would get accomplished); of a scientist capable of grasping many issues—political as well as technical—and analyzing them; of a wheeler-dealer interested in getting the best deal possible in pursuit of long-range environmental goals; of a patient, sensible, trust-worthy person protecting the goods of the Earth. A role model incorporating these qualities provides a shining image of how to act and be the environmental professional for all seasons, perhaps the "rational person" of Walter Lippmann.

Analytical Models or Paradigms

Images or role models do not give concrete directions or approaches to individual problems. Professionals generally accept analytical or disciplinary models and paradigms that place the day-to-day problems into a framework, which illuminates possible solutions. Forest or resource managers, for example, utilize conservation economics as their model. The model espouses the "wisest," most efficient use of natural resources over the longest period of time. A pioneer of the field, Bernhard Fernow, provided a rough notion of the model in his *Economics of Forestry* (1902). Fernow argues for government responsibility in limiting the rights of private parties of natural resources and managing them for the long-term public good of society; thus, he outlines proposals for the economic management of natural resources in general and of forest resources in particular. Gifford Pinchot followed his lead, as have dozens of government resource economists since the turn of the century.

The engineer's disciplinary model is mathematical. His training in mathematics, the physical sciences and engineering sciences enable him to solve basic design problems, and often enable him to work on technical machinery based on technical reports of operating systems. Increasing specialization and mathematical applications have been responsible for monumental changes in the natural and built environments. The mathematical model of engineering has led to revolutionary changes in the use and control of energy and natural resources; transportation, communications, computers and information networks; the expansion of space programs and military hardware systems; and new genetic engineering in the biomolecular field. These advances have resulted from basic quantification and specialization in mathematics and the physical and biological sciences.

The basic model for the environmental professional also is derived from the sciences but more closely connected to the ecosystems approach. Academic disciplines are organized according to bodies of scientific knowledge: inorganic material in the physical sciences; organic material in the biological sciences; socio-cultural material in the social sciences. Within each of these broad categories there are divisions and subdivisions, and from the scientific disciplines there are applied sciences, such as medicine, environmental science, public administration, even law and business. No one can master it all. To advance knowledge, scientists stay in one reasonably secure area and attempt to understand one minuscule section of it. The more one moves into several broader areas, the more possibility of error in solving a problem that cuts across them. Thus, science has opted to study problems as tiny independent components, separated from other components. The scientific method is derived from this view of experimentation and data collection.

Most environmental problems are generated in human socio-political systems and have impact on the physical/biological sphere. The shock waves of these problems are vast, from macroecosystems to microsystems and back again. Understanding the possibilities and implications of natural and industrial systems requires a new paradigm that ecosystems studies have attempted to provide. Ecosystems specialists isolate the components of a system, often through computer analysis, and study interrelationships of the smallest atom to the universe as a whole.

The components that all environmental professionals deal with are first of all scientific, particularly those pollutants that have an impact on human health and the environment; technological, in the sense that technology is responsible for a great number of those pollutants and technology is called upon to correct those problems; regulatory, because regulations are the means by which environmental problems are supposed to be solved; economic, because regulations have an enormous impact on the economic system and on industry in particular; socio-political, because politics and the public play a large role in what and how much will get done nationally and locally.

The model that the environmental professional constructs to solve day-to-day problems is put into his or her work context. Industry specialists need to work with large teams of lawyers and engineers and demand special skills of technical negotiation and project management. Agency and environmental specialists need to know processes of their own offices as well as of those in industry.

The assumption of the process of technical negotiation as well as the ecosystem model is that no one can solve an individual problem without the assistance of others in the system. Such a proposition is obvious from material already covered in this book. When industrial managers ignore everything except profit-loss, they overlook consequences like leaking toxic waste drums, waste discharges or fugitive chemical emissions. When bureaucrats look only at the letter of the law, the validity of the science, technology and economic impacts may be overlooked. Environmentalists who say numbers do not count, only individual lives, often forget society does not have an infinite pot of dollars, and money spent to save lives on the environmental sector could save four times as many in another sector; we have to look at dozens of applications of a given investment to determine the full array of benefits.

As Robert Morison of Cornell University once said, "One automobile crossing the empty Dakota Bad Lands changes the composition of the air; one privy on an Appalachian hillside pollutes the Ohio River. The practical question remains: When does the pollution become intolerable?" What does this pollution mean for the regional ecosystem, the country? Who is responsible for it? Should it be cleaned up? By whom? How?

No single theory, model or paradigm has been developed for the ongoing use of an ecosystems approach. Environmental professionals need specialized training in a number of disciplines, experience in team-analysis and management of environmental problems and policy decision-making, and special understanding of spillover effects (externalities) and alternative courses of action. Environmental professionals commit themselves to lifelong learning in the context of practical experience and theoretical formulations within an ecosystems framework. This standard will remain always out of reach, of course, since it encompasses all knowledge.

Professional Training

Goals, images and models are powerfully transferred to students through professional training, where role models present the standards and a glimpse of what it is like to work in the field, what needs to be known in it and what values are held by its professionals. Schools of forestry and engineering and other professional schools socialize entrants into the profession as they build a subculture by presenting knowledge they believe is important for their potential colleagues. Foresters, engineers, physicians and others develop their own language and ways of thinking in professional schools and carry them into the world where they join other card-carrying professionals.

Although a number of environmental interdisciplinary courses of undergraduate study (environmental studies, environmental planning or design, environmental health, conservation) exist for interested students, people with these undergraduate degrees rarely attain industry positions, and only occasionally jobs in agencies. The EPA and Labor Department *Environmental Protection Careers Guidebook* (1980, p. 8) does not specifically recommend an environmental undergraduate degree. Noting that private and public sector employers usually hire people from traditional fields, the authors suggest a student hedge his or her bets in case the environmental field is full. Less than 11 percent of this study's sample noted a background in environmental studies or a similar interdisciplinary course of study.

The environmental field has become a melange of specialties: botanists, wildlife experts, analytical chemists, engineers, modelers, economists. Consulting firms want specialists for specific contracts, such as hydrogeologists for groundwater contamination work, engineers for various design tasks,. For permitting or other regulatory work, no special training is seen as necessary. Often young people are hired into an industrial position or agency, then promoted into the field from within. Thus, people in the field hold widely disparate commitments, disciplinary backgrounds, understandings of their goals. A community of interest might exist among those who maintain connections with mainline environmental groups, but it's not usually related to professional concerns or personal development. A lively environmental commitment is not necessarily an advantage among other professionals already working in environmental departments in industry and agencies.

Beyond the notion that a great deal of specific knowledge and a model of understanding that knowledge (ecosystems) are crucial for environmental professionals, professional training is needed to enculturate them into a community of concern that can deal with problems in the profession. This community is not necessarily described by the language of environmental groups or the theoretical generalities of environmental studies curricula in the universities. There are tens of thousands of environmental specialists working on problems never alluded to in the standard texts describing pollution in the United States: What kind of production processes are polluting and why? What specific technical solutions for waste reduction or recycling of hazardous waste exist, and what hinders their implementation? What are the difficulties in sampling and monitoring of air pollution? How reliable is analytical equipment?

It is not difficult to list the kinds of knowledge that environmental specialists should possess. Chemistry seems to become more important every year, as new pollutants cause new interactions and impacts on health and the environment. The complex meteorological interactions of acid rain or biochemistry of carcinogenesis, even mundane calculations of groundwater contamination and remediation, all presuppose a solid background in chemistry. Yet the majority of college chemistry departments entertain little interest in a sequence of courses in environmental chemistry on either the undergraduate or graduate level. Engineering schools, from which most environmental professionals are hired, require only a few courses in basic chemistry, nothing that would teach the complexities of environmental sampling analytical instrumentation techniques.

Mathematics and engineering are important, of course, because environmental professionals work mainly with numbers and need to know what the numbers mean. Most environmental assessments are expressed through numbers, and analysis involves drawing conclusions through numbers. But quantitative analysis assumes that the numbers provide an accurate measure of the problem and that the problem has been framed accurately. Analysts need to be taught the broader significance of the problems beyond number crunching, especially since numbers are used to settle environmental disputes because they seem neutral. Numbers, of course, are neither more nor less neutral than qualitative statements. They are limited to the significance of what they represent, e.g. parts per million of a pollutant, board feet of timber, BTUs.

For example, after the nuclear meltdown disaster at Chernobyl in the Soviet Union, scientists had to decide what kinds of radiation to monitor, where and when to monitor it, and how to analyze and report the information. The media then picked out what seemed important to them (a critical point in the democratic process), and reported that to an understandably frightened public. A wide range of interpretations were circulated at the time about eventual deaths that could come from the accident, from a few thousand to over 100,000 depending upon how one read the radiation numbers.

A solid background in math, science, engineering, social sciences and the liberal arts all are necessary so the environmental specialist can think critically. Ecosystems thinking mostly involves careful analysis of an infinite combination of variables. Technical training in the sciences and engineering (enough to teach the scientific bases of environmental problems, but not much more than half of an undergraduate program) should provide the background of a more generalized liberal and environmental studies. Applied courses should come at the end of undergraduate training or, better, in graduate school.

To develop a sense of professional training in environmental management, a six- or seven-year program is optimal. After a solid program in the basic sciences, engineering and liberal arts, some specialized courses to gain entrance into the field, graduate training can fine tune professional training with further courses in applied science and a research project. The primary difficulty with majors exclusively in science or engineering—the bread-and-butter background of the field— is that they do not yet see their disciplines as parts of larger systems.

Fritzjof Capra (1982) has shown how the traditional Cartesian paradigm of science, the study of isolated units of matter, now cannot be considered theoretically sound for any disciplinary study. Einstein and subsequent quantum mechanics physicists have illustrated in many ways how all molecules, atoms and subatomic particles cannot be studied in isolation. Even the researcher affects the study of a system, as do all its other surroundings. Again, in academic life as in the practical world, one must study as many interrelationships, alternative views and impacts of a system as can be handled in the study. Capra provides many examples of the inadequacies of the mechanistic model of studying isolated units in the physical and biological sciences as well as the social sciences, psychology, economics and engineering.

More than the knowledge of these disciplines, it is important for students to take courses in the way environmental scientists and managers integrate the knowledge in specialized courses in air and water quality, hazardous waste, energy, land use and environmental health. Interactions must be seen on micro and macro levels among the physical and biological processes, the social and political (legal/regulatory) processes, and the technological or engineering processes that change relationships among natural and human systems.

Professional Standards

The unclear standards and contradictory role expectations of environmental specialists interviewed in this study stem from the unclear, fragmented state of the profession itself. Goals depend on the often shortsighted aims of the work place; images are limited to the role models of business or the environmental movement; paradigms and models are defined by the confined views of scientific disciplines or engineering mores; and professional training has not yet been developed.

A clear identity as a technical negotiator would greatly enhance the morale and professional development of those working in environmental management. It would affect the institutional standards as well. This professional identity would announce to society what the environmental specialist does in his or her work. A clearly defined role that is generally accepted by government and industry employers would add a new dimension that goes beyond the short-term interests of business and the confined institutional structures of government and environmental groups. If institutionalized, the environmental negotiator could act as an integrating force in a divided and fragmented field.

C.S. Calian (quoted in Lebacqz, p. 69) reviewed eight codes from widely different professions; from these it is possible to describe the professional standards of environmental specialists, to present a picture of the kind of people other professionals would expect them to be: They would incorporate an environmental commitment and an ideal of service to the larger community. They would understand the importance of knowledge, analysis, continued study and technical negotiation for the purposes of environmental protection. They would cooperate with colleagues in this goal along with lifelong learning about the many ways that lead through complex situations, a habit that leads to the maintenance of high-level performance standards in the field. They would avoid all conflicts of interest that would jeopardize the standards and ethical goals of their work. These professional responsibilities above all reflect the kind of integrity expected of the environmental professional.

Rationality and the Public Interest

Whose rationality and which public interest? This is the central problem of one who assumes professional responsibilities that demand technical negotiation and objectivity. This is also a central theme of political philosophers in Western society from the time of Plato and Aristotle to the present, because dissensions and divisions have characterized social groups at least since the Peloponesian states. A mountain of literature has been produced on the subject especially in the last few centuries. Utilitarians like Jeremy Bentham noted that communities were actually "fictitious bodies" whose many different interests define them; Karl Marx saw social conflicts arising from division of labor and the ruling classes' possession of the means of production. Factions, strife, wars are described by all of these writers. Hobbes even claimed that without government, no one's life would be safe, so people wisely formed political unions. The framers of the U.S. Constitution prepared a document that would attempt to protect the public good from the destructiveness of factional interests, through a system of checks and balances, democratic participation and consent of the governed.

It is not unknown that sectarian divisions, arbitrary use of political and economic power, prejudice and transient political passions are messy facts of life. It is not always clear, however, that what is described as "the public interest" by lawmakers, regulators, community leaders, industry spokesmen and environmentalists encompasses the good of all. Of course, there are many public interests, all dependent on the economic or social interests of the groups, as well as such variables as time, geographic location, sometimes even religion. Factories built along rivers (for discharging waste—later with tall smokestacks), interstate freeways running through cities, and nuclear energy not long ago were agreed upon as representing the true public interest.

In its report on financing public interest law in the United States, *Balancing the Scales of Justice* (1976, p. 209), the Council for Public Interest Law provides an important insight into the meaning of "public interest": "What distinguishes public interest lawyers from other legal practitioners is that their clients are unable to obtain adequate legal services in the normal commercial marketplace. Public interest law rests on the conviction that the public interest is likely to emerge and the legal process function more effectively if all sides to a dispute are represented." If the environmental professional is to represent the public interest he or she must see to it that all sides of the question are represented, including possible future ramifications, and help negotiate a practical "rational" solution.

In the *Public Philosophy,* Walter Lippmann (1955, p. 42) said the "public interest may be presumed to be what men would choose if they saw clearly, thought rationally, acted disinterestedly and benevolently." Though it is now agreed it is extremely difficult to solve problems without some bias, even in the pursuit of knowledge (there is no value-free literature), objectivity in science and the professions is still recognized as an ideal to be pursued.

A degree of objectivity in environmental management professionals is possible because regulatory norms that go beyond special interests have been established as societal guidelines. Scientific norms also provide guideposts for action, and the experience of several generations of environmental management give further directions. These norms and the many experiences of professionals in the field have produced an awareness that is the result of no one special interest group, one that looks to the needs of future generations, an ethical concern considered in Chapter 7.

Conclusions

One reason for the societal difficulty in establishing a tradition of environmental protection in the United States is the assumption that standards are developed to be fought over by teams fielded by various special interests. The special interest teams are in the same game, but because they have been divided by many disciplinary and social forces, they have not developed their own professional identity, image, training, codes of behavior, subculture. These elements of professional culture could act as an integrating factor and greatly improve the quality of performance and ethical standards so necessary to maintain gains in environmental protection.

Bibliography

Part of this chapter was inspired by notions in Chapter Three of Karen Lebacqz, *Professional Ethics: Power and Paradox* (Nashville: Abingdon Press, 1985). Two related books are by Dorothy Emmett, *Rules, Roles and Relations* (New York: St. Martin's Press, 1966), and Michael Bayles, *Professional Ethics* (Belmont, CA: Wadsworth, 1981).

For material on related professions, see *Profession Without Community: Engineers in American Society* by Robert Perrucci and Joel E. Gerstl (New York: Random House, 1969); Edwin T. Layton, *The Revolt of the Engineers* (Cleveland: Case Western Reserve University Press, 1971); David F. Noble, *America by Design* (New York: Alfred Knopf, 1977); and Herbert Kaufman, *The Forest Ranger* (Baltimore: Johns Hopkins University Press, 1967). Alston Chase's cogent study is titled *Playing God in Yellowstone: The Destruction of America's First National Park* (Boston: Atlantic Monthly Press, 1986). Walter Lippmann's *Essays in the Public Philosophy* (Boston: Little, Brown, 1955) and Fritjof Capra's *The Turning Point* (New York: Simon and Schuster, 1982), on scientific paradigms, both provide useful background reading for the work of environmental professionals.

CHAPTER SEVEN

Ethical Responsibilities

Because environmental specialists in industry, agencies and environmental groups have established the rules of their own game with their own inward-looking values, ethical responsibilities of the profession are often nonexistent. In the conflict of environmental battle, survival dominates morality. Yet, as noted previously, when a specialist did have an "environmental" ethic from earlier commitments and training, carrying out his or her duties often caused personal conflicts that led to moral compromises. The following 11 cases are examples of those ethical dilemmas:

- A young man with experience at a state agency was hired by a medium-size firm to handle environmental regulations. During the hiring interview he was asked whether he was on good terms with state enforcement officers, but he did not suspect he might be asked to influence their judgments. After he was hired, he found out the company was in compliance with very few environmental regulations, and he was expected to find ways around the laws and keep the costs of his section to the minimum. He realized many companies were in similar circumstances and he did not want to give them a competitive advantage over his own; he also wanted to get his company into compliance. He was considering a position with another firm, but wasn't certain his decisions would be easier anywhere else in industry.

- Another person was asked to take care of regulations at the least expense. She knew it was possible to obtain a variance and prepare a suitable compliance plan that would not cost much, yet would be acceptable to the state. She also knew that little progress would be made in treating toxic waste streams.

- A man who mixed chemicals for a company for four years was promoted to assistant environmental manager under the production engineer. He was aware of many instances of illegal disposal of wastes into streams and other shoddy environmental practices. He said he just did what he was told but wished he was not in the job because it meant suppressing information demanded by regulatory agencies.

- An agency staff person complained about sweetheart deals between his supervisors and industry people. He believed the deals ran counter to the spirit and the letter of the regulations and he was considering giving his information to a local environmental group.

- Another federal worker resented his agency's blatant disregard for EIS documents that warned against several projects the agency approved. Noting that his work was being disregarded, he wanted to take some action that would re-establish the goals of NEPA but felt his work would become even less effective if he complained to Washington.

- An environmental specialist knew her supervisor was deliberately changing her monitoring data when he entered them into lab reports. She decided to quit her job rather than make a fuss about it.

- An environmental manager found out that toxic waste underground storage drums were leaking, reported it to the company and asked for money in the budget to do the cleanup. Company officials said they were in no position to perform remediation, and would tell him when they were. The manager believed they would stall indefinitely. He did not consider reporting the company to government agencies but quit a year later because no action was taken. He regretted he did not tell the company why he left.

- Another manager knew his firm's treatment system was often inoperative and it would cost a great deal to bring it up to an efficient standard. Since he did not have an obligation to file reports on the system, he said nothing about it to the company, realizing the higher-ups would not welcome his message. Anyway, he said, he didn't think they were violating the law.

- A worker complained about toxic dust from a machine he worked on to an industrial hygiene specialist who also was the environmental manager. The manager referred the matter to the nurse on duty who said there was no health problem involved, but the environmental specialist thought there might be. In the company, however, he was required to speak only to the nurse about health problems. He said he did not want to inform the union or OSHA or even the employee who had complained because he did not want to get into trouble.

- An environmental specialist falsified regulatory documents because he had assured the plant manager he could handle the job without problems from the agencies. He said he was afraid he would be fired if the agencies made any demands on the firm.

- A low-level environmental specialist in a company knew about a hidden pipe that flushed sewage water mixed with toxic waste from the factory into a nearby waterway. The pipe was hidden because the company had no NPDES permit. He knew he would lose his job if he told anyone about it, yet felt guilty about concealing the information.

Ethical Roles

Clearly, environmental specialists suffer from the lack of ethical codes based on their role in society. Because the subject is not discussed in professional schools and journals, ethical confusion contributes to lower standards in all sectors of environmental management practice.

People's roles in a profession dispose them to act in a particular way: doctors, lawyers, engineers. Society also expects them to "live up" to their standards and tends to be shocked when they do not. Professional standards become codified, and sometimes sanctions (disbarrment, professional exclusion) are imposed upon those who violate the standards. Professional responsibilities are ethical in nature because they cover professional behavior, and the rights of employers, clients and society at large. They define the values, or what the profession believes to be important in their relationships among themselves and with others.

I do not attempt to specify "normative" ethics, what kinds of behavior are "really" right or wrong and why, or the universal principles that might apply as rules of behavior for environmental professionals. Yet such principles are implied since moral judgments are made about why it is proper for all professionals to act in a prescribed manner. The implications of such conduct transcends explicit or implicit contracts that any professional has with employers, clients or society.

For example, the term "responsibilities" has both negative and positive connotations. A person can be held "responsible" or liable for causing some harm, a negative connotation connected to legal obligations. The term also implies an understanding of a universal norm; e.g., a moral person is held by society to be "responsible," someone others can count on to competently perform duties with honesty and integrity. The implication here goes beyond professional integrity, although it includes the notion, plus something akin to Kant's categorical imperative ("Do unto others . . .") of respect for all persons. It means a person can "respond to value," understand something of value beyond one's own personal good and act on the external value because of its intrinsic worth, for other humans, all life, all of nature. It is not my purpose, however, to inquire into the reasoning by which these normative ethics are established—as do Kant and others—but rather to concentrate on the concrete ethical responsibilities of environmental professionals, as established by the ethical codes of scientific and engineering societies.

In Chapter Six, I discussed the public service responsibilities of environmental professionals to mediate among regulatory, economic, environmental and public health demands of various constituencies; to be prepared for this task with as much education and experience as possible; to assume a stance that might have to include the immediate demands of employers, agencies and the long-term health of people and the environment—to personify Lippmann's ideal of a "rational" person. The obligation to uphold professional standards includes both an intellectual and affective (willing or behavioral) side. By examining existing ethical codes in professional scientific and engineering societies, we can learn whether these documents could answer questions of more specific ethical dilemmas of environmental specialists.

Professional Ethical Codes

Ethical codes in professions have evolved from several sources. Initially, the motive might have been derived from an effort to "protect" the public from "unqualified" people working in a profession. For example, physicians trained in Western science gradually have been able to monopolize the field by establishing certification procedures that emphasized their own tradition and codes of behavior. The rationale has been developed to protect unknowing patients from unqualified practitioners. Most occupations, including plumbers, lawyers, electricians, engineers, starting with medieval guilds centuries ago, have established similar kinds of certification that limit entering practitioners.

A second source of codes has been new political movements. The Progressive movement subsumed new occupations into its ideals of professional codes. Political and scientific leaders called on professionals in engineering, agriculture, geology, physics and biology to contribute their knowledge toward developing a better society in the public service. After World War II, when most in the nation were preoccupied with new houses, highways, highrises and consumer goods, a few groups of scientists who advocated a stronger sense of social responsibility for their professions began to warn of the dangers of military technology, particularly nuclear bombs and atomic energy.

Then, in the late 1960s, a new movement of scientists, including groups such as the Scientists' Institute for Public Information, Science in the Public Interest and later Physicians for Social Responsibility, became more militant, particularly in universities, in their opposition to military research and nuclear weaponry. The movement's influence has increased and its interests broadened. Many distinguished scientists have contributed to studies on the "nuclear winter" and acid rain. Thus, from the time of the Progressives, when science was regarded as a shaper of public policy, to the present, when science is often used to criticize public policy, the notion of public service has evolved. Many "progressive" notions, like conflict of interest rules or the need to work for the public good, have found their way into scientific ethical codes.

Consequently, traditional groups such as engineers and chemists have updated their professional codes by acknowledging the need for public service, and by testifying in legislative and public hearings. Although conservative in their approach and conclusions, their entry into the public arena has institutionalized the notion that science and engineering provide the knowledge from which legislation is developed and, therefore, the professions have special obligations to society. Indeed, the media and the professionals themselves often assume the role of "guardians of the truth." The professional codes enumerate professional and ethical duties to their members and to society.

In 1980, the American Association for the Advancement of Science published a study on professional ethics activities in the scientific and engineering societies, *AAAS Professional Ethics Project,* "to identify the range of professional ethics activities conducted by the societies affiliated with AAAS; and to describe ethical principles, rules of conduct and ethics programs adopted by the affiliated societies." (p.1) AAAS defined professional ethics as "those principles that are intended to define the rights *and* responsibilities of scientists and engineers in their relationship with each other and with other parties including employers, research subjects, clients, students, etc." (p.6)

The survey covered 146 engineering and scientific societies representing 1,872,412 members as well as 1,008 institutions (universities or other professional societies), an impressive range of individuals and activities. To the question, "Has your society adopted any statement of ethical principles?" 114 societies responded (p. 21); 46 replied that they have adopted ethical statements, representing 958,442 scientists and engineers, or 51.2 percent of the members in the 146 societies. Another 468,862 members subscribed to codes of other societies, totaling 1,427,304 members (76.2 percent of all members in the societies) who are governed by ethical rules. From survey data it is not possible to determine why the other groups do not spell out ethical rules.

The survey (p. 135) also classified ethical statements of the codes into the following categories: 1) *member-directed*: members' conduct and rights and privileges; 2) *profession-directed*: responsibilities to colleagues and the profession; 3) *employer/sponsor-directed*: responsibilities to employers and those who finance their work; 4) *client-directed*: responsibilities to clients, employees, patients, research subjects (animal or human), students; 5) *society-directed*: responsibility to the community in which they live and work or to society in general, and other generalized responsibilities.

The following statements typify those that are "member-directed" (pp. 136-137). The number of societies that list it in their codes are in parentheses:

- Members shall avoid and/or discourage sensational, exaggerated, false and unwarranted statements. (21)
- Members shall not give a professional opinion, make a report, or give legal testimony without being as thoroughly informed as possible. (9)
- Members shall strive to maintain an appropriate level of professional competence. (24)
- A member's professional responsibility shall take precedence over personal interests. (12)
- Members shall expose to authorities other members who engage in unethical, illegal or unfair practice. (11)
- Members shall preface public statements by clearly indicating on whose behalf they are made. (8)
- Honesty, integrity, loyalty, fairness, impartiality, candor, fidelity to trust and inviolability of confidence are incumbent upon every member. (1)

In rights and privileges to members section:

- Members are entitled to a safe and efficient work environment. (2)

In the "profession and employer" sections are a variety of statements indicating loyalty and service ("shall perform services with unqualified loyalty to the employer," as three societies put it), protecting employers' interests (11), information (16), and "advising employers of possible consequences of the work in which they are involved." (10). And finally, "Members should report to their employers any matter which they believe represents a contravention of public law, regulations, health or safety or professional ethics." (7)

Following is the remainder of the full list of society-directed statements:

- Members should speak out against abuses in areas affecting the public interest. (6)
- Members should safeguard the public against members deficient in moral character or professional competence. They should expose illegal or unethical conduct. (7)
- Members should observe all laws and cooperate with legal authorities. (7)
- Members shall strive to protect the safety, health and welfare of the public. (11)
- Members shall use their knowledge and skill for the advancement of human welfare and contribute to public education and charitable and other non-profit organizations. (21)
- Members should strive to meet the needs of the disadvantaged for advice. (1)
- Members should donate a portion of their services for no pay. (1)

The statements are self-explanatory and what they profess is good for their societies: maintaining competence, respecting the rights of others, advancing the public good. Of course, many code statements are contradictory because a large number say the employers' interest is to be protected at all cost and at the same time regulations and legal authorities are to be observed. Loyalty to regulations or public health needs might conflict with an employer's environmental practice. A few rules even imply the professional has a duty to "blow the whistle," while at the same time maintaining loyalty to the employer.

Ethical Responsibilities

Even if we applied the specific directives of the established professional codes, it is not certain that any clearly defined course of action must necessarily be taken in many of the ethical dilemmas facing environmental specialists described at the beginning of this chapter. Although many professionals in scientific and engineering societies express doubt that the ethical codes have any practical effect, the codes continue to be discussed in their journals and mentioned in court cases and the media. In the space shuttle *Challenger* disaster of 1986, wide public discussion about the role of engineers at Morton Thiokol (and their knowledge of the defective O rings) followed the investigation.

Can the codes be applied to the cases listed above? In a few cases, the problems had more to do with exercising mature judgment than ethics. For example, a few of the specialists had accepted positions they should have known would involve compromises with personal ethics. One respondent who worked in an agency said she did not seek a job in industry because she believes the strictest regulations should be maintained everywhere at all times and she knew most companies might not appreciate her fervor.

Is it necessarily unethical to "just do what you are told" regardless of the environmental consequences? In my interviews, the majority of those who rated high on the "environment" (vs. profit) index indicated they were doing as much as they could, did not want to appear overzealous in efforts to force compliance, and were waiting until they might have more influence in the firm or agency.

What about company practices that could lead to a worker or public health problem? There clearly is a responsibility in these cases at least to inform higher management and the worker, both to protect one's employer and the public in the short and long term. Nonetheless, I found very few clear-cut cases in which an obvious response was called for because of harm to an individual or the natural environment. The nurse who brushed aside the problem of toxic dust merely told the worker to wear a mask, and informed the environmental manager she had been investigating the literature on the dust for a generation. The burden of proof and ethical responsibility fell on the environmental manager (trained as an industrial hygienist) to research the issue himself before he took further actions. When an environmental manager complained about toxic discharges in a waterway, his supervisor told him the company's permit allowed these discharges. Should the manager then complain to the state (and lose his job) because he knows that the waste killed marine life in the area? Is this an ethical responsibility? Obviously, it is not a black-and-white situation, nor are there only two ethical options.

Among the more interesting discussions I had was with the person who knew about the hidden pipe illegally discharging toxic waste. He told me he had discussed the matter with the senior engineer, who dismissed the infraction as unimportant. "That stuff is diluted as soon as it hits the river," he told the young man. "The farmers in the valley pour more pollution into the water from their crops (runoff from fertilizers and pesticides) every day than we do in a year." Two justifications for their actions were given: one based on the longstanding engineering conclusion that dilution is the solution to pollution; and the second based on a perceived inequity of the law, giving farmers more political benefits than small companies. It was clear in the engineer's comments that he considered the rule infractions on the same scale as running a red light with no cars in sight.

In the majority of ethical conflicts in industry presented above, managers knew that their firms avoid decisions that might cost them money. It is clear that in the vast majority of companies, environmental protection outlays are filtered through economic lenses. The more farsighted believe they will receive tangible and intangible returns on their investment. In the rest, practices range from falsifying documents or cutting corners on environmental affairs to doing only the minimum required, to performing functions they believe are adequate to protect health and the environment.

Ethical problems for environmental managers are not unlike the ethical pressures felt by most middle managers to save money for the firm. Because so many environmental managers work under or with production engineers, whose job is to meet corporate goals on or below budget, environmental specialists are expected to cut costs to the bone to protect corporate goals that can be extremely unrealistic. One illuminating conversation with an environmental manager who had worked his way up through the ranks illustrated his dilemma:

Everybody here has been around long enough to know what happens to division heads who lose money. We aren't around for the big meetings that set goals for the company, and the people at those meetings forget that the environmental budgets are shoved into division budgets. So the guy I've been working with for nine years comes to me and says our division is losing money and we have to cut back on environmental monitoring. What he's really saying is that if I can't make money I'll lose my job. Heck, there are a lot of ways you can fool the agencies and save money, so you're tempted to help your co-workers out.

Under pressure to save money, most managers can justify their cost-cutting measures. Even in the seamier cases, the great majority of those in charge of environmental affairs, including engineers and scientists, sincerely believe no harm is being done to the natural environment or human health. Therefore, they are not interested in arguing with younger personnel over an issue they regard as petty or inconsequential in terms of what is good for the company. If the younger people remain with the firm, they eventually will stop "kicking against the goad."

In fact, there are many points of latitude in which the environmental manager can work. Sometimes the companies have permits or variances from strict compliance. In other cases, managers might believe the spirit of the law is being kept, so strict adherence is not necessary in every case. A laboratory supervisor, while agreeing that environmental regulation is necessary, said sometimes "the regulatory limits are often arbitrary and inflexible, not taking into account the uncertainties of analytical and sampling techniques. If the pH limit is 7.0, and the lab reports 7.1, should that be reported as a violation, or should it be considered as within specification? No real harm will result from the discharge of pH 7.1; should one interpret the letter of the law, or be flexible in interpretation? If the analytical precision for chromium analyses is plus or minus 0.005 ppm, and the laboratory reports a value that is 0.005 above the allowable limit, is it a violation?"

Several points can be made regarding this comment. First, most regulatory agencies do insist that these readings be reported as violations even if the amount is minuscule. Second, sampling techniques and instruments are often unreliable and uncalibrated so the numbers at many firms might be wrong in the majority of instances. This problem is an undiscussed conundrum among environmental professionals everywhere. Third, within experimental error a great deal of variability is possible; i.e., 18 and 24 parts per billion are really the same number (statistical bias of data judged from standard reference materials, though it is difficult to explain this point to media reporters). The fourth reason is that agencies tend not to accept anything but the letter of the law because environmental managers have not gained the credibility in the field that would allow them to make prudent judgments in these matters.

These issues fall in with countless others: Does the public have the right to know of any potential catastrophe? Would divulging such information cause needless panic? Should the environmental manager "blow the whistle" under certain circumstances? What is the best way to do this? Such problems demand the prudent judgment of environmental managers based on technical knowledge, weighing the facts, judgment, collaboration with other involved parties, decision, action.

Ethical conflicts are built into the environmental policies of firms that do not allow the environmental manager to make decisions based on the long-term good of the firm. The environmental manager must have the authority to mediate among corporate officials, stockholders, lawyers, regulatory personnel, consultants, environmental groups, fellow workers or unions, and the budgetary representatives of the firm. Agency personnel may face conflicts among supervisors, fellow staff, industry representatives, environmental groups, even interested friends. That is, this model assumes that professional and ethical conflicts exist and must be resolved in a prudent, reasoned manner.

The field has to set itself apart by approaching problems objectively, and by manifesting integrity or responsibility, the "ability to respond" to the facts of the situation. One environmental specialist complained that his co-workers and his firm, "didn't give a damn about anything except themselves." I heard virtually the same comment from an agency employee, where political infighting is often confused with ethical corruption. The implication of the professional codes first of all is that those in the profession "give a damn" about their own competence, the natural environment, the long-range good of their employers, and the good of society. This quality of mind establishes a profession, in whatever work situation, able to make decisions about ethical questions, more than individual rules or regulations, far more than "doing what you're told" or moving up the ladder on the fast track.

Environmental Problems and the Media

During the 1960s and '70s, the common rallying cry of public interest groups was that only business could influence public opinion because only business had the funds to sustain long media drives to inculcate its point of view. The point is fairly obvious: Public opinion affects profits; therefore, those who want greater profits will seek to influence public opinion. The National Association of Manufacturers, as do all specialized trade groups, takes out advertising, writes canned editorials and sends them to hundreds of newspapers, writes speeches for individuals to give (such as a PR firm for the American Tobacco Institute wrote for physicians to deliver), but mostly use television. Even sponsoring public television helps project a corporate image that might influence public opinion positively for the firm. The fact that industry employs the media in many ways and during the 1980s has emphasized its commitment to environmental quality is so well understood that the point need not be stressed.

Less often discussed is the use of the media by environmental groups or the way the media professionals themselves present environmental news. To even the score with industry, environmental groups attempt to influence public opinion through the media by demonstrations, press conferences to publicize environmental pollution problems or threats to the public health, articles in journals, documentaries on environmental subject matter, and so on.

In a discussion with a veteran environmentalist, I brought up a few issues that local groups were working on and asked whether the good ends of environmental groups justified questionable means to accomplish those ends. It seemed to me that playing up to the fears of the public by overstating the possibility of a cancer epidemic because of insignificant or scarcely calculable amounts of contamination in water (one part per billion) was irresponsible. It seems to me that it is unethical, I told him, to bring up inconclusive studies and quote biased authorities. Of course there is a serious problem with contaminated groundwater, but why exaggerate it and compare the situation with Bhopal or other "toxic time bombs," I asked him? These were a few of his remarks:

> *No, our situation is not as bad as Bhopal, but it could be. And it is possible that our* (state epidemiological) *studies are close to the mark. We have to use the media to get the attention of the public. Unless we bang everybody over the head with this stuff they don't pay any attention to us. We have to remind everybody that they might be poisoned and their kids might be poisoned if they drink well water or live around a lot of these places that are not careful about their toxic air emissions. Then we can make some other important points about the need for open space and wilderness, and how development is responsible for a lot of these troubles.*
>
> *What you don't understand is how strong the opposition is. If we don't use all our ammunition on them, they'll blow us away. It's like that guy on "Hill Street Blues"* (popular television program) *used to say, "We've got to get them before they get us." Every time we try to reason with these guys we come out with nothing but egg on our face.*

In a society that is adversary by nature, inconclusive scientific studies are used as acceptable science, and the media rarely make sophisticated distinctions. In the campaign he referred to, the study's conclusions made banner headlines, with the news story containing interviews with several local families that had health problems and two health authorities who were "worried" about the problem. Two environmental leaders called for mass demonstrations. At the time of the meeting, local industry was already spending millions of dollars in remediation of groundwater contamination and public health agencies were doing extensive testing in the area. It seemed to me that some people were attempting to get public support for a round of lawsuits.

Couldn't the technical specialists who work for environmental groups apply the same kind of honest judgment that we expect from professionals in industry and the agencies? And cannot similarly trained environmental professionals in different institutions relate to a sincere common attempt to solve pressing community problems? Isn't it possible to maintain the commitment, even strong passion, for the issue without resorting to the rhetoric that colleagues in the sciences recognize as bordering on the dishonest? May we not expect environmental professionals to clarify the issues rather than confuse and frighten just to gain attention? It is not necessary to compromise one's position to be accurate and honest about the meaning of scientific data.

Our environmental agenda should not be set by the dramatic presentations of *Quincy* or *Lou Grant* (TV shows of the 1970s that dramatized problems of toxic waste) or even docudrama portraits, however laudable it is to alert the public to significant societal problems.

Ethical Responsibilities of Media Professionals

It is significant that both industry and environmentalists regularly criticize the media for inaccuracies and prejudice. The subject came up regularly in my interviews with industry personnel. In the 1980s, industry has tended to be more critical of the media than have environmental groups, perhaps because the public opinion pendulum has shifted away from their power center and the media have largely been responsible. During the 1960s, the civil rights movement benefited from wide media exposure, and the war in Vietnam was taken to the nation's living rooms. In the late 1970s and '80s, the media have taken up the issue of toxic wastes.

Lippmann said about the power of the media: "The casual fact, the creative imagination, the will to believe, and out of these three elements, a counterfeit of reality to which there (can be) a violent instinctive response." The reality created by the media is mythic in the sense that it exists in the mind of the reader, the listener, the viewer, depending on the way "the casual fact" is structured and presented. There can be a violent instinctive response if the media succumb to the temptation to titillate rather than inform, stress the dramatic rather than the reality—if the media are not ethically responsible for an honest, reasoned presentation of the event or fact.

Following are three recent examples of the manner in which the media have handled environmental data. They are not the worst examples of media bias, nor the best cases of responsible journalism, rather they indicate a propensity for the dramatic instead of objectivity. Similar examples can be regularly found in each mass medium—print, radio, and especially television.

Titillation

The first case comes from the perennially popular TV news "magazine," *60 Minutes*, in the show on December 12, 1985. Diane Sawyer interviewed the major parties involved in an investigation by an Alabama district attorney, Larry Evans, who was looking into possible improprieties of Gov. George Wallace's son-in-law, James Parsons. Parsons had purchased a piece of property to use as a toxic waste dump, got the necessary government permits for its use as a Class I site (for hazardous waste) and sold it to a large waste management firm. He kept royalty rights so that he would receive further payment depending on the amount of waste dumped there each year.

Speculating that Parsons stood to make millions, even tens of millions of dollars, Evans said he believed the public's health was jeopardized by the arrangement. Sawyer questioned a hydrogeologist who said the thick clay soil would keep any chemicals from moving into the groundwater for at least 10,000 years. Rather than obtaining another opinion on the subject and inquiring into the necessity of strong plastic liners over the clay, Sawyer simply asked, "Yes, but would you want one of these landfills in your back yard?"

A further exchange took place with Parsons' lawyer, who said there was nothing wrong with landfills, in fact, Southerners were being patriotic in their willingness to help solve a national problem. Evans answered that Alabama is turning into the "pay toilet" of the industrial Northeast: "What's patriotic about burying chemicals in your soil?" The strong implication was that the community would suffer health and economic damage at the hands of an outside company, paying off a local politician to dump somebody else's toxic waste near their homes.

There *is* a national problem with siting all kinds of waste treatment, incineration and landfills, and at the moment it may be patriotic to accept them provided strict safety measures are maintained. No community wants a site "in their back yard," no matter how many of the products the community uses contribute the wastes. With her comment about the site, Sawyer did not enlighten people about toxic wastes or dump sites, rather she played along with the prejudices of the investigator and the fears of the public in general. Whether or not we like the fact that Gov. Wallace's son-in-law is making lots of money, he is making money because very few states are able to have legitimate sites permitted to handle hazardous wastes, however safely they are transported and disposed of.

We never found out the answer to the big question: Should all toxic dump sites be outlawed everywhere? Neither did we find out how safe the site in question was for the containment of wastes or for the townspeople. How far is it from the community, where are the roads, which way does the wind blow? What are chances for accidents, or how much risk is the community exposed to? How much money did the community get? The reason for the unfocused journalism was not bias but rather the penchant of the media to dramatize and titillate. Sawyer focused in on the eyebrow-raising aspects of the case, not the questions that could have performed a genuine public service of responsible journalism. The program, it should be noted, is billed as an in-depth investigative report.

Propaganda

The second case indicates the need for media editors and directors to recognize the difference between propaganda and balanced presentations. If someone places a story on a complex, controversial subject that blatantly represents a position of advocacy, the editor has a responsibility to present an alternative viewpoint or show the original piece to someone knowledgeable enough to explain how it might be fallacious. The more important the issue, the more incumbent the responsibility. It is not enough to sympathize with the intentions or view of the author.

The controversy was raised over the need and desirability of ocean incineration of toxic wastes. Free-lance writer/environmentalist Gar Smith wrote an article entitled, "The Burning Question" for *This World,* a Sunday supplement magazine of the *San Francisco Chronicle* (May 12, 1985). The article presented a melange of episodes designed to show the danger of burning toxic wastes at sea, and was pegged on a bill by a local legislator that would ban burning of toxic wastes at sea for three years. Smith set up a few of the arguments in favor of recent EPA recommendations on procedures for allowing testing and burning, but presented them in a way they could be easily knocked down by juicy quotations from his authorities. Much of the case was built on the fact that one of the companies doing ocean burning had been fined by EPA for past illegal disposal activities. (Were the people responsible for the violations still making policy for the company, or did more recent history tell a different story? Smith was not interested in these questions.)

To illustrate the type of argument Smith presents, a few quotations that exemplify his mode of argument follow: "Europeans call them 'leper ships'" [The "leper ships" have had no accidents in 13 years of operating and have kept toxic wastes out of European groundwater.] The possibility of doing ocean burning after EPA Administrator Burford lessened emission requirements "set dollar signs dancing in the eyes of U.S. businesspeople." [Smith does not mention that requirements were soon restored to earlier ones.] Referring to the lack of pollution control devices on the vessels, Smith orates, "It would be much cheaper to let the hydrochloric clouds and toxic metals pour, untreated, into the seas." [Of course, this is just what was done with the toxic wastes until the late 1970s; they were dumped into the oceans and waterways; ocean incineration destroys at least 99.99 percent of the wastes at 2,400 degrees Fahrenheit and, according to EPA tests, the residue had no impact on the environment. Because of the extremely high temperatures, scrubbers were not required to clean the exhaust of hydrochlorine gas.] After EPA risk assessments using computer predictions showed one spill for every 1,200 operating years, Texas Gov. Mark White is quoted approvingly: "No one ever believed the Titanic could sink... until it happened." [Incineration ships are equipped with collision avoidance radar, double hull, 12-tank steel construction with pumps to stabilize the load or transfer wastes out of a leaking tank. EPA officials accompany all burns and monitor procedures.]

An environmental educator living in the San Francisco area read Smith's article and called the feature editor in charge to complain. He told her all the data are not in on ocean incineration, but EPA has been researching the matter for 10 years. His main problem with the article was that it was distorted in a way that prohibited calm overview. He said Smith led readers to believe that more dangers are associated with ocean incineration than land incineration, which Smith recommended, even though public health problems actually might loom much larger on land, depending on conditions. Furthermore, he pointed out, Smith had ignored the larger questions of wastes at Superfund sites that are contaminating groundwater and the 264 million metric tons of hazardous wastes in the country generated each year. The 1984 amendments of RCRA banned from land disposal certain hazardous wastes after a period of time, and their disposal must be planned for. Smith's recommendations for recycling or less waste generation were not helpful or even possible in the case of many wastes, particularly in the short term. Land incineration has not even been an option because local communities have rejected their construction. Basically, the environmentalist complained, the article was propaganda, not helpful journalism.

The editor invited the caller to write a response to Smith's article and guaranteed that it would be published. He wrote about 1,000 words, mainly outlining the problem of what needs to be done quickly, what kind of long-term solutions can be phased into environmental management as they become practicable, and what risks are involved with ocean incineration as an interim solution. He noted that the site Smith found so abhorrent, 200 miles from the California coast and encompassing 2,116 square miles, had been recommended by an independent consultant to EPA as "one at which ocean incineration can be carried out without fear of impinging upon use of the sea, of detracting from the value of human amenities or of jeopardizing human health." It was far from fish breeding grounds, far from migration routes of sea animals and birds, far from shipping lanes, recreational fishing and sailing, and enjoys favorable weather. (S.F. *Chronicle*, April 2, 1984) Finally, he wanted it known that the National Wildlife Federation supported ocean incineration at least as an interim solution "under carefully controlled and tightly regulated conditions" because of the toxic waste crisis.

Two weeks later, a six-sentence summary of the educator's response was printed in the "letters" section of *This World*, taken from the first and last paragraphs of his article. He wrote a strong letter of protest to the magazine's editor, saying the generalities that the editor chose from his response were almost as useless as Smith's original article. Six weeks later he received a note from the editor, saying she had reviewed the articles in question and felt he had been treated fairly.

The editor's response revealed that she believed the issue lay in their willingness to present an opposite opinion, not the merits of the question of ocean incineration or their responsibility to provide balanced journalism for the public. Smith's colorful phrases and gossipy anecdotes and quotations from the halls of Congress and public hearings fit into their format of "interesting" writing.

Cancer-mongering

In the third case, incompetent reporting combined with the media's penchant for the dramatic created some undue alarm-ringing. In the fall of 1985, the Consumer Products Safety Commission released a study by a panel of scientists that concluded that the use of DEHP, Di(2-Ethylhexy)Phthalate, a plasticizer that is mixed with polyvinyl plastics as a softening agent, could provoke liver cancers in children under a "worst" case scenario. The chemical is used in pacifiers, plastic diapers and some baby toys.

Within a few days, NBC's *Today* show reported the study, saying, "Pacifiers meant to calm and soothe, squeaky toys and smiling elephants meant to bring joy and laughter could be hazardous to your baby's health. . . ." The CBS *Morning News* reported similar horror tales of "possible health risks" in "millions" of baby products.

Robert J. Samuelson, economics columnist for the *Washington Post*, was concerned about the report because it suggested pacifiers and other plastics products in his own home threatened his infant daughter. He decided to investigate the report's conclusions and found out that the "worst" case scenario meant 0.003 percent danger of additional cancer, and then only if the baby regularly used plastic baby pants, teethers, toys, pacifiers and slept in a plastic crib. What are the chances that an infant would absorb enough of the chemical for a long enough period that could approximate the commission's study done on rats? Not much, perhaps as little as zero risk. Dr. Richard Griesemer, chairman of the panel, told Samuelson, "The chance of children getting liver cancer is very little." Samuelson was relieved but irritated with the journalistic irresponsibility. He told his story in the *Washington Post* on October 9, 1985, to assuage the concerns of other parents and complain about irresponsible television commentators as well as incomprehensible writing in the reports.

It is difficult, however, to convince the media to be certain of their material, albeit socially significant and very dramatic, before they needlessly frighten millions of parents who for decades have been using pacifiers with their children.

It should be noted that it is possible to present informed, balanced reports, even on extremely difficult and controversial subjects. For example, in February 1986, the Public Television Network aired a *Nova* report, entitled "Toxic Law Trials," discussing the toxic tort case of citizens of Woburn, Massachusetts, against firms believed to have contaminated the city's water supply. The citizens sued because clusters of children in East Woburn who drank from the contaminated wells developed leukemia.

The program's strength came from its balanced viewpoint and because its writers clearly showed by the angles they developed that they were trying to find out the truth of the situation: Is there a link between contaminated water and human health? Was the link established in this case? What does all the statistical evidence mean? How could it be biased? Do statistical correlations actually mean that direct physical causation could be proved? Could residents be certain that the source of the contamination involved the sued companies? The program was a marvel of solid environmental education, and although it left the major questions unanswered, viewers certainly were more informed about a few of the central environmental questions of the day.

Responsibility to Future Generations

Although this chapter has not primarily focused on normative questions of value (whether absolute criteria can be established that would help answer questions related to environmental ethics), such norms continually suggest themselves. What ethical stance should we have toward the natural environment and future generations? The question concerns not only waste discharges, those who generate the waste and environmental managers, but also those who throw their garbage in the trash or flush it down the toilet. One reason industry personnel, whether in small or large firms, do not seem affected by ethical concerns is that environmental degradation does not result from single instances of pollution, but rather from the cumulative impact of many firms discharging wastes over time. Similarly, it is easy for individuals to dismiss their own minuscule impact on the environment, no matter what they consume or throw out.

A central theme of environmental ethics in recent years has been whether those now living have a responsibility to those who will live after them. In a negative, legal sense the answer is clear: Our estate can be sued for damages for which we are liable. Simply because we happen to die, or not stay around for good or evil deeds to have their impact, does not mean we are absolved from responsibility. The common sense appeal to graduates every June—"to leave the world a better place than you found it"—indicates how entrenched the concept is. National parks and forests, trust funds, charitable donations and foundations all attest to people's interest in future generations. The obvious general application of the notion of this book is that environmental specialists in industry, public agencies and environmental groups have a special duty to future generations because of their professional obligations.

"Responsibilities," described here, refer to respect for others, wishing them well, furthermore, not doing them harm. Again, simply because we do not know who and how many will comprise these future generations does not mean they won't be affected by what we do today or that they are not due our respect. We can assume they will have similar, if not identical, needs for food, water, shelter and a full natural environment. We have been given a reasonably healthy environment and society because our ancestors left the world a better place than they found it, which argues for continuing the tradition. In the words of Martin P. Golding (Partridge 1981), "Future generations are members of our moral community." Though they might be remote from us in time, many contemporary thinkers and leaders argue that future generations are bound to us in rights and obligations as a part of the same moral community.

Ronald M. Green (Partridge 1981, p. 89) presents these responsibilities in three ethical axioms:

1. *We are bound by ties of justice to real future persons.*

2. *The lives of future persons ought ideally to be "better" than our own and certainly no worse.*

3. *Sacrifices on behalf of the future must be distributed equitably in the present, with special regard for those least advantaged.*

The third statement needs some explanation: The poor of this generation, particularly the urban poor, have enough difficulty simply surviving and common sense dictates that extra demands should not be put on their shoulders to protect future generations. For example, if EPA closes down smelters around the country or shuts plants that make aerosol sprays for present and future environmental benefit, society has an obligation to assist those whose own immediate future is jeopardized by the action.

The axioms, of course, generate dozens of further questions: What specifically are our responsibilities; i.e., what kinds of environments are we duty-bound to preserve or create for our posterity? What are we duty-bound to forgo? Is it possible to anticipate the needs of future generations? Is it realistic to assume that nations around the world will care or bother with these questions? What can be done?

Most basic environmental problems should be placed on the table for discussion, as they were at the International Stockholm Conference in 1972, and at a 10-year anniversary conference sponsored by the Royal Swedish Academy of Sciences in 1982: acid rain, disposal of hazardous waste, the ozone layer (its erosion because of continued use of chlorofluorocarbons), carbon dioxide buildup because of continued increases in industrialization, groundwater depletion and contamination by toxic chemicals, continuation of farm practices that cause soil erosion, rapid cutting of tropical forests which portends drastic climatic changes, loss of wilderness and subsequent wildlife that depend on integral ecological habitats. The responsibilities to future generations include preservation of the natural environments not only because of temporary considerations of human health, but because that is a precondition of the survival of all species, including humans.

Perhaps the most important question is whether enough people care about posterity, whether individuals and nations "give a damned about anyone but themselves," in the words of one of my respondents. In the *New York Times Magazine* (January 19, 1975, reprinted in Partridge 1981, p. 191), Robert Heilbroner presents the problem in this way:

> *Will mankind survive? Who knows? The question I want to put is more searching: Who cares? It is clear that most of us today do not care—or at least do not care enough. How many of us would be willing to give up some minor convenience—say, the use of aerosols—in the hope that this might extend the life of man on earth by a hundred years? Suppose we also knew with a high degree of certainty that humankind could not survive a thousand years unless we gave up our wasteful diet of meat, abandoned all pleasure driving, cut back on every use of energy that was not essential to the maintenance of a bare minimum. Would we care enough for posterity to pay the price of its survival?*
> *I doubt it.*

The title of Heilbroner's article, "What Has Posterity Ever Done for Me?" about sums up the cultural problem. The unspoken rules of the game of Western society are contractual. We give in proportion to what we receive. But we already have received from our predecessors in culture, science, technology, the goods of the earth, and more. Again, simply because we were an unknown future recipient of goods and services does not exempt us from the implied contract to continue its terms. The ethical principle extends the contract and is derived from that which deals with "respect for persons" of ages to come, of the ability to respond to the value that future generations represents.

In a previous chapter, I noted that enlightened environmental management in industry is characterized by its recognition that it is necessary to plan for future risks, to do more than the minimum required by law, to continually audit its facilities for health, safety and the environment. Whatever the motive—protection against future liability claims, good public relations, employee health and morale— these practices represent a practical concern for future generations. They also offer leadership to others in industry, and even many in agencies and environmental groups who might become fixated on short-term goals.

In any event, if we are to protect future generations by protecting the environment, we must learn as much as we can about the physical and natural world. Thus, our focus is shifted once again to politics, political organization and the possibilities of a national research program.

Bibliography

The material on ethical codes was taken from Rosemary Chalk, Mark S. Frankel, Sallie B. Chafer, *AAAS Professional Ethics Project: Professional Ethics in the Scientific and Engineering Societies* (Washington, D.C.: American Association for the Advancement of Science, 1980). Note also the books by Lebacqz and Bayles, cited at the end of the previous chapter. The excellent anthology on *Responsibilities to Future Generations* was edited by Ernest Partridge (Buffalo, N.Y.: Prometheus Books, 1981). Clarence C. Walton's *Corporate Social Responsibilities* (Belmont, Calif.: Wadsworth, 1967) not only provides models of responsibilities but traces important historical trends as well. *Corporations and the Environment: How Should Decisions Be Made?*, edited by David L Brunner, Will Miller and Nan Stockholm (Palo Alto: Graduate School of Business, Stanford University, 1981) applies ethical and practical concerns to cases in environmental decision-making. Among the many good books on the impact, messages and ethics of the media are Daniel Pope, *The Making of Modern Advertising* (New York: Basic Books, 1983) and Todd Gitlin, *The Whole World Is Watching* (Berkeley: University of California Press, 1980). Gitlin's book is especially interesting because he shows how Students for a Democratic Society, a radical-left group of the 1960s, came into the spotlight of CBS and the *New York Times,* which soon were responsible for packaging its message for the country and even the group itself, because its members played to that spotlight in an effort to publicize their ideology.

CHAPTER EIGHT

The Federal Role

T he two basic obstacles blocking progress in environmental protection are the adversary relationships among the major institutions of environmental management and within the environmental work force itself, and the lack of professional identity, educational or career path, cultural codes or even societal recognition for workers in the field of environmental management.

Environmental specialists normally receive career definition and rewards from their employers' special interest and viewpoint, rather than the professional demands of environmental protection. Therefore, the even more basic problem of the values conflict among these institutions must be addressed to make further advances in behalf of environmental quality. Even with societal status that cuts across the barriers of industry, agencies and environmental groups, the environmental professional's work would remain seriously impaired without some way to bring together the adversaries at the beginning of the process of setting laws, rules, standards, criteria. Scientific research must be combined with values clarification among factions at the federal level. It is unrealistic to assume conflicts can be avoided, but the endless stream of lawsuits, criteria revisions, legal amendments and enforcement disparities can be curbed by addressing fundamental differences at the federal research and rule-making level—before obstacles become too difficult to overcome.

Furthermore, the critical aspect of the federal role in environmental protection is the government's responsibility toward future generations. Our discussion of how industry, agencies and environmental groups are beating their separate paths toward the future will explain the federal role in assuring an efficient, equitable, healthful and environmentally secure future. Each sector can justify its own position on environmental protection policies in the short term, but short-term justifications cannot lead to a solid future for environmental quality in the nation or the world.

How has each of these interest groups justified its short-term policy? Corporations have spent tens of billions of dollars for pollution control equipment since 1970. They have spent even more on lobbying, court battles over standards and liability, and public relations. The industrial sector has taken precious little leadership on establishing good environmental legislation, but rather maintains its tunnel-vision perception of shareholders and profits as it fights off pesky environmental attacks from the rear and regulatory mandates from the side. Although corporate compliance seems to be growing, the environmental bottom line remains shaky.

Government agencies, mandated to enforce the law, face court battles with industry and environmental groups. Agencies often are slow to set standards because they know someone will sue as soon as the standards are published. Agency specialists want to be certain they can defend standards in court, so they also need to know which way the political wind is blowing. They often delay permits, especially if there is controversy, causing justified uncertainty and chagrin in industry ranks. State and local agencies often lean favorably toward local industry, thus exposing themselves to attacks from environmental groups or politicians. Agency bureaucratic culture tends to be cautious, sometimes paranoid.

Environmental groups strive toward idealistic standards and, even in an age of scientific uncertainty, usually can find scientific studies to back their demands for stronger protections. They learned rhetoric and community organizing from civil rights activists in the 1960s, with lots of tips from David Brower, the Sierra Club director responsible for many court victories during the Fifties and Sixties, and Ralph Nader, whose moral passion and research techniques informed the activity of public interest groups of the Seventies. They have enlisted a committed group of scientists and tens of thousands of volunteers to their ranks. Environmental groups have been conditioned into distrust of industry, developers and anyone who wants to compromise. They have learned that if they start from a "middle" position, they get dragged even further to the "right," so they begin bargaining from far to the left of center. Yet they lose more battles than they win, mainly because of unreasonably high expectations in a world of finite resources and scientific uncertainty about real risks vs. perceived risks.

Environmental Progress

These positions, hardened on the anvil of struggle, have in large measure hindered environmental legislation from achieving its intended results. Two General Accounting Office reports imply the Clean Air and Clean Water acts are not working well. In 1979, the GAO reported that 72 percent of the air-monitoring stations it examined around the country were improperly sited and 58 percent had improper equipment. In 1982, the office reported that 82 percent of major industrial facilities were not in compliance with their water discharge permits at least once in an 18-month period, and 31 percent were in serious violation at least 50 percent of the time. After four years of interviews in the trenches of environmental management, I am not surprised at these numbers. They may even be optimistic in some regions of the country.

Data from yearly reports of the Council on Environmental Quality indicate spotty improvements of water quality in the nation's rivers and streams, with little change in average water quality. In fact, many studies of air and water quality indicate only modest improvements since the mid-1970s, with new problems looming: groundwater contamination, acid rain and toxic air pollutants, including those innocently generated inside private homes. Lawmakers and agency officials originally did not always pick the most important air or water pollutants to regulate in terms of impact on health and the environment; newly isolated hazardous substances, in both air and water, are far more difficult to regulate.

At a lecture at the University of North Carolina (Oct. 25, 1984), EPA Administrator William Ruckelshaus said that when the environmental laws were passed, policymakers assumed they actually knew which were the harmful pollutants, how they could measure and develop standards for these pollutants, and what their health and environmental impacts were. None of these assumptions turned out to be accurate, according to the former administrator. They didn't know most of the major pollutants, didn't know how to measure them, and their knowledge of the health and environmental impacts was primitive by today's standards.

They also thought they could regulate the pollutants without great economic impact and that when more information was gained, standards could be reset. These assumptions were especially errant, and the three factions have wasted many of their resources in court and in the media, their positions becoming more entrenched. The arena of these battles is omnipresent in local, state and federal politics.

The task of regulating pollutants and their millions of possible impacts, as well as the tens of thousands of polluters, is so multidimensional and complex, with overlapping regulatory and enforcement agencies, that the notion of putting some simplicity and rationality into the process seems too ambitious to consider. But in this chapter I present a program that represents the broad conclusions of my study; it especially takes into consideration the main complaints of the respondents. The major national problem concerns setting standards and priorities for regulatory agencies. Local and state problems involve control and enforcement questions. This chapter focuses on establishing national environmental objectives and priorities through structural changes in the federal research agenda by including different scientific and economic viewpoints in the process.

National Standards and Priorities

Even before EPA was organized, J. Clarence Davies in 1970 accurately presented the problem of environmental management in his first edition of *The Politics of Pollution* (pp.147-48):

> *Although man has been making major changes in the natural order for at least a hundred years, we are still remarkably ignorant about the effects of such changes on natural processes or on human beings. We do not know whether the many chemicals which man dumps into the air, water, and soil are injurious to health. There are good grounds for believing that some of them are, but we do not know how much of which ones are injurious. We do not know whether the burning of fossil fuels is producing irreversible changes in the composition of the earth's atmosphere and, if it is, what the ramifications of such changes are. When we build dams, drain swamps, or irrigate large areas we do not know the full effects of such projects on water, soil, fish, or wildlife.*

It is necessary to know the effects of pollution if one is to formulate a rational program of control. Until we know the effects of a pollutant it is difficult to determine whether it should be controlled and, if so, how stringent the controls should be. If, in fact, emissions from the burning of fuel are permanently changing the amount of carbon dioxide in the atmosphere, and if such a change will result in an increase in world temperature, the melting of the polar ice caps, and consequent flooding on a massive scale, then clearly extraordinary efforts are warranted in controlling such emissions. If, on the other hand, such a chain of events is not likely, and if, in addition, the health effects of low levels of carbon dioxide are discovered to be insignificant, then control of carbon dioxide emissions becomes a low-priority matter.

Almost 20 years after he wrote these words, hundreds of billions of dollars spent on research and pollution control, we still are guessing about the impact of pollutants on health and the environment. How could this happen?

First of all, environmental legislation with its all-encompassing goals of the early Seventies—improved health, visibility, less ecological impact, more recreational opportunities, reduced materials damage— were swept in under the assumption they would cost less than the critics claimed; and even if they were more expensive, the country was optimistic about the strength of its own economy. President Lyndon Johnson reflected the views of the vast majority of Americans in the 1960s when he called a "guns and butter" policy realistic. America could take care of all its domestic needs and fight a war in Vietnam to save the world for democracy.

Thus, early criteria for environmental regulations were as stringent as politically possible, based on available ecological and health studies. The standard for photochemical smog, for example, was based on one report, a 20-year study of respiratory problems of nurses in Los Angeles; the study was challenged many times, criticized for faulty methodology. When a second study did not produce additional evidence of significantly reduced lung function, EPA lowered the standard, but only slightly. Most people did not want the standard changed, especially those who lived in large cities where they did a lot of wheezing and sneezing. Furthermore, people with asthma and emphysema were not considered in the studies, a group that may be large enough to warrant stronger regulations.

The rationale for a new smog ruling in 1978 was not scientific. It was economic. At the time, the country was reeling from soaring inflation, fueled by the steep rise in oil prices that affected the entire economy for years, unemployment and recession. Chairman of the Council of Economic Advisers Charles L. Schultze told EPA Administrator Douglas Costle that new Clean Air Act amendments "would impose substantially higher costs on business than is necessary."

Meanwhile, the Occupational Health and Safety Administration, under Eula Bingham, was resisting any efforts to lower standards that protected the work place from carcinogens. Economic duress was not considered an acceptable argument at OSHA, though the agency also was mandated to ensure that its standards did not impose undue economic hardship on industry.

The trend toward cost-benefit analysis of regulations officially began in 1976 with an executive order by President Gerald Ford, requiring government agencies to prepare cost-benefit analyses before putting into effect or changing any federal regulations that might have an impact on the economy. Presidents Carter and Reagan have reissued Ford's order. The Toxic Substances Control Act, also passed in 1976, stipulates that health risks be balanced against economic factors and other "public impacts." Since that time, scientific and economic studies (combined with risk assessments) have been used by competing sectors to fight regulations, go to court and carry on an ideological war through academic journals and the press. Television has stuck to the dramatic aspects of the issues.

The history of environmental regulation underlines the deep conflict of values over public health and economic progress. In 1958, the Delaney amendment was passed; since then, the Food and Drug Administration has been charged to ban any food additive shown to cause cancer in animals. The assumption is the additive also will cause cancer in humans, so that error will fall on the side of safety no matter how unlikely that the cancer would develop. The Delaney amendment has provided a standard for much environmental legislation, and certainly has been defended by most environmental groups.

Before 1981, federal environmental standards typically were set to reduce the risk of disease to one person in a million, or sometimes 1 in 100,000. Since the beginning of the Reagan administration, when economic concerns took priority, several standards regarding radiation (uranium tailings, uranium mills) were lowered to 1 in 1,000. In the rule-making on benzene in 1984, EPA noted that its standards were based on cost-effectiveness; the standard was set at the point on the cost curve where the greatest number of health benefits would accrue per dollar invested. However, this brought loud protests that human health benefits are not measurable in dollars. Thus, one reason environmental progress is so slow is the conflict in public policy that allows strong differences of opinion about criteria for standards: How much safety for human health and the environment at what cost? How safe is safe enough for the cost?

Problems with Risk Assessment and Management

Political leaders have turned to risk assessment studies to help them out of these policy conundrums. The studies are meant to determine how to establish reasonable norms of safety for health and the environment at a time when resources, especially public goods, are scarce. Risk assessment has been designed to help decide how to set standards on chemicals, food additives, radiation and other substances people ingest and absorb.

The Committee on the Institutional Means for Assessment of Risks to Public Health has provided basic definitions of the risk assessment/risk management process for the National Research Council (1983, p. 3). The committee defines risk assessment as "the use of the factual base to define the health effects of exposure of individuals or populations to hazardous materials and situations." And risk management refers to the "process of weighing policy alternatives and selecting the most appropriate regulatory action, integrating the results of risk assessment with engineering data and with social, economic, and political concerns to reach a decision." On first glimpse, risk assessment appears to deal with the scientific basis of risk management policy decisions, especially regarding standards. The committee makes it clear, however, that even in the scientific aspects of risk assessment, value judgments are made that infer the quality of risk to human health. That is, although risk management deals with policy decisions after scientific risk assessment measures are taken, risk assessment judgments, which include various scientific value options, have caused as much controversy as risk management decisions.

The committee shows that the process of risk assessment includes four steps (p.3):

- *Hazard identification:* The determination of whether a chemical is causally linked to particular health effects. Four classes of information are used in this step: epidemiologic data, animal-bioassay data, short-term studies such as the mutagens tests that indicate the possibility of carcinogenicity, and comparisons of molecular structure, which compare an agent's chemical or physical properties with agents whose properties are linked with known carcinogens. Currently, animal-bioassays represent the strongest evidence of hazard identification.

- *Dose-response assessment:* The determination of the relation between the magnitude of exposure and the probability the health effects in question will occur.

- *Exposure assessment:* The determination of the extent of human exposure before or after application of regulatory controls. Here, as in the preceding steps, available evidence may be minimal or lacking so that analysts must make inferential judgments.

- *Risk characterization:* The description of the nature and often the magnitude of the risk, including attendant scientific uncertainty.

The process has been refined over the last decade. Scientific studies usually depend on laboratory experiments with animals that are given extremely high doses of the hazardous substance being tested, and often end with computer calculations that estimate the level of exposure that will cause no more than one in a million lifetime risk of cancer in humans, or economic calculations to determine the cost of a specific regulation.

The risk assessor assumes it is possible to extrapolate results from animals to humans, and that the mathematical models are accurate. Most scientists agree that the extrapolations and other risk-assessment techniques are still too primitive to tell us what Clarence Davies wanted to know in the late 1960s: how much harm the substance will cause.

Using animal studies in risk assessment demands a twofold extrapolation: 1) from an extremely high dose in a short timeframe to a protracted low dose that reflects actual consumption; and 2) from animal to human. It is virtually impossible to replicate actual human ingestion of a substance in a laboratory, or to calculate all the possible synergistic combinations that would affect the outcome.

It is even difficult to come to conclusions with one simple extrapolation. In an often-quoted 1972 article in *Minerva* magazine (10: 209), Alvin Weinberg pointed out that we could be reasonably certain of the effects of low-level doses of radiation on animals only by experimenting on 8 billion mice. One significant problem with huge doses of a substance, as commonly performed on animals, is that they would overwhelm the normal protective measures a human body takes to detoxify hazardous agents at lower doses; further, the high doses introduce metabolic pathways nonexistent at lower doses. Some studies have illustrated this problem, notably the classic example of nitrilotriacetic acid (NTA), the chemical introduced in the 1960s to replace highly polluting phosphates.

There are other problems with the tests. Humans have different diets, lifestyles, drink more alcohol and, most of all, have different predisposing genetic makeup upon which the hazardous substance works. Different people with different lifestyles complicate the picture immeasurably. If it is difficult to extrapolate conclusions within the same species—e.g., rats and mice—how much more difficult to extrapolate from rats to humans. Furthermore, the National Academy of Sciences declares there is no methodology to assess the long-range effects of toxic agents. The latency period for cancer can be 20 years or more.

All the data are contestable. Epidemiologic studies are somewhat less controversial, but demand large population groups that cannot be subjected to scientific controls. When large, relatively homogeneous groups are studied with controls that show connections among environmental factors such as exposure to chemicals, tobacco smoke or radiation and cancer or other diseases, the evidence tends to be accepted. But when the latency period is 20 years, it is extremely difficult to track down an exposed group of individuals, even if the affected population is huge.

Furthermore, critics of animal studies have noted that such studies indicate far more serious carcinogens synthesized by plants are eaten by humans every day. For example, Bruce Ames, who in the 1960s developed one of the first short-term tests to identify chemicals that might be carcinogens, also has identified many toxic chemicals that plants have synthesized as defense against predators and are regularly eaten by humans. He also identified mold carcinogens such as aflatoxins—1,000 times more potent as a carcinogen in rats than the pesticide EDB—that are found in peanut butter, corn products and apple juice; and burned and browned material from frying foods like hamburgers as well as high fats and high intake of alcohol (*Science* 221: 2256, 1983).

Ames' point is not that these foods are dangerous, though they could be if eaten in great quantities, but that they are no more dangerous than the chemicals for which we are setting one in a million standards. Finally, many of the dread hazardous substances, such as PCBs and solvents, would be toxic indeed if ingested or bathed in, but sealed with oil in a transformer do not present serious problems unless mishandled.

Driving without a seat belt and smoking are 1,000 to a million times riskier, depending on the circumstances. Indeed, sitting in our car, a few feet from the gas tank, as all of us do after we step into our automobiles, represents a much bigger risk than many environmental risks causing public outcries.

Questions of Value

Thus, scientific controversies about the levels of acceptability—doses of chemicals or radiation a person can safely absorb—impede the setting of standards acceptable to all concerned. Just about everything a person does involves risk, but calculating the precise degree of risk is enormously difficult. There also are value questions and questions of equity. Most people differ on the level of risk they are willing to accept. Many people smoke cigarettes, knowing very well that the risk of smoking is one of the few positively proven health hazards. Other people build homes on earthquake faults knowingly and willingly, others on riverbanks or below dams. And many people would involuntarily accept risks if it meant keeping a job.

K.S. Shrader-Frechette (1985) has noted that a number of value decisions are made in the calculations in risk assessment studies. In policy-makers' attempts to develop a method to rationalize their process, they often quantify their values into the same units; e.g., lives saved per dollar expended. Shrader-Frechette calls this method of risk assessment the "commensurability presupposition," or "the assumption that the marginal cost of saving lives, across opportunities, ought to be the same." (p. 55) Dollar values cannot account for individual needs of high-risk population groups, such as people with asthma, bronchitis or emphysema, pregnant women and small children, or those who live next to or work in nuclear plants or copper smelters. Similar ethical arguments can be directed against "probability" methodologies of traditional risk analysis. Simply because there is a greater or lesser degree of probability of a risk or accident in society as a whole does not mean the risks are distributed equitably or ethically.

Because it is all but impossible to determine risk preferences of social groups, the setting of standards, which presupposes the ability to determine the quality of risk to people and the environment, has been chaotic. Scientists are subject to methodological biases, even those who are not employed by a group that influences their judgment. Furthermore, scientists in consulting firms and laboratories, who perform work for industry, as well as agency scientists, who are battered by the political winds, and of course, environmental group scientists, who exclude many economic goals as they pursue those that often amount to zero risk—all are influenced by considerations beyond their discipline. Even academics are connected to funding sources in industry and the federal government. Most people, scientists included, are conditioned by economic and ideological biases that affect the way they perceive risk.

Economists who try to do "value-free" cost-benefit analyses not only are limited by the goal of the analysis, which is to reduce all values to dollars, but also by primitive methodology and insufficient data. They are supposed to make connections between reduced emissions of industrial pollutants and human health or environmental costs, without knowing countless environmental variables. For adequate analysis, they would have to make the informational links between the change in technology, to the emission of pollutants, to the changes in the ambient environmental quality, the effect on people, plants, animals and ecological systems. Such models do not exist and if they did, information is simply not available to make them work.

Political Decisions

With or without adequate scientific data, policy-makers will make decisions, which will depend on the politics of the moment. Earlier chapters have indicated how serious environmental "events" have led to legislation (with or without adequate enforcement), as in the passage of the Clean Air and Clean Water acts, and, more recently and more spectacularly, "Superfund" after Love Canal, and new emphasis on chemical plant safety after Bhopal. This crisis mode of environmental concern has been the pattern of legislation and action since at least the end of the last century when typhoid provoked local action for water treatment. The primary motivation for environmental legislation and enforcement has been the concern about health, and the support of the environmental movement in the preservation of wilderness. When public support wanes, environmental action and research flounders.

Recently, public concern has centered on toxic substances because the media have dramatized their role in inducing cancer. Thus, through environmental groups and politicians who have seen it as a good election issue, legislators and agency officials have been pushed into establishing priorities around toxics rather than long-term problems such as wetlands, coastal protection, noise pollution problems, population pressures in the Third World. Events such as Bhopal and Love Canal play the role disasters always have played. Bhopal caused EPA to divert many of its research resources for a year to compile a list of the 403 chemicals considered "immediately dangerous to life and health." Meanwhile, research on problems of ecological toxicity has been neglected since the late 1970s because of such on-going demands for visible results and continued budget cutbacks.

A 1987 EPA internal report suggested that the agency might be overtaxing its resources on hazardous wastes and cleanup of chemical waste dumps and underfunding high risk/low priority items like ozone depletion, urban and farm runoff pollution (especially pesticides) and indoor air pollution from radon, formaldehyde, heating and cooking appliances and other sources. The report also gave EPA's rationale: relative risk from pollution is only one of many factors that determine agency policy. Others are statutory requirements, public demands, technological and economic feasibility and, of course, scientific uncertainty.

It will no doubt take many years to unravel the entanglements of environmental conflicts built up during the past generation. There are agencies that do the same kind of research as other agencies but may not view the problems in the same way. For example, although EPA is the largest regulator of toxic substances that can cause cancer, the Food and Drug Administration (responsible for drugs, food, cosmetics, medical devices, TVs and microwave ovens), the Consumer Products Safety Commission (monitors consumer items like children's clothing, patching compound and aerosol sprays), and OSHA (hazards in the work place) all have become heavily involved in risk assessment studies, on their own and with each other.

To factor in the costs and benefits of proposed safety regulations in their risk studies, each agency has its own formula for determining the value of a human life (Cf. *Fortune* Feb. 3, 1986). At OSHA, it is $2 million to $3 million; EPA values one life at $750,000 to $1 million; the Federal Aviation Administration puts the value of a life at $750,000. Economists disagree about which factors (lost income, distress to families, etc.) should be included in the formula. The agency administrators do not have to cooperate to reach regulatory consistency. There is little interagency coordination of goals, programs and research. Several presidents have attempted reorganization, but with little success because of strong opposition from the agencies and their powerful lobbyists.

One reason for these problems is that individual agencies have been delegated responsibility for national policy, not for developing an integrated national policy. The problem is structural because it deals with the need to coordinate the activities of a number of government departments and agencies into an integrated system with unified objectives and priorities. There are hundreds of examples of uncoordinated agency actions that have compounded the difficulties of implementing environmental laws over the past decade. (Cf. Davos 1984)

For example, the Clean Air Act required a scrubber technology that made it more difficult to comply with the Clean Water Act and the Resource Conservation and Recovery Act, which shifted the disposal of the waste. EPA banned agricultural uses of ethylene dibromide after a 10-year debate at the same time the Occupational Safety and Health Administration announced and then withdrew its standard on the pesticide. Because of the separate charges of the dozens of federal, state and local agencies, industry often has to obtain dozens to hundreds of permits for one project. The SOHIO oil pipeline project in the late 1970s required more than 700 permits.

These agencies eventually get to comment on new EPA rules. And industry and environmental groups comment on standards during the external review period after the process has gone through the phases of initial review, working party review, and steering committee review. During external review, everybody gets into the act: the Office of Management and Budget, which attempts to substitute less costly alternatives; regulated firms and trade groups, which have their own science advisers to debate health and environmental costs; congressional committees; other affected agencies; and, finally, the public and environmental organizations. Public hearings are held throughout the country. It takes at least four years for each rule to clear these hurdles. No wonder it took four years to implement the first rules of the Resource Conservation and Recovery Act. By the time every group spoke its piece, nobody was satisfied with the rules, the agency or environmental quality in the United States. And, of course, each step costs a huge bundle of money.

National Research Center

A national interagency research center needs to be established to coordinate short- and long-term projects with special emphasis on intermedia research and programs on pollution-control technologies. A more refined risk-assessment model could be developed and standardized among the agencies, one that would take into account strengths and weaknesses of scientific studies, highlight points of scientific inference and incorporate corrections for value biases. A board with specialized committees should be formed, comprised of experts representing scientific viewpoints in and out of the departments, able to make policy decisions that would not be shaken by temporary heavy political and media winds.

An interagency research unit could help put some organizational order into the current practice of environmental management. For example, at the federal level responsibility for control of toxic pollutants is spread over numerous agencies: besides EPA, OSHA, FDA and CPSC, mentioned above, there are the U.S. Forest Service, which uses pesticides to control forest pests, the Army Corps of Engineers, Water Resources Council, National Oceanic and Atmospheric Administration, Fish and Wildlife Service, and many smaller offices. Each agency has its own charge, its own rules and, in most cases, has appealed to different research units to justify its regulations.

A coordinated interagency research effort could lead to a consensus on environmental and health regulations. Rule-making is the central focus and is problematic for environmental specialists, whatever their position in industry, agencies or environmental groups. Regulations depend on research, which nowadays is scattered, far-flung and conflict-ridden.

Dozens of departments, agencies, bureaus, councils, commissions, boards, services and administrations relate to environmental and conservation goals but have nothing to do with with each other in practice or in national planning. What do the Forest Service, Army Corps of Engineers and EPA do together in planning environmental impact research methodology, aquatic studies and erosion reports? Today, very little, yet all are involved in this work through legislative mandate. Congress' mandate, for example, includes concerns and research programs for ecological stability. Yet each agency has its own lobbyists, legislative friends and detractors. Dozens of agencies work at cross-purposes, usually on short-term projects to satisfy some constituency or the demands of some new national media hype. The bureaucracies have no reason to find out what is going on elsewhere because there are plenty of mouths to feed in their own stables. A coordinated research program would give the public more bang for their tax dollars, and offer more possibilities for protecting the environment for future generations.

Fragmentation has led to waste and lower-quality basic and applied research in the environmental field. Most large departments and agencies have adequate research budgets for applied research, but never enough for basic research on vital environmental questions. Under time and political pressures to produce results, the agencies contract out work that is not reviewed thoroughly by peers in the sciences. Applied research often is done and accepted for use in setting standards before scientific models have been scrutinized by peers. Many lawsuits have been filed and won because the research methods have been suspect, even in such fields as toxicology where animal bioassays have determined standards for toxic substances. The accuracy and reliability of quantitative data, stringent quality assurance/quality control programs, and even such basic questions as the need for modern analytical instruments, remain unsettled throughout the agencies. Some states, including New York and California, have decided to establish their own standards based on their own admittedly inadequate studies.

There is no shortage of research information, good and bad. Thousands of research institutes at universities, agencies, private consulting firms and laboratories, as well as large laboratories at corporations and trade group consortia churn out billions of bits of information. Much of it is filed in data retrieval information systems and available to libraries around the world, but a great deal of it is not because it was gathered under contract to private industries or trade groups. The National Technical Information Service cannot even account for much of the scientific work done by the agencies and their contractees. Nor are the tens of thousands of laboratory studies funded by industries like the chemical and drug manufacturers to determine safety and toxicity able to be coordinated and utilized for further studies of similar chemicals.

Because these studies lack accountability and peer review, scientific confidence in the results is lacking. Government agencies have the authority to investigate laboratories that are conducting industry studies for fraud and flawed techniques but cannot look over researchers' shoulders while they perform the experiments. Duplication of effort causes monumental waste, while fundamental research is neglected. Again, the issue is that each faction is solving its own short-term problem to achieve short-term political or ideological gain.

These uncounted thousands of studies, based on differing statements of the problem, dissimilar data and assumptive values or methodologies, are used to prove different hypotheses. A new interagency National Research Center could benefit first of all by establishing objectives and priorities among its own agencies and sharing research budgets to avoid overlap. Internal competition, judged by review of fellow agency workers, would be healthy, especially in a scientific sense. These research priorities would then be extended to include studies, past and current, of private research institutes, which could continue their ancillary contractual role. Most important, the national center would include scientific and financial resources from industry and environmental groups.

In spring 1984, the National Science Foundation reported that in 1983 private industry had spent $44.3 billion in research and development, for the first time in 20 years surpassing government R&D expenditures, $39.6 billion that year. It always has been in industry's interest to do its own private research because it can apply the results to increase profits. In many industries, this may no longer be the case. Most manufacturing industries realize it now costs much more to produce toxic chemicals and waste than it did a few years ago.

Companies can be forced to pay chemical taxes to fund future emergencies, they are liable for damages both to workers and communities in case of accidents, and in many instances they are regulated by "right to know" laws and must inform workers and outsiders about possible hazards at the work place.

It is in industry's interest, and in the interest of environmental groups, to join government agencies in trying to define and control hazards and to develop production technologies that generate less waste and utilize cheaper pollution control equipment. If they do not cooperate, they could wind up in a position of great liability or at least in a less advantageous economic position. For example, they would not have the advantage of knowing which chemicals are likely to be banned if they do not help define the problem, thus, they could not plan the orderly phaseout of the offending manufacturing processes and ineffective pollution-control equipment. By participating in the research and planning, they could help establish timetables for ordered transition into new technologies or less hazardous products. Billions now spent on lawsuits, lobbying and private research could be saved and put into enlightened environmental management.

Industry and environmental groups must enter the policy-formation process at the research level so they can help establish priorities and rule-making from the beginning phases of environmental management practices. Their only role has been to attack policy from the outside, at great expense and with much chagrin. But growing economic pressures on all concerned precludes continuing to forge policy through conflict. More rational procedures also could lower the heavy stress levels and work loads of local agency personnel.

The MITI Model

Since 1968, Japan has solved many of its research problems cooperatively through the Ministry of International Trade and Industry. MITI was established to promote industrial cooperation, and it oversees a joint industry/government research fund along with a government-sponsored clearinghouse of technological information. Billions of dollars from government and industry are poured annually into cooperative research projects. One obvious research project needed in the United States is a common, comprehensive and unified program for the regulation of carcinogens of all types and by all modes of exposure: food, water, air, drugs and cosmetics, consumer goods. Such a project requires the cooperation of all involved agencies, industries, environmental groups, labor, consumer groups. With ample long- and short-term funding, a program could be established involving the world's leading scientists operating under a realistic timetable not shackled by the evening news or political rallies. A balanced, unified program reflecting scientific consensus among all parties could lead to strong, credible legislation and regulation on carcinogens.

Other countries must become involved in the national center, for many reasons not the least of which is that we have common concerns and sometimes we even share responsibility for each other's pollution and health problems. Canada, for example, might have had different national research priorities during the 1970s if it had been involved with

U.S. research on acid rain and asbestos impacts. And all sectors—industrial, government, environmental—might have initiated different postures had the research been done cooperatively since the mid-1970s when the problems became apparent.

Everyone engaged in the acid rain debate agrees there is a problem but, because of its complexity and inconclusive evidence, disagree about what course of action is possible and desirable. The scientific community is still not certain about the magnitude of the problem, the exact relationships among acid sources (power plants, autos, refineries, smelters) and their receptors (lakes, streams, forests), nor about the chemical (especially meteorological) mechanisms and combinations of air pollutants that do the damage and rates of decline of either watersheds or forests. There have been more hearings in Washington on the acid rain problem than any other scientific issue, but resulting in neither scientific nor political consensus. Quite the opposite.

Scientists do agree that damage is accelerating so rapidly that emission of sulfur dioxide and nitrogen oxides must be controlled as soon as possible. But with the cleanup estimated to cost hundreds of billions of dollars, it would be unwise to single out any source of acidification—such as power plants in the Midwest—for massive expenditure of funds if concomitant action is not taken at the same time to cut automobile pollution and other pollutants such as volatile organic compounds and heavy metals. The gaps in knowledge are huge, and a central focus of research priorities could save money and avoid duplication. As it is, Canada, EPA, the Electric Power Research Institute, which is the research arm of the power companies, European governments and other international institutes are setting their own research priorities.

Canada especially should be involved in a U.S. national research center because so many of its products cross the border and are affected by U.S. regulation. Some of the biggest asbestos mines in the world are in Canada, and the Canadian government has a significant ownership and interest in them. After EPA banned asbestos from U.S. products, the Canadian asbestos industry lost many of its major markets. The Canadian government then began to fund research to prove that the risk is exaggerated and that it can be controlled (CBC radio, *Sunday Morning*, Feb. 9, 1986).

In the debate about acid rain as well as about asbestos, the definition of the research and its findings can clarify many issues. EPA researchers focused mainly on the microscopic asbestos fibers that are produced in factories and shipyards, substances that reach the most sensitive sections of the lung; Canadians are more interested in the cruder fibers that come from mining the material. Many U.S. acid rain researchers, for example, noted complex atmospheric interactions that implicated nitrogen oxides from autos; Canadian (and many U.S. environmentalist) researchers wanted to indict primarily and almost exclusively the Midwest power plants. Obviously, much time, money and effort could be saved through joint research and common framing of the research problem.

So much basic environmental and ecological research needs to be done worldwide, yet so little is spent on research that it is increasingly imperative that new, less wasteful institutions are found. According to Colin Norman of Worldwatch Institute in Washington, D.C., only about 5 percent of the global research and development budget, including the United States', is spent on pollution control and even less on basic ecological research. Yet, despite the extraordinary number of private and government research institutes around the world, one strong and well-funded group could coordinate their activities, which would save them all money as they solved common problems cooperatively.

Research Agenda

In a speech to the Natural Resources Council of America that was reprinted in *EPA Journal,* (Sept. 1985), EPA Administrator Lee M. Thomas emphasized that environmental problem-solving cannot be confined to individual media—air, water, waste, and so on. The problems are connected so intimately that it is possible to regulate a water problem and end up with an air problem. He said that a large source of toxic air pollution may come from industrial volatile organic compounds, which evaporate at municipal sewage treatment plants. Again, the major source of several toxic metal pollutants and PCBs in the Great Lakes is air deposition. Acid rain starts out as air pollutants from industrial sources and automobiles and ends up hundreds to thousands of miles away, killing fish in lakes and leaves on trees, even toxifying soils. Some toxic metals are removed from the airstream of an industrial process, put into the wastewater stream, treated and converted to sludge, put in an incinerator and returned to the air.

The moral of the story is that in environmental research whole systems need to be analyzed. Ecologists have learned how difficult this process can be in trying to account for environmental change even in the simplest of systems. It also is challenging to examine the many pathways of pollutants in and through land, water and air media. In factories, it is very difficult to perform mass balance studies and account for total volume of, say, chemicals that are processed and escape into the atmosphere out the vents, and made into products while waste is being combined with water, treated and disposed of. Yet, until whole systems studies are organized industry by industry, it will not be possible to answer such important questions as how much pollution is going into air and watersheds, and how much is buried, stored or burned. Each state and federal regulatory program has its own regulatory requirements and standards.

Ecosystems studies are packed with so many kinds of information from different disciplines that they cannot even be termed a field of study. Each area of inquiry requires different kinds of information from different disciplines. The work is more like an integrating concept than a theory of knowledge or something that can be systematized and repeated in study after study. It is interdisciplinary but even this term is too generalized to assist in developing a standard methodology. It is what Lynton Caldwell calls a "metadiscipline" because the results of these environmenal studies could achieve a new level in the integration of knowledge. The methodological perspectives of different researchers allow them to approach problems through different paths as they grapple with the enormity of very large ecological or technological systems.

Risk Assessment

Among the most difficult of the new research responsibilities is the development of an acceptable methodology of assessing risk, one that incorporates quantitative measures of risk with qualitative corrections and explicit value inputs. In spring 1985, the President's Council on Environmental Quality released a report on long-term environmental research and development. In it, several of the panels addressed the problem of quantitative risk assessment and the need for research on basic biological processes (pharmacodynamic and environmental mechanisms of toxic effects) and the extension of a solid methodology to include human health effects other than cancer, such as systemic toxicity. Hundreds of factors beyond carcinogenicity might be involved in toxicological analysis.

The Risk Committee of the National Research Council (1983, p. 6) believes the risk assessment process can be improved substantially by: a) utilization of all available scientific knowledge with diversified approaches for specific regulatory needs; b) standardization of analytic procedures among federal programs through development of guidelines that spell out how inferences are made in the risk assessment process; and c) the creation of an institution that will ensure continuing review of risk assessment methods as scientific information expands.

Despite the widespread criticisms (often for political or ideological purposes) of animal bioassays for assessing carcinogenicity in humans,

Elements of Risk Assessment and Risk Management

(Courtesy, Committee on the Institutional Means for Assessment of Risks to Public Health, National Research Council, 1983)

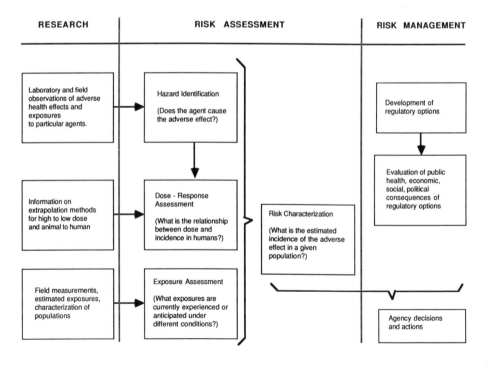

most scientists agree that, all things being equal, animal studies provide a strong indicator of cancer in humans. Of the 30 chemicals listed by the International Agency for Research on Cancer as human carcinogens, all but two (estrogens and smokeless tobacco) have been found in animal bioassays to be carcinogenic. But when these indicators are translated into economic risk assessment equations, such ethical considerations as involuntary acceptance or other unknown factors are ignored, as K.S. Shrader-Frechette (1985) has noted. These methodological questions have to be worked out in new risk assessment models. It is difficult to separate the fact and value questions because values are incorporated into the facts (by method, choice of quantitative data, ideological preferences).

In a keynote address to the First International Risk Seminar in London in 1983, William W. Lowrance suggested we "develop ways of intercomparing sources of risk, comparing risks against risks, weighing risks against the benefits they accompany, and appraising the societal return from reducing risks." Such a model could incorporate quantitative data such as toxicity, infant mortality, actuarial data, frequency and severity of hazards, possible less hazardous alternatives (an extremely important variable), and true cost-benefits, including pollution control cost and damage cost for the whole country (admittedly difficult to determine), health costs saved, productivity enhanced, disruptions delineated, all of which now have numbers ascribed to them since clean air, auto safety and other standards have been introduced. Even the ethical issues can be weighted and included in the model along with such factors as societal functions, geographic area, product classes, contributions to a specific illness and mortality. A wide array of risks, from chemicals and consumer products to potential waste dump sites or land use decisions, could be analyzed if such a model were developed and refined. Risks could be defined and compared regarding their significance and acceptability with qualifications. Values would be made explicit and clarified in the analysis. This, of course, is no small research task, and would need the participation of many interest groups.

Decision-making

The final decisions about environmental policies, regulations, standards do not come from computer models, however superbly they might clarify the options. Decisions are made by the people who represent many interest groups, scientific positions and political ideologies. A policy-making board should include related government agencies as well as representatives from industry, environmental groups, labor unions. A good model that has factored in data that many interest groups agree are important provides a beginning to the negotiation. The negotiating process demands some scientific understanding but not so much that would preclude citizen participation in the policy-making process.

Experience under the first Reagan administration with Secretary of the Interior James Watt and EPA Administrator Anne Gorsuch Burford has taught policy-makers that national decisions for environmental protection have to be safeguarded from short-term political disruptions. The short-term election cycle has greatly interfered with long-term environmental problems in the past because politics generally is concerned with immediate issues and constituencies. Therefore, it has become necessary to establish a policy board with responsibility for long-term developments, supported by the staff of experts from a national research center.

The policy board could weigh reports for the research center and decide on short- and long-term risk management strategies. If a national research center had come to such a board in the late 1970s, when it was apparent that acid rain was a problem in North America and Europe, such short-term decisions as liming lakes or treating them with nutrition-enriching sludge and phasing out old power plants on a timetable could have been made, while more specific information was gathered by the research center to determine future action. By the 1990s, many Midwest power plants would have introduced new, less polluting technologies at far less cost than the $50 billion proposed by legislators and environmental groups for retrofit measures during the acid rain debates of the early 1980s. As it happened, factions developed with their own studies and media blitzes, and after 10 years of huge expenditures of money, the continent has little to show for its investment.

Decision-making has always been tense when parties with conflicting interests are jawboning, but comparative risk analysis, based on credible and legitimate science, can assist in the negotiating process. In the real world we are always balancing out risky ventures, from the moment we step out of bed in the morning. That risk does not involve other populations, like asbestos workers or asthmatics, so that its value can be recognized as individual. Some risks, like driving automobiles and flying airplanes, generate benefits for society, which has agreed they are worth the societal risk at least until a better alternative comes along. The policy board needs to clarify the risks, identify the parties that might be especially concerned, and establish rules as equitably as possible, including future generations. Societies must act but, according to most political constitutions, they must act responsibly and equitably.

At the bottom of many environmental policy conflicts often lie expectations for zero risk that can be unreasonable in contemporary society. For example, although chloroform shows up as a carcinogen and a mutagen in laboratory tests, chloroform also is produced when chlorine interacts with organic matter in the chlorination of drinking water. Because of chlorination, modern society has been preserved from the hundreds of epidemics from infectious diseases that plagued cities until recent times. Most scientists suspect that chloroform in drinking water might contribute to increases in cancer rates. But until the linkage is positively made and alternate methods of purification are found, we prefer to live with the possible risk of slight increases in cancer than to return to far greater risks of contaminated drinking water.

Local Implementation and Enforcement

Although consistent and credible national policies are important to establish common rules of the game, local practices ultimately will determine the effectiveness of those policies. Given some recent improvement in environmental protection activities, local practices are still uneven or inequitable at best and chaotic or ineffective at worst. States are unusually out of sync in their implementation and enforcement practices. In regions where compliance has been uniform, there have been strong monitoring and control programs. Federal agencies must be provided enough resources to strengthen their oversight of local enforcement.

There is some hope for compliance mainly because data management systems have become more and more sophisticated and the federal agencies gradually have become geared to their use. Now they need to make their information and implementation practices available to state and local agencies.

Until very recently, agencies have been buried by industry information: permit applications, manifests of hazardous waste disposal, reporting data. But slowly, some agencies are putting these data on computer files and making the information more accessible. A great deal of enforcement can begin at a computer terminal, proceed to letters of inquiry regarding faulty information or discrepancies, and finally lead to site visits. Most firms have become sophisticated enough to know what information, useful or misleading, to give enforcement officers during site visits, and a computer can help agencies equalize the relationship.

Local enforcement depends on the interest, competence and determination of local agencies. When these are lacking, industries have a number of creative ways to circumvent the law, far beyond just dumping waste into sewers, still a common practice. Some companies forge manifests, give their wastes to midnight dumpers, find convenient swamps or waterways, and so on. These practices anger firms that comply with the law because they give the lawbreakers an unfair economic advantage. For firms that consistently evade regulations by illegal means, stiff fines are necessary; in serious cases, the threat of a jail term. Some enforcement agencies have begun to apply these stronger means of pressure, especially where district attorneys have sought to grab the public's attention swiftly and dramatically. The media assist with all things dramatic.

Regional state compacts are necessary to deal with various environmental problems of coordination. In the Northeast, six New England states and New York formed the New England Regional Commission to track down industries not in compliance and to develop a data base to plan for future hazardous waste treatment and disposal facilities. Since most companies must send their wastes out of their region or state for disposal, the states need a check on where it goes, and whether it reaches its destination. A common computer system records the manifest (hazardous waste form) from the generator and does not "approve" the transaction until it receives the duplicate from the disposer. For illegal activity to occur under such a system, there would have to be collusion among the generator, the transporter and the disposer. It is essential that all hazardous waste generators are on this system, but other kinds of efforts can bring in recalcitrant industries.

What is important about these kinds of information systems is that information about toxicity, "right to know" data, and other emergency response procedures can be included for local fire departments, law enforcement officers and agency personnel. The computer can be a useful health protection tool as well as an enforcement arm.

Other coordination problems can be solved by creating new "authorities" that would manage environmental problems now controlled by cities, counties and specialized local governments, perhaps by offering financial inducements. Because it has been so difficult to find sites for treatment, incineration or disposal of hazardous waste, the representatives of five Southern California counties and two cities formally signed a joint powers agreement that created the Southern California Hazardous Waste Management Authority. Each county and city has agreed to find sites for new hazardous waste facilities in proportion to its own share of waste generation.

Environmental Protection Managers

The human glue that binds the entire process of environmental management is the people who work in the field, from local laboratory supervisors and environmental managers in industry or agency personnel to environmental group scientists and national researchers and policy makers. All need an extraordinary sophistication in their knowledge; moreover, they need a quality of professional behavior that keeps them above the factionalism that is the major deterrent to environmental progress. Clear conclusions from federal cooperative research units would greatly help fulfill their professional charge.

The pressures of competing interest groups have torn apart this nation that has been able to generate material wealth and a strong national tradition largely because social classes and interests have cooperated to serve a broad national purpose. Unfortunately, this cooperation and benevolence seem to depend on prosperity and a limitless supply of natural resources. As long as there was enough economic growth to satisfy the needs of the special interests, they joined together on the big issues. But this happy state has disintegrated. There is no better example that the cooperation no longer exists than that of the environmental protection movement. All sides are willing to spend enormous sums of money in court and through the media to make tiny points in the face of the opposition.

John W. Gardner, founder of Common Cause, called this problem of government "the special interest state," where a wide range of legitimate interests, private and public, bring pressure and influence action that will stalemate important national goals. Gardener spoke about the problem during spring 1976, at a meeting of the American Society for Public Administrators: "The sheer range and variety of interests cancel each other out and the system lies paralyzed. . . . The fragments of government have no effective way of working together or thinking together."

It is proposed here that the fragments of environmental protection in the United States can be pulled together by an integrated national policy and a committed group of people, who with intention and responsibility set themselves to protect the health and environment of those who live in the present and those who will live in the future.

Bibliography

William W. Lowrance's quotation on risk assessment comes from the Proceeding of the First International Risk Seminar, Royal College of Physicians (London: Libbey & Company Limited, 1983). His *Modern Science and Human Values* (New York: Oxford University Press, 1985) covers a wide range of topics on science-related subjects and professionalism, ethics, risk assessment and policy-making. A solid treatment of the scientific and policy functions of risk assessment comes from the Committee on the Institutional Means for Assessment of Risks, National Research Council, *Risk Assessment in Government: Managing the Process* (Washington, D.C.: National Academy Press, 1983). Kristin S. Shrader-Frechette approaches some of the same subjects from a philosophical viewpoint in *Science Policy, Ethics, and Economic Methodology* (Boston: D. Reidel, 1985); and *Risk Analysis and Scientific Method* (Boston: D. Reidel, 1985). Another more technical treatment is Paolo Ricci, *Principles of Health Risk Assessment* (Englewood Cliffs, N.J.: Prentice Hall, 1985). In *Knowledge and Discretion in Government Regulation* (New York: Praeger, 1984), Ted Greenwood clarifies the problem of using scientific knowledge in a political environment as well as the practical complications that arise when public policy is developed in such a tradition. In "Environmental Management: Can We Afford Established Trends," *The Environmental Professional* 8 (1986):4, 305-10, Climos A. Davos has developed a strong argument for changing past methods of environmental management from segmented to an integrated environmental policy based on cooperation and "social codetermination." Many of Lynton Keith Caldwell's books and articles on environmental policy have been pioneering and informative in the past generation, most recently *Science and the National Environmental Policy Act* (University, Ala.: University of Alabama Press, 1982); and *International Environmental Policy: Emergence and Dimensions* (Durham, N.C.: Duke University Press, 1984).

What Can Be Done

The purpose of this book has been to examine the context of environmental protection in the United States, how it has developed historically and what systems govern its functional dynamics today. I identified three sectors—industry, government agencies and environmental groups and their historical antecedents—that have established an adversary action/reaction dynamic on both a "macro" level in society at large and on a "micro" level in the work place and in local communities.

The process has become deeply entrenched in society, grooving itself into a syndrome of escalating demands as an extremely costly, inefficient way to solve environmental problems. The basic difficulty with continuing such an adversary approach, with its short-term, quick-fix, litigious mechanisms, is that problem-solving by action-reaction creates new problems or environmental disorder. Industry cuts the best deal it can with agencies or takes them to court over legal standards, in the process spending much money that could be invested or used for more constructive, environment-enhancing activities. Agencies compete over turf battles or become immobilized because any activity could threaten their budgets, or any of a variety of other political ensnarements. Environmental groups sometimes reach for the moon in their demands or become prone to battle their "adversaries" on principle rather than on the scientific or social merits of the case. To make a very long story short, the syndrome has dealt a heavy blow to continued progress in environmental quality, despite hundreds of billions of dollars spent in the past generation by all three groups of adversaries.

Wherever the solution to environmental problems is found, the approach must integrate all three sectors, since solutions will follow only actions that account for the values of each. Even environmental mediation, which resolves conflicts by outside parties, falls short of integrative mechanisms because the process is based on adversary premises. The structures of environmental management must integrate human action with a common perception of environmental standards and planning for the future.

The notion of respect for future generations, fundamentally an ethical concept, in this book has been applied to environmental management at all levels—in industry, which must protect itself and its resources for its long-term survival; at agencies, whose charge is to protect the quality of the natural environment for future generations despite political pressures; and to environmentalists, whose strategies must be realistic enough to protect the environment for generations to come.

Specifically, this ethical notion has been used in reference to everyone who has an interest in environmental progress, particularly environmental specialists working in the three sectors. If society would identify environmental professionals and charge them with the mission of doing "good work," as the late E.F. Schumacher put it, those in the field could integrate the sectors by maintaining high professional standards. Firms and agencies that fall short of those standards would be marked by workers who know what they should be doing. Environmental professionals, particularly "in the trenches" of industry and enforcement agencies, remain divided about short-range goals, long-range objectives, procedures, values and a host of other processes. The reasons lie in their training, work subcultures, career goals and the lack of professional schools that agree on what is needed for their educational development. The integrative power of such a large group of well-trained and motivated professionals remains an unrealized possibility.

The integrative possibilities of a federal planning and research role also remain largely unrealized, for obvious political reasons. But the power of the federal government reorganizing its research units would be able integrate diverse scientific, economic and political points of view in the United States and worldwide. Organized with an adequate combined budget from contributing agencies, a National Research Center could arrange scientific and political purposes consonant with priorities. Again, the pressing need is to avoid continued unplanned environmental deterioration by planning around such disorder. If industry can be integrated into the policy-making process to the extent that it can plan the required operational changes, companies may be willing to stop manufacturing risky products, change production methods, and phase in effective pollution control equipment. It is the random, haphazard nature of contemporary policy planning that leads to wasteful litigation and inaction on important problems. Most of all, such a powerful federal agency could be the forum for creating shared values that can lead to enlightened environmental management.

The recent past, despite all the conflict and wasteful expense, surely suggests reason for optimism about the future because environmental protection has taken its place as a premier subject of national debate. The relentless efforts of hundreds of environmental groups and committed individuals have made ordinary people aware of the major elements of the discussion, and the public has shown its concern by voting overwhelmingly for increased environmental protection. This contemporary phenomenon is unique in America's environmental history.

The opportunity has arrived to attempt to solve the traditional dilemmas by applying integrative mechanisms, even more than the few suggested here. Under the weighty baggage of ineffective, musty institutions, the nation has been slogging painfully toward an anxious future long enough. Perhaps with redesigned systems we can move efficiently and feel secure about the fate of future generations.

In her Sonnett No. CXL, Edna St. Vincent Millay highlighted the challenge:

> *Upon this gifted age, in this dark hour*
> *Rains from the sky a meteroic shower*
> *Of facts—they lie unquestioned, uncombined,*
> *Wisdom enough to leech us of our ill*
> *Is daily spun, but there exists no loom*
> *To weave it into fabric.*

The meteoric shower of scientific, social and political facts and opinions from adversary factions lie around us. With federal enlightenment, environmental specialists can act as the integrating loom to weave wisdom into a mantle of environmental protection.

AAAS client-directed ethical codes, 151, 152
AAAS employer/sponsor-directed ethical codes, 151
AAAS member-directed ethical codes, 151
AAAS profession-directed ethical codes, 151
AAAS Professional Ethics Project, 150
AAAS society-directed ethical codes, 151, 152
acid rain (precipitation), 82, 117, 162, 178, 179
agency culture, 104
Air Pollution Control Association (APCA), 48
Alaskan pipeline, 48
America by Design (Noble), 146
American Association for the Advancement of Science (AAAS), 150
American Medical Association, 23
American Petroleum Institute, 53
American Statistical Society, 23
American Tobacco Institute, 155
Ames, Bruce, 171
analytical models, 136, 139
animal studies, 170, 171
Animas River, radioactivity, 43
Anmoore, W. Va., 115
Apostle of Cleanliness, 25
Arab oil embargo, 53
Army Corps of Engineers, 48, 102, 103, 130, 134
Arnott, Neil, 17
asbestos, 54, 178
aspirational commands, 65
auto emissions, 52
auto industry lobby, 51, 52
auto pollution, 31
baby pacifiers, 160
Bentham, Jeremy, 17, 144
benzene, 54
best available control technology (BACT), 64
best available technology (BAT), 46, 76, 116, 119
best practicable technology (BPT), 46, 76
Bhopal tragedy, 33, 63, 118, 121, 156, 173
Bingham, Eula, 168
biochemical oxygen demand (BOD), 46
Brower, David, 47
"bubble" policy, 64, 116, 119
Budd, William, 28
Bureau of Reclamation, 40, 41, 47, 102
bureaucratic inertia, 100
Burford, Anne Gorsuch, 56, 57, 95, 181
Cagney & Lacey TV show, 122
Calian, C.S., 144
Calumet Canal, 28

Calvert Cliffs legal case, 118
Canada, 178
carbolic acid, 27
carbon monoxide, 54
carcinogens, 171
Carson, Rachel (*Silent Spring*), 43
Carter, President Jimmy, 56, 113
catalytic converters, 53
categorical imperative (Kant), 149
CBC Radio, 179
CBS Morning News, 160
Chadwick Report, 17, 32, 130
Chadwick, Edwin, 17, 23
Chernobyl nuclear disaster, 63, 142
Chevron penalties, 119
chlorine, 30
cholera, 17, 23
citizen suits, 47
Citizens Committee on Natural Resources, 111
Citizens for a Better Environment (CBE), 9, 116
Clean Air Act and amendments, 50, 52, 53, 54, 56, 131, 173, 174
Clean Air Coalition, 110
Clean Water Act and amendments, 54, 55, 57, 100, 119, 131, 173, 174
clean water crusade, 47
colonial period, 14, 15
commensurability presupposition, 172
computers in environmental management, 79, 183
Conservation Directory, 112
Conservation Foundation, 123
Conservation, Environmental Response, Compensation and Liability
    Act of 1980 (CERCLA) Superfund, 62, 132, 159
construction grants, 42
Consumer Product Safety Commission (CPSC), 160, 173
consumerism, 33, 41
conventional pollutants, 46
Corbin, Alain, 16, 19
corporate culture, 82, 88
cost-benefit analysis, 54, 172
cost-effective technologies, 82
cost-effectiveness in risk studies, 169, 172
cost-oriented environmental management, 76-79
Council on Environmental Quality, 56, 166, 180
crisis-oriented environmental management, 72-75
Cuyahoga River fire, 45
Davies, J. Clarence, 50, 68, 107, 167
deep pockets laws, 118
DEHP, 160
Delaney amendment, 169
Dickens, Charles, 16
dilution of pollution in rivers, 20
disinfection, 28

Donora, Pa., disaster, 49
dose-response, 170
draining and paving streets, 15
drilling, wastes, 99
dysentery, 16
Earth Day, 45, 47
Echo Park controversy, 40
EDB (ethylene dibromide), 171
effluent limitation guidelines, 76
Eisenhower administration, 42
Electric Power Research Institute (EPRI), 179
electroplating companies, 74
Energy Supply and Environmental Coordination Act of 1974, 53
enforcement problems, 96
engineering ideology, 135, 141
engineering societies, 129
enlightened environmental management, 79-82, 84, 89
Environmental Agenda for the Future, 123
environmental audits, 79
Environmental Defense Fund (EDF), 9, 53, 109, 119, 120, 123
environmental goals, 134, 135, 136
environmental group effectiveness, 121
environmental heroes, 138
environmental impact statements, 48, 130
environmental law activist groups, 110, 116
environmental management history, 129-131
environmental manager study, 7, 8, 71
environmental managers, definition, 129
environmental mediation, 140
Environmental Protection Agency (EPA), 48, 53, 173, 174, 175
Environmental Protection Careers Guidebook, 137
environmental steward, 139
environmentally oriented managers, 84
epidemiological studies, 171
Epstein, Dr. Samuel, 58
ethical cases, 147, 148, 152-154
ethical codes, 149-151
ethical responsibilities, 149
ethical roles, 148
exposure assessment, 170
extrapolation problems, 171
fecal coliform bacteria, 46
Federal Water Pollution Control Act, 42, 47
Federal Water Pollution Control Association, 44
Fernow, Bernhard, 129, 139
Flannery Decree, 54, 76, 119
Food And Drug Administration (FDA), 169, 173
Ford, President Gerald, 169
forest managers, 130
Forest Ranger, The (Kaufman), 134
Friedman, Frank B., 89, 92

Friends of the Earth (FOE), 9, 109, 111
"fundamentally different factors" (FDF) variance, 56
future generations, responsibility for, 161 ff.
Gallup poll 59
garbage collection, early, 21
Gardner, John, 51, 184
Gaskell, Elizabeth, 16
General Accounting Office (GAO) reports, 166
General Motors, 114
germ theory, 27
Gibbs, Lois, 113
Glen Canyon controversy, 47
Grace, W. R. Co., 3, 118
Grand Canyon controversies, 47
grass-roots environmental groups, 110, 113
Great Depression, 32
Green, Ronald M., 162
Griscom, John C., 23
Harington, Sir John, 19
Harris poll, 59, 120, 122
Hawkins, David, 52
hazard identification, 170
health reformers, 15-17
Heilbroner, Robert, 163
Hering, Rudolph, 25, 28
horse wastes, 21
human life, value, 174
ideologically committed specialists, 106
immigrants, 14, 15
implementation plan, 46
industrial revolution, 16, 21, 22
INFORM, 91, 92
institutions of environmental management, 123
intermedia pollution, 179
irrigation ditches, 19
Izaac Walton League, 34, 43, 109
Johnson, President Lyndon, 47
joint and several liability, 118
Kay, Philip, 17
Kennedy, President John F., 43, 50
Ladies' Health Clubs, 30, 34
Ladies' Protective Association, 24
land application of sewage, 19, 28
Lavelle, Rita, 94
Lawrence Experiment Station, 27, 28, 41
League of Women Voters, 44, 123
Lebacqz, Karen, 134, 145
legal standing, 117, 118
Life magazine, 41
Lippmann, Walter, 121, 145, 157
Lister, Joseph, 27

Los Angeles smog, 49
Lou Grant TV show, 122
Louisville, Ky., laboratory, 28
Love Canal, 49, 57, 62, 121, 122, 173
Lowrance, William W., 181
manifest system, 62
Manville Corporation, 89, 118
media ethics, 155
Metamorphosis of Ajax, 19
miasma theory, 10, 16, 27
Ministry of International Trade and Industry (MITI), Japan, 177
Mize, Verna, 113
3M Company, 91
Morison, Robert, 137
Muskie, Sen. Edmund, 44, 46, 48, 51
Nader, Ralph, 111, 114
Nader's Raiders, 114
National Association of Manufacturers, 155
National Audubon Society, 9, 34, 43, 109, 112, 123
National Board of Health, 25
National Council of Mayors, 44
national environmental organizations, 110
National Environmental Policy Act (NEPA), 45, 47, 102, 129
National Forest Products Association, 123
National Oceanic and Atmospheric Administration, 175
National Pollutant Discharge Elimination Systems permit (NPDES),
    46, 54, 55, 56, 57, 73, 131
National Research Center, 175, 176
National Research Council, 170, 180
National Science Foundation, 176
National Technical Information Service (NTIS), 176
National Wild and Scenic Rivers System, 47
National Wildlife Federation, 9, 34, 43, 109, 112, 123
Natural Resources Defense Council (NRDC), 9, 54, 109, 119, 120, 123
New Deal, 34, 42
New York Times/CBS poll, 59, 120
Newsweek, 41, 115
nitrogen dioxide, 54
Nixon, President Richard, 46
normative ethics, 149
Occupational Health and Safety Administration (OSHA), 174, 175
ocean-based waste incineration, 158
off-peak pricing conservation mechanisms, 120
Office of Management and Budget (OMB), 56, 98, 174
Office of Technology Assessment (OTA), 62
"offsets" policy, 64, 116
Oil Pollution Act of 1924, 42
Opinion Research poll, 120
organization of environmental sections, 80, 88
ozone layer, 162
ozone standards, 54

Passaic River pollution, 43
Pasteur, Louis, 27
PCBs, 59, 171, 179
Pennsylvania Health Department, 30
performance standards, 129, 143
permits for effluents, 46, 76
pH, 46
Philosophic Radicals, 17, 32
photochemical smog standards, 168
Physicians for Social Responsibility, 150
Pinchot, Gifford, 129, 139
Playing God (Chase), 135
political appointees, 94
politics in agencies, 94, 95
"Pollution Prevention Pays," 91
Pollution Probe Foundation, 91
Poor Law Commission, 17
population growth, 15, 22, 39
pragmatist specialists, 105
pretreatment standards, 56, 119
primary ambient air standards, 54
probability methodologies, 172
professional culture, 143
professional goals, 134
professional images, 134, 138, 141
professional roles, 133
professional training, 132, 133, 137, 142
profit-oriented managers, 84
Progressive Movement, 23, 29, 135
Public Health Act (England), 18
Public Health Service Act of 1912, 29, 41
public health surveys, 18
public improvement groups, 24, 25
public interest groups, 110
public interest, 144
public opinion polls, 59, 120
public-owned treatment works (POTWs), 54
Public Philosophy, The (Lippmann), 145
quarantine, 27
Quarles, John, 52
Quincy TV show, 122
"rational person" (Lippmann), 145
Reader's Digest, 43
Reagan administration, 56, 169
reasonably available control technology (RACT), 64
receiving water standards, 46, 57
refinery operations, 81
research and development, 176
Restoring the Earth (Berger), 114
Resource Conservation and Recovery Act of 1976 (RCRA), 62, 96, 98, 174
resource recovery of waste streams, 76, 78

Revolt of the Engineers (Layton), 135
right-to-know laws, 63
risk assessment, 169, 180, 182
risk characterization, 170
risk management, 169, 181
risk preferences, 172
risk-averse specialists, 105
Rivers and Harbors Act of 1899, 41
Rivers Pollution Act (England), 20
Roosevelt, Pres. Franklin D., 34
Roosevelt, President Theodore, 25
Ruckelshaus, William D., 49, 53, 111, 115
rule-making, 98, 167
sampling requirements, 73
Samuelson, Robert J., 160
San Francisco Bay pollution, 116
San Francisco Chronicle, 158, 160
sanitary engineering, 27, 130
"Sanitary Question," 18
Santa Barbara oil spill, 45
Saturday Evening Post, 41
Saturday Review, 43
Sawyer, Diane, 157
Scenic Hudson Preservation legal case, 117
Schlesinger, Arthur, 16
Schultze, Charles L., 168
Schumacher, E.F., 188
Schurz, Carl, 129
Science in the Public Interest, 150
Science magazine, 56
science model of EIS, 103
Scientists' Institute for Public Information, 150
Scrap v. United States case, 117
secondary ambient air standards, 54
Sedgwick, William, 24
Seeger, Pete, 59
semiconductor plants, 77
septic systems, 101
sewage disposal, colonial, 15, 23
sewage treatment, early, 27, 28
sewage, colonial, 15, 24
Shattuck, Lemul, 23
Shrader-Frechette, K. S., 172, 181, 185
Sierra Club v. Morton case, 117
Sierra Club, 9, 41, 47, 109, 111, 112, 119, 123
Sixty Minutes TV program, 157
slums, 15, 22
Smith, Southward, 17
smoke pollution, early, 30, 31
Southern California Hazardous Waste Management Authority, 184
Sports Illustrated, 43

states rights vs. federal regulations, 95
Stoner, Dr. J. B., 31
sulfur oxides, 54, 119
sulfur standards, 51
sustained yield, 129
Tarr, Joel, 21, 28, 38
tax-deductible status, 111
Taylor, Serge, 103, 107
technical negotiation, 135, 138, 140
technology-based standards, 46, 57
technology-forcing regulations, 46
temperature inversion, 49
Tennessee Valley Authority (TVA), 119
The New Yorkers (Smith Hart), 14
Thomas, Lee M., 179
Time magazine, 58
Times Beach, Mo., 58
Today TV show, 160
Torrey Canyon oil spill, 45
total suspended solids (TSS), 46
Toxic Law Trials documentary (*Nova*), 161
Toxic Substances Control Act (TOSCA), 169
toxic torts, 118
transportation innovations, 20
Turning Point, The (Capra), 143, 146
TV environmental coverage, 58
typhoid fever, 23, 27
U.S. Civil Service Commission, 95
U.S. Constitution, 94, 144
U.S. Department of Agriculture, 134
U.S. Fish and Wildlife Service, 175
U.S. Forest Service, 48, 102, 103, 130, 134, 175
U.S. News and World Report, 43
U.S. Park Service, 102
U.S. Public Health Service, 42, 44, 49
Udall, Stewart, 44
unconventional pollutants, 46
Union Carbide Corp., 63, 115, 118
Unsafe at Any Speed (Nader), 114
urban congestion, 40
urbanization, 15
utilitarianism, 17, 34, 71, 130, 144
Valley of the Drums, Ky., 58
Villareme, 18
voluntary compliance, 97, 99, 100
Wall Street Journal, 115, 120
Wallace, Governor George, 157
Waring system, 25
Waring, Col. George E., 25, 26
Washington Post, 160
water closet, 19

Water Quality Act of 1965, 44
Water Resources Council, 175
water works systems, early, 24
Watt, James, 56, 181
Weinberg, Alvin, 171
Wilderness Act, 41
Wilderness Society, 9, 41, 112
Woborn, Mass., water contamination, 118, 161
Worldwatch Institute, 179
Yellowstone National Park, 135
young environmental specialists, 86, 87

NOTES